TELEVISION AND SEXUALITY

Regulation and the Politics of Taste

Jane Arthurs

OPEN UNIVERSITY PRESS

Open University Press
McGraw-Hill Education
McGraw-Hill House
Shoppenhangers Road
Maidenhead
Berkshire
England
SL6 2QL

email: enquiries@openup.co.uk
world wide web: www.openup.co.uk

and Two Penn Plaza, New York, NY 10121–2289, USA

First published 2004

A catalogue record of this book is available from the British Library

ISBN 0 335 20975 0 (pb) 0 335 20976 9 (hb)

Library of Congress Cataloging-in-Publication Data
CIP data applied for

Typeset by RefineCatch Limited, Bungay, Suffolk
Printed in the UK by Bell & Bain Ltd, Glasgow

For Minnie and Colin Arthurs in recognition of how much I have learned from their unfailing wisdom and generosity.

For Jonathan, Jessica and Joseph Simmons for their love and support.

CONTENTS

SERIES EDITOR'S FOREWORD

Looking across the array of ongoing public debates concerning television, it is striking to note how fiercely contested the ones revolving around human sexuality and its representation tend to be. From one society to the next, alarm bells are recurrently being sounded, not least by those intent on holding television culpable for undermining what they consider to be proper moral values or standards of taste and decency. Typically, much is made of the perceived power of television to influence public attitudes unduly in this regard – witness, for example, the extraordinary furore ignited when singer Janet Jackson's 'wardrobe malfunction' left her breast briefly exposed on US television. 'It took the Bush administration 10 months to launch an inquiry into the apparent failures of intelligence in the lead-up to the war on Iraq', remarked journalist Marina Hyde at the time. 'It took them less than eight hours to launch a full-scale probe into the apparent failure of Jackson's undergarments in the course of a televised performance during the Super Bowl halftime' (*Guardian*, 7 February 2004).

Jane Arthurs's *Television and Sexuality* is a welcome exploration of this hotly contested terrain. It succeeds in drawing together disparate strands of critique into an innovative interpretive framework, always with an eye to engendering fresh insights into the cultural politics of sexuality. In the course of showing how – and why – the boundaries demarcating what it is appropriate for television to depict are fraught with tension, Arthurs devotes particular attention to the ways audiences are addressed as both sexual citizens and sexual consumers. Accordingly, she examines how different television genres – including comedy, drama, news, current affairs, science documentaries and 'soft-core' pornography, among others – legitimize, to varying degrees, certain uses and pleasures for imagined communities of taste within the constraints of wider regulatory codes. Television in a digital age, she argues, has a crucial role to play both within the personal sphere in the formation of our sexual selves and as a public sphere that contributes to political debate about sexual practices and their representation. Indeed, it is in unravelling the connections between the personal and the public, she believes, that television's impact can be most effectively discerned for analysis. In charting ways forward, *Television and Sexuality* seeks to challenge familiar assumptions about sexual citizenship in ways that resist the dangers of state paternalism without, at the same time, capitulating to the narcissistic individualism of consumer culture.

The *Issues in Cultural and Media Studies* series aims to facilitate a diverse range of critical investigations into pressing questions considered to be central to current thinking and research. In the light of the remarkable speed at which the conceptual agendas of cultural and media studies are changing, the series is committed to contributing to what is an ongoing process of re-evaluation and critique. Each of the books is intended to provide a lively, innovative and comprehensive introduction to a specific topical issue from a fresh perspective. The reader is offered a thorough grounding in the most salient debates indicative of the book's subject, as well as important insights into how new modes of enquiry may be established for future explorations. Taken as a whole, then, the series is designed to cover the core components of cultural and media studies courses in an imaginatively distinctive and engaging manner.

Stuart Allan

ACKNOWLEDGEMENTS

This book developed out of a course I have been teaching since 1996 at the University of the West of England, called *Gender and Sexuality in Film and Television*. I would like to thank all the students with whom I have discussed the programmes and issues included here. Their insights and diversity of responses have enriched my own thinking enormously. I have shared the teaching of this course with several people over the years and to them I would like to extend my thanks for their enthusiasm and intellectual engagement. They have helped to shape my thinking in numerous ways and we have had a lot of fun working together. Paul Ryan's work on gay representation in television drama helped me to get started on Chapter 7. Sherryl Wilson's (2003) work on talk shows helped to stimulate the interest in confessional television that emerges in Chapter 4. Helen Kennedy's work on girl gamers has kept me updated on the gendering of new media technologies and their transgressive pleasures. Suzy Gordon's work on psychoanalytic theory and feminist film studies has helped to maintain my own interest in the relevance of these approaches to television, and she also read and commented on early drafts of almost all of the chapters. Nils Lindahl-Ellio, with whom I have taught a course on Environmentalism and the Media, has been an important influence on my approach to wildlife films in Chapter 5. Finally, I would like to thank Stuart Allan for recognizing the potential for a book on this topic, and for his continuing encouragement and advice in the development of the project.

The School of Cultural Sudies at UWE has provided ongoing financial support for the book's completion, especially in awarding the research leave in 2000 to 2001 that enabled much of the research and writing to be done, and then again at the end of 2003 for bringing the project to fruition. The School also financed Sherryl Wilson's work on collating the database of documentaries that I draw on in Chapter 6. I would like to thank her for doing this time-consuming research in such a meticulous and good-natured manner, and Phillip Hargreaves for providing technical training and computer support for the software used.

The School's Gender and Culture Research Group has been a valuable source of advice in helping to polish the final version. Richard Hornsey, Helen Kennedy and Gillian Swanson, in particular, contributed detailed comments at this stage. Jon Dovey also gave detailed advice and I would like to thank him for having been a colleague with whom, over the years, I could discuss television of various kinds with such enthusiasm and insight.

Thanks also go to the organizers of the conferences where I have given papers on my research, and to the Faculty of Humanities, Languages and Social Science for financing my attendance: Visible Evidence X1, UWE, Watershed Media Centre, 2003; Media in Transition 3: Television, MIT Boston, USA, 2003; Global Village or Global Image, BFI/ITC/BSC, Institute of Education, London University, 2001; Television: Past, Present and Futures, The University of Queensland, Brisbane, Australia, 2000.

A very warm thanks to those who first taught me how to study television, namely Manuel Alvarado, David Buckingham, Philip Drummond and Robert Ferguson at the Institute of Education, London University, where I completed an MA in 1984. But the seeds of this book were sown even earlier at a summer school organized in 1982 by the BFI Education Department entitled 'Who Does Television Think We Are?' A special thanks to David Lusted in whose seminar group I learnt how to take television light entertainment seriously without sacrificing the fun.

Material included in Chapter 8 was published as 'Sex and the City and consumer culture: remediating postfeminist drama', in Feminist Media Studies, 3(1). I would like to thank the journal for permission to publish a revised version here.

INTRODUCTION

1

Cultural transformations

This book looks at how sexuality has been represented on television over recent years. The past decade has witnessed a marked transformation in the diversity of these representations as a result of changes in the economic and cultural context within which programmes are produced and distributed. Given these changes, which I will be examining in relation to examples drawn primarily from television in the UK and USA, what kinds of sexual practices and identities are now visible? The 'implied viewer' to whom television is addressed is central to my analysis. This is the 'you' to whom producers imagine they are speaking in policy statements, continuity announcements, programme trailers, channel branding, scheduling practices and targeted advertising, as well as in the programmes themselves. Producers may be informed by audience research, but they also act on embedded assumptions about who is watching, what kind of programmes they like and what forms of address are appropriate. In the past, television has been criticized for its conservative address to a 'family' audience, while excluding marginal identities that fall outside this traditionalist norm. This address is also tied to changing assumptions about what television is *for*. How is this changing as we move into the multichannel digital era? Television emerges, then, as a complex set of localized and historically specific practices that are produced out of changing definitions of its audiences and purposes. My central concern is with how these institutionalized definitions and practices have influenced the forms of sexual representation during this period.

Television is a mass medium whose institutional routines were formed in the 1940s and 1950s within a set of practices and regulations that assumed a middle-class family audience with traditional patterns of gendered behaviour. These households were imagined as nuclear families, with one television in the sitting room that the family watched together, except during the day when the husband and older children would be out at work. Explicit representations of heterosexual activity, or even the mention of other more 'deviant' sexual behaviours, were unthinkable for a medium that transmitted the core values of the society from the public domain into the private sphere of the family home. By the end of the century, however, the degree of transformation in this mode of address can be exemplified by the global broadcasting of meticulous and detailed descriptions of US President Bill Clinton's illicit sexual activities. These descriptions of oral sex with a young intern in the White House would have been regarded as far beyond the boundary of taste and decency even in the recent past. News reports in 1998 presented us with an interrogation of the legitimacy of certain forms of sexual behaviour, questions concerning the use and abuse of power in sexual relations, the questioning of the boundary between private as opposed to public morality and a full exposure of the legal hearings, on television and the Internet, to establish the truth of Clinton's sexual exploits. This culminated in what came to be the impeachable issue, a disputation over what counts as 'sexual relations'. People's responses to these revelations polarized between the fundamentalist Christians' condemnation and the liberal tolerance of the majority. This left many feminist commentators unsure and ambivalent, marking perhaps a retreat from the certainties of 'politically correct' discourses of sexual behaviour. It also led to many parents complaining about the invasion of family television by detailed sexual information.

One year earlier, in 1997, television was similarly saturated with one big news story, the death of Princess Diana, which in turn led to numerous evaluations of her life. Similar questions arose about the gap between the public rhetoric about 'family values' and the 'truth' exposed in the media about the private behaviour of Prince Charles and his mistress, Camilla Parker-Bowles. A television interview given by the Princess on *Panorama* in 1995 was a key moment in this history of scandalous revelation. After this interview she had been portrayed not just as a wronged individual, but as the victim of an outdated patriarchal institution in which wives are only important in order to produce the male heir. She was championed as an inspiration to those in positions of relative powerlessness who through a new political awareness find the strength to remake themselves as independent women. Other commentators, however, labelled her as either manipulative or mad and therefore an unreliable witness to the truth.

These two examples, which I explore further in Chapter 4, serve to underline the more general case that television discourses about sexuality are increasing not only in quantity but also in the range of moral and ideological positions from which events and issues are debated and evaluated. This is a sign of the profound changes that have transformed the way in which people inhabit their gender in advanced capitalist societies (Giddens 1992; Bell and Binnie 2000; Beck and Beck-Gernsheim 2002). The old standards no longer seem to apply, but new ones are still in the process of formation. Some people want to hang on to the past; others are impatient with the slow pace of change to a new set of relations in which the certainties of the patriarchal social order no longer hold sway. Television is a primary public forum for the conduct of this debate across both fictional and factual genres, in news, documentaries, current affairs programmes, talk shows, sitcoms and drama. They address issues such as:

- sexual morality in the public and private spheres – adultery, child sexual abuse, sado-masochism, homosexual rights, sexual harassment, prostitution;
- changing patterns of family life – the rise in the number of single-parent families, cohabitation, working mothers, gay and lesbian parenting;
- the limits of sexual representation in a deregulated media market – people's right to privacy, the effects of pornographic images.

These cultural transformations are linked to the legal status of sexual behaviours and the recognition of identity rights arising from successive waves of political campaigning by the 'new social movements' – bohemian, feminist, gay and lesbian, queer – and the growing concern for children's right to sexual safety and education. In other words, they are concerned with questions of 'sexual citizenship'. There has been a flurry of legislation in the UK around sexual matters that hasn't been seen since the 'permissive' legislation of the 1960s. Then it was the recognition of homosexual rights, legal abortions and liberalized divorce laws, alongside the contraceptive pill, that was credited with creating the conditions for the sexual liberation movements of the time. Following the 'family values' backlash that dominated the conservative politics of the 1980s and first half of the 1990s, a new political agenda on sexuality has emerged from 1997 with New Labour in power. The recognition of homosexual citizenship rights, in, for example, the equalization of the age of consent, has been accompanied by attention to children's sexual rights, with new laws to protect them from adult abuse in response to the paedophile scandals of the 1990s (The Sexual Offences Act 2003).

The digital revolution

There is a widespread agreement that we have entered into a third era in television (Ellis 2000). The first era was based on a very small number of networks addressing a relatively undifferentiated, mass audience within national boundaries. The second was an era of expanded 'choice', with multichannel systems from the mid-1970s in the USA and the 1980s in the UK, offering more minority interest programmes. This happened gradually in the UK: the mainstream BBC and ITV channels were supplemented by BBC2 in 1963, Channel 4 in 1982 and Channel 5 in 1997, while cable and satellite channels also increased capacity from the mid-1980s. Digital technology in the 1990s brought a new era of 'abundance' in which the number of channels has multiplied and extended their global reach, while new interactive and storage capabilities are now being added. Although not yet universal, this new era has been gathering pace as digital access has spread to more than 50 per cent of the 24.5 million homes in the UK by the start of 2004. This has been boosted by the provision of Freeview alongside the existing cable and satellite subscription services (the complete replacement of analogue television is planned for 2010). The full implications of this transition, alongside other changes such as convergence with other digital media such as the Internet and mobile handsets and the integration of television companies into large, global media conglomerates, is the focus for industry and policy discussions. New models for financing television and new regimes of government regulation are being developed to accommodate these changes (Siune and Hulten 1998).

Technological developments have also changed the processes of production. For instance, the miniaturization of digital cameras has made possible the confessional diaries and intimate portrayals that have exposed previously hidden aspects of everyday life (Dovey 2000). In turn, these generic innovations have produced a wider and more diverse audience for documentary, bringing them into the schedule as a commercially oriented ratings strategy. Technological developments have also driven the expansion of the commercial sex industry, with the Internet allowing for cheap and effective marketing and distribution of sexual services and products. Not only has this in itself become a topic for journalistic investigation, it has also changed the context within which television competes for its audience. The restrictions on erotic content on television that were enforceable in the past no longer seem as justified or, indeed, possible when it comes to the supranational footprints of satellite television.

The effects of technological and economic changes in the television industry are not inevitable but the result of the ways in which people respond to the potential they offer. It is a political process in which competing institutionalized **interests** are in play across the industry and government. Over the past twenty years in the UK, for example, this has produced a recurring debate over the relative claims of 'public service' versus 'the market' as able to deliver a 'quality' television system that provides for minority as well as majority tastes and interests. Among those minority but culturally powerful interests is a concern to preserve television as a democratic 'public sphere'. In constructing the audience, therefore, in whose name the political wrangling over purposes is conducted, the two key rhetorical figures to emerge are the 'citizen' of a nation state and the 'consumer' in a global market. These are not static categories but are open to redefinition as, for instance, new claims for citizenship emerge or new markets are exploited for profit. Neither are they entirely separate, as increasingly citizenship has become redefined in consumerist terms, with governments merely providing the conditions within which private enterprise can deliver the services for which consumers pay.

The increasing fragmentation of the audience undermines established ways of understanding the political economy of television and its cultural significance. It has been argued that the 'era of abundance' in the digital age has changed television's ideological role, reducing its power to delineate the centre and the margins, to influence the shared assumptions of a national culture. Instead it is suggested we should now think in terms of 'diversity' (Ellis 2000), and a questioning of the 'myth of the centre' that television claims for itself (Couldry 2003). The notion of individual consumer control has entered into the rhetoric of the 'imagined audience'. 'A more interactive, service demanding model is emerging for whom "content" must be tailored. Narrow-cast audiences are no longer "objects" of mass marketing but "subjects" of choice' (Hartley 2002: 63). An advertising campaign at the end of 2003 for 'Sky Plus', a digital 'personal video recorder' linked to satellite television services, had the slogan 'Create Your Own TV Channel' as a way to sell its computer-based recording and playback system. Interactive, digital services allow multiple uses for the TV set, including the kind of information-seeking we previously associated with print or computer media. Internet websites also allow 'communities' of viewers to construct meanings and uses for programmes that extend as well as respond to the television text (Hills 2002).

One of my central questions, then, discussed more fully in the following chapter, 'Sexual Citizenship in the Digital Age', is what effect these shifting conceptualizations of the audience have had on how *sexual* citizenship and *sexual* consumerism have been redefined within these larger categories. What assumptions about sexual 'identity' underpin the address to citizens and consumers? How does this determine what can or cannot be shown, who is visible or invisible, what is considered normal or abnormal, legitimate or illegitimate, true or false, good or bad? Moreover, what kinds of sexual 'interests', in both senses of the term, are the citizen and the consumer assumed to have? In other words, what kinds of sexual information and education or pleasures does television now provide across the multiple genres and 'platforms' of the digital age?

Pleasure and risk: researching television and sexuality

Before we go any further, I need to clarify my conceptual approach to these questions and the 'disciplinary discourses' from which they are derived. This is a complex task because of the diversity of disciplinary influences on the study of television (see Miller 2002 for discussion of this fact). Moreover, there is an equally diverse literature on sexuality on which I also draw (Bristow 1997; Segal 1997; Bell and Binnie 2000; Bhattacharyya 2002; Weeks 2003 for overviews). Inevitably, then, this account will be highly selective.

To begin, I want to clarify my use of 'sexuality' as a term. To what exactly does it refer and how is it to be distinguished from the related terms of 'sex' and the adjective 'sexual' when used in phrases such as sexual difference, sexual identity, sexual desire, sexual orientation or sexual relations? In my usage 'sexuality' is taken as a more general term that encompasses these other terms. It refers to the cultural expression of the sexual in specific contexts and as such its meanings are discursively produced. Different contexts produce different meanings because terms are defined in use and might overlap or extend into new areas as practices change. 'Sex', for instance, is used in some contexts to mean erotic encounters that may or may not involve sexual intercourse. What kinds of behaviour are included in this definition are open to debate and can even be a matter of legal dispute in, for example, sexual abuse cases of various kinds. In feminist sociology, on the other hand, 'sex' refers to the biological differences between men and women, as compared to the cultural differences that are denoted by 'gender'. A distinction that was established to counteract the assumption that male and female behaviour is biologically determined was itself overturned in 'queer theory'. 'Sex' became problematic as a biological term when it was argued that these biological binaries are as socially constructed as any other aspect of gender.

This complexity is indicative of the extent to which 'sexuality' is the focus of intense social and political struggles over meaning. The stakes are high in that these struggles determine not only what we 'know' about 'sexuality' but also the legitimacy of the identities and behaviours to which it refers. This approach to sexual 'discourse' as a form of 'regulation' is drawn from Michel Foucault, whose influence on the study of sexuality in cultural and media studies cannot be overstated. His *History of Sexuality, Volume 1, An Introduction*, first published in 1976, but widely available in translation from the beginning of the 1980s, was responsible for the subsequent proliferation of work on the discursive construction of sexuality, and is an important influence on the form of this book. In the space available here, I want to sketch in some main conceptual ideas, then signal the key discursive influences on the regulation of sexuality on television.

'Discourses' are ways of talking, thinking or representing a topic that produce meaningful knowledge about it. In this perspective it is not the case that discourse about sexuality merely describes a pre-existing thing; instead, it is constructed through the very discourses that seek to study, describe and regulate it. The production of discourse is something we do; it is a practice that has effects in the real world, on our behaviour. The knowledge that a discourse produces is a kind of power over those who are known, who are 'subjected' to the discourse. Since the Enlightenment, discursive power has depended on the accumulation of evidence through the scientific methods of observation, investigation, classification, labelling. The population is thus divided according to the documenting of the normal against which deviance and abnormality is measured. Every society has ways of regulating sexuality, of determining what is normal and abnormal, legitimate and illegitimate; these fall into 'who' restrictions and 'how' restrictions but the details and contents of these regulations differ widely. Hugely powerful institutions have developed out of these 'discursive practices'. The knowledge they produce has the power to define what is true as well as what is normal. Together they constitute the 'discursive formation'; that is to say, the combined network of discourses that characterize a particular historical period.

One of the characteristics of Foucault's work has been its very broad historical sweep in his tracing of the discursive shifts that instituted the modern period. Subsequent writers have developed his account of the dispersed and pluralistic forms of power in modern cultures to examine the localized interplay of power and resistance that regulates sexuality in very particular historical times and institutionalized places (this book included). Ken Plummer (1996), for example, seeks to explain why specific 'sexual stories', as he terms them, have specific times, while others do not. In Plummer's view the post-war period is deserving of special attention in that it was a period in which the sexualization of modern capitalist societies and a growing 'democratization' in intimate relationships gathered momentum. The growth of the mass media is one of the main reasons for these changes, alongside the expansion of an affluent, consumer society. Various responses to these conditions have emerged, some very critical of the increasingly individualistic, narcissistic and confessional culture they have encouraged. These negative responses have had the effect, Plummer argues, of amplifying the amount of sexual discourse in circulation. The process of regulating sexuality, as Foucault noted, has the opposite effect from that which is usually assumed. Rather than the amount and range of sexual expression being restricted, it proliferates instead. Condemnation of deviance has the effect of being an incitement to perversity, and everyone involved can partake in the pleasures of examination and confession. This process is explored in more depth in Chapter 4, which considers the way that media scandals work simultaneously to reinstate and exceed sexual boundaries.

Foucault also argues, in contradiction of the beliefs held by many sexual radicals, that this proliferation of discursive practices cannot be conceptualized as a 'liberation' of sexuality; instead it is a more precise means by which to regulate sexual behaviour through the creation of new forms of sexual 'subjectivity'. All discourses produce subject positions for us to inhabit that are embedded in power relations of domination and subordination. Thus the feminist, gay and lesbian liberation movements that have challenged the previously dominant discourses of liberal and conservative regulation have in their turn been criticized for 'policing' the boundaries of desire by subsequent 'queer' movements. Although queer arguments for indeterminate and fluid identities might appear to have arrived at the point where sexuality finally escapes the disciplinary effects of discourse, some critics, who regard them instead as complicit with the requirements of capitalist markets, regard this as illusory. A never-ending process of division into diverse and changing niche markets ties these seeming outsiders into the heart of ideological regulation of consumerism (Bourdieu 1984: 370; Hennessy 1995; Seidman 1995). It was the puritan restraint of old that offered the greatest obstacle to this capitalist 'exploitation'.

Although Foucauldian cultural studies have been criticized for prioritizing discursive power over economic forces, in my view this is a false dichotomy. Powerful legitimating discourses enable the economic and technological developments in the television industry that constitute the material conditions within which programmes are made. The most powerful in the current context is the discourse of **neo-liberalism**, in which it is argued that the diverse tastes of individual consumers will be best catered for by a 'free market' in television.

Genre, taste and discursive regulation

The structure of this book is based around genres, with each chapter focused on a single or closely related group of generic categories within which specific issues around sexual representation are explored. Indeed, it is a central assumption of my approach that genres are a key form of discursive regulation of sexual representation on television. They are defined in the history of the relationship between the industry and television audiences.

Genre, in this perspective, is best conceived not as a fixed set of endlessly reproduced textual conventions, but as a dynamic network of discursive connections that work to regulate aesthetic forms and their circulation. 'Defining the genre is a process of connecting the various discourses shaping the genre, of constantly going out from the text to other discourses and their institutional sites' (Juffer 1998: 28). Genre as a system legitimates certain 'uses' and 'pleasures' for an **imagined community** of taste (Altman 1999). Social hierarchies that serve to define these communities are thereby linked to a finely differentiated hierarchy of genres and aesthetic conventions (Bourdieu 1984). These cultural distinctions are in constant flux and renegotiation. Moreover, as Mark Jankovich (2001: 7) points out, drawing on Bourdieu, 'sexual tastes are not only amongst the most "classifying" of social differences, but also have "the privilege of appearing the most natural" '. This is reinforced by the often visceral reaction of disgust that is provoked by the taste cultures of groups to whom we do not belong. For broadcasters, therefore, it isn't simply a case, as is often asserted, that 'sex sells'; instead it is a case of customizing sexual discourse to particular social groups in the audience in order to maximize their pleasure while minimizing the offence to others. This customization process is enhanced by the shift to multiple channels so that, in the digital era, whole channels can now be branded around a single generic category, whether it is documentary (Discovery Channel) or pornography (Playboy Channel). While mainstream networks still have to accommodate a range of taste cultures, their generic mix is crucial in establishing a brand identity for a channel. Mixed genre channels can become identified with a small part of their output. Channel 4's upmarket, youthful brand, for example, is strongly linked to its promotion of imported US 'quality' drama (McCabe 2000; Jankovich and Lyons 2003) and Channel 5's with downmarket 'soft porn' (see further discussion in Chapter 3).

Television production and its critical reception are also regulated by these 'quality/ trash' distinctions in taste that work to legitimate the tastes of the more powerful. In the American system 'quality' is determined by the economics of the market. 'Quality' television is profitable television addressed to affluent niche markets, as defined against the mass market (Feuer 1995). But even in the mass market there has always been a commercial incentive to present 'aspirational' images of middle-class life to encourage consumer buying. Charlotte Brunsdon (1990) demonstrates how in the UK, in discussions about the need to protect 'quality' television from the ravages of the free market, different assumptions are made about what television is for, and more particularly what certain genres are for. Public service ideals have been based on the assumption that television could improve the tastes of the masses and thereby encourage middle-class values and behaviour. Within the general injunction that public service television should educate, inform and entertain, Brunsdon shows how these functions are also ordered in a hierarchy of taste linked to class and gender. Factual genres that inform and educate are regarded as intrinsically more worthwhile than fictional genres whose main purpose is to entertain. The same hierarchy operates within fictional genres, so that drama which is intellectually demanding or in some way educational and informative in a realist mode is more worthwhile than **popular** melodrama that works on the emotions. Mass market television is often dismissed and reviled as 'trash TV' among an intellectual elite who don't share the tastes of the majority. Popular tastes, and women's preferences, reverse this hierarchy of value.

Within the industry, different quality criteria will come into play depending on the context, especially the balance between commercial and political pressures. In the 1990 Broadcasting Act in the UK, for example, the regulatory pressure to maintain middle-class criteria of quality was still a force to be reckoned with, despite the free market rhetoric of the Thatcher government, backed up as it was by a panoply of statutory measures. This included a 'quality threshold' for the allocation of commercial franchises, and the setting up of the Broadcasting Standards Commission to monitor standards of taste and decency. By the time of the 2003 Communications Act legislation, however, priorities had shifted towards the profitability of the commercial industry in a global market, although public service ideals remain in the rhetoric of 'citizenship' and 'diversity'. Along with other cultural influences there has been a loosening of restraint and a greater desire to appeal directly to 'popular' tastes, dispensing with **normative** values to address a culturally more diverse audience. This has had a major impact on the way that sexual discourse is handled.

Effects studies

The dominant tradition of academic research on television and sexuality has been carried out by psychologists and sociologists who use 'content analysis' of texts and 'effects' research on audiences. Government and industry sponsors of various kinds, and also advocacy groups promoting specific religious agendas, have funded these in the main. This is an important tradition of research because of its long-standing influence on television policy and regulation, despite liberal commitments to freedom of speech (see Chapter 2). Barry Gunter's (2002) book *Media Sex: What Are the Issues?* provides a thorough overview of these traditions, while a more critical assessment can be found in Sarah Bragg and David Buckingham's (2002) review in *Young People and Sexual Content on Television*. The limitation of this approach is in the way that it conceptualizes the relationship between television and sexuality. It is locked into a narrow definition of the issues in terms of the presence or absence of explicit sexual talk and display. Moreover, the continuing influence of **Puritanism** places all the emphasis on the risks rather than the potential pleasures of sexual portrayal. Concerns over the effects of television on sexual identity and behaviour are entirely normative; that is to say, oriented towards the prevention of 'deviant' behaviour and the promotion of traditional 'family values'.

Multiple problems of research validity arise, ranging from the impossibility of isolating television as an influence, to doubts over the textual meanings assumed in the decontextualized coding practices used in 'content analysis' (Gunter 2002: 240–66). In content analysis programmes are recorded over a specific period such as a whole week and then analysis focuses on scenes in which sex is either talked about or portrayed visually. These scenes are then given coded descriptors to classify their 'content'; that is, the type of sexual activity, whom it involves, its levels of explicitness and its moral perspective and meaning. This can then be summarized in statistical form and compared with previous studies to show what the trends are in sexual portrayal. For example, a study in the USA, where the majority of this research is conducted, found that:

> Over a 20-year spell from the mid 1970s sexual depictions became increasingly prevalent on network television programs during the mid-evening time slot, with 43% of programs containing any sexual material in the 1970s and 75% doing so in the 1990s. Although network TV in the US rarely goes beyond showing kissing and cuddling there has been a marked increase in explicit talk on controversial matters such as rape, incest, and homosexuality. . . . This overall increase in sex on mainstream television was largely attributable to a greater amount of talk about sex in situation comedies and drama series.
>
> (Kaiser Family Foundation 1996; cited by Gunter 2002: 25)

The emphasis on the increasing *amount* of sex in this account derives from concerns that too much sex on TV is a potential problem and needs to be monitored and regulated, alongside public opinion on this issue. This is not just a question of frequency, but is also linked to concerns over increasing explicitness, which has the potential to embarrass or offend television viewers and also, in so doing, upset advertisers.

Any emphasis on sex for pleasure is also considered potentially harmful to the morality and/or health of the nation from the 'family values' perspective that dominates this tradition, in which the sanctity of marriage is paramount. Gunter (2002: 37) summarizes several studies over many years which:

> have indicated a tendency for television to represent sex as a largely hedonistic pursuit rather than as part of a loving, established, and long term romantic relationship, and one publicly sealed through marriage. Instead sex is frequently depicted as an activity indulged in more often by unmarried than married couples.

Worries are also expressed over the tendency in television fiction to emphasize the pleasures rather than the risks of sexual activity from a social reform perspective in a concern to promote sexual health. 'Contraceptives are rarely referred to or used, yet women seldom get pregnant, and men and women rarely contract sexually transmitted diseases unless they are prostitutes or homosexuals' (Gunter 2002: 37). This question of harm is taken up by 'effects' studies that try to measure the impact on people's sexual behaviour and attitudes. In particular, impressionable young people are perceived as being at greatest risk of copying these portrayals. No account is taken of potential variations in viewer's responses or interpretations beyond identifying which groups might be most 'vulnerable' to bad influences.

My approach in this book challenges this normative framing and the narrow concern with 'explicitness' and 'protecting' the child audience from sexual knowledge, which dominates the 'effects' tradition. Nevertheless, I am not arguing that television has no effects on sexual practices and identities. Indeed, I want to emphasize the crucial role it plays as sexual **pedagogy**. Buckingham and Bragg (2003, 2004) pursue a similar agenda through a more sophisticated form of audience research that is designed to inform cultural policy in the lighter regulatory context of the future. They argue that this needs to be linked to a better understanding of textual meanings that moves beyond the simplistic assumptions of content analysis. This book contributes to that agenda by identifying the modes of address and forms of sexual discourse mobilized across a diverse range of genres and how these have arisen from historical shifts in the regulatory context.

Public sphere debates

Suspicion of sexual pleasure has often characterized 'left-wing' public sphere debates as well. They frequently assume that a proliferation of sexual discourse is an unquestionably bad consequence of the effects of neo-liberalism, convergence, globalization and deregulation on the 'quality' of television provision. Understood as 'dumbing down' or 'tabloidization', these changes are seen to accompany the increasingly commercial priorities that regulate output. The citizen's democratic right to information and education has been squeezed out of the schedules, to be replaced by pleasurable entertainment for the consumer. Politics is marginalized in new infotainment formats by the growing emphasis on personal, emotional and sexual concerns of confessional culture (McChesney 1998; Dovey 2000; Sparks and Tulloch 2000; Winston 2000). The most important limitations to the 'dumbing down' perspective are as follows. First, it depends on a narrow conceptualization of citizenship that derives from a puritan form of left-wing critique suspicious of sexuality and entertainment as a distraction from 'real' politics. This is no longer convincing, in my view, in the wake of the **new social movements** and their politicization of the private sphere. Feminist writers, for example, have drawn attention to the radical uses of scandalous publicity and the gender hierarchy that gives men more power than women to draw the line between the public and the private (Fraser 1995). Second, the category of 'quality TV' depends on a hierarchy of taste that masks the preferences of a male elite in the guise of a universal value. This view has come under sustained attack, again from feminist critics, who point to the way that generic innovation has enabled subordinated 'others' to come in from the margins of representation on television. These debates are discussed further in relation to concepts of sexual citizenship in Chapter 2, news reporting of sex scandals in Chapter 3, science documentaries in Chapter 4 and current affairs documentaries in Chapter 5.

Arguing against this emphasis on cultural decline, other writers welcome the diminishing power of governments over content regulation, arguing that demands for recognition and equity linked to citizenship and identity politics have been delivered by a 'consumer democracy' delivered by the **market** (Hartley 1999; McNair 2002). Television's integration into global capitalism has meant a relative decline in the regulatory power of the patriarchal nation state. Moreover, the concept of 'lifestyle', it is argued, has replaced a fixed sense of identity as people reflexively fashion their sense of self through their consumption practices. In a context where traditional forms of authority, such as the church, have declined as an influence on sexual morality and sexual behaviour (although not absent from the discursive 'mix'), people have to find a set of moral and practical solutions to 'the good life' for themselves. The social conditions of 'intimate relations' have changed. A growing individualization is a feature of the 'risk society' in which the certainties of tradition no longer hold sway, and this has had a particularly destabilizing effect on gender relations and identities (Giddens 1992; Beck and Beck-Gernsheim 2002). In this context, it is argued that the media function as a source of materials from which to fashion a sexual ethics for oneself out of the diversity available. New channels and genres have developed to cater for emergent tastes and values, acting, therefore, as a 'progressive' force for change from an authoritarian sexual culture towards a 'democracy of desire' (Hartley 1999; McNair 2002).

In some ways this is a convincing case, and this book contributes to a map of these emergent taste cultures and their 'progressive' sexual ideologies. Yet there are also several problems with a perspective that simply celebrates the pluralism of the commercial media. First, it relies on a selective account in which only those programmes that support the thesis are included. The continuing presence of 'traditionalist' sexual politics and moralities at the centre of the schedules is overlooked, in news and current affairs or science documentaries, for instance. Second, television as a commodity form has its own regulatory effects that limit the kinds of meanings and audience pleasures it produces. The sexual 'freedoms' encouraged by a consumer society cannot replace the need to engage in debate about sexual ethics and the politics of representation. Indeed, it makes it more urgent as sexual representations proliferate not only in the programmes we watch but also in the ubiquitous advertising by which the majority of television is financed. Foucault's concept of 'technologies of the self', on which these theories draw, emphasizes that these techniques work to produce ever finer distinctions in the formation of an ethical self. It is those contexts in which there is apparently the most sexual freedom (the example Foucault cites is the relationship between adult male citizens and young boys in Ancient Greece) that generate the most detailed instructions on sexual conduct (Foucault 1988). As we move further away from traditional moralities, attention needs to be paid to the multiple disciplinary discourses that replace them.

My argument, therefore, is that there is a legitimate 'public interest' in the forms of sexual representation made available; it isn't something that can be left to market relations but neither is it simply 'trash' to be got rid of. Television has a significant role to play in the development of sexual citizenship and should be a forum and stimulus for political debate and education, as well as a source of personal meaning with fragmented audiences pursuing their individual desires. What kind of role should we be asking of television in this respect that goes beyond the puritan restrictions of the past? In addressing these concerns my intention is to combine questions of policy with identity studies and widen the scope of both areas of debate.

Feminist cultural theory

Without a doubt the most significant academic tradition of research in the analysis of sexual representations on television has been feminist cultural studies. From the early 1980s a rich diversity of approaches has been developed that, initially drawing on feminist film studies and feminist sociology, but then on a wider field of black, gay, lesbian and **queer** studies, has contributed enormously to the direction taken by television studies as a field of study. From an initial concern with textual issues of gender equity drawing on semiotics, **psychoanalysis**, theories of ideology, the analysis of mainstream stereotypes and 'progressive texts', it soon took on a wider cultural agenda with research into audience pleasures, the politics of taste and the integration of television into the routines of everyday life. The analytic approaches taken in this book draw extensively on this history as a source of critical approaches to the evaluation of the gender politics of sexual representations on television, and as a means to identify the influence of feminist cultural critique on these 'popular' discourses of gender. These contribute to an 'integrated approach' (D'Acci 2002) combining detailed textual readings with a contextualized understanding of the political, economic and cultural influences on their production and reception. The following overview identifies how key feminist issues in textual analysis, the politics of taste and philosophical questions about the cultural determinants of 'sexual difference' are mapped across subsequent chapters.

From 'progressive texts' to 'postmodern ambivalence'

The influence of feminist campaigning for equal citizenship rights in the 1970s brought concerns over sexual equality on to the cultural policy agenda. The concept of sex role stereotyping is now widely used to criticize media representations and provides impetus to calls for more 'positive' images of women, especially in television advertising. Content analysis of sex role stereotyping has reported on over thirty years of underrepresentation, subordination and sexual objectification in the representation of women on television, although during the 1980s the effects of the women's liberation movement began to influence portrayals. These changes meant that the aesthetics of the 'progressive text' dominated feminist media studies in the 1980s. In these debates, located primarily in film studies and adapted to television, the ideological meanings embedded in the genre conventions of popular forms were of central importance. It was these that reproduced the status quo, and it was therefore these conventions that had to be transformed. When it came to drama it was the question of role reversal that dominated. It was considered important for women to be in central roles as active goal-oriented protagonists whose desires drive the narrative and whose point of view the audience is encouraged to adopt. It was in relation to women's role in crime series that these issues first emerged. Whereas women had been confined to peripheral roles in crime series, as either victim of the crime or girlfriend to the main male characters, once made central, it was they who were shown in control of the technologies of detection and law enforcement – the car, the gun, the surveillance technologies. Theirs was the active, controlling gaze and it was their knowledge that established the narrative truth. They therefore became the guarantors of the law that underpins social organization.

The important issue here is the limitation in simply reversing male and female roles. Role reversal might allow women characters to escape their stereotypical roles as appendages to men, but the demand for narrative 'equality' for women was also criticized as a means to encourage women to slot into the world of work without there being any need to make any changes to accommodate them. **Hybridization** of crime shows with the conventions of the soap opera went some way to answering these concerns. In *Cagney and Lacey* (CBS 1982–88), for example, the first police series to be based around a team of two female police detectives, it was an essential step in allowing a feminist critique of the abuse of women's sexuality to emerge on television crime series. It invited audiences to engage with the politics of sexuality through the crimes they encountered in their professional roles (such as rape, underage sex, domestic violence, pornography and prostitution). It was the women's discussions about these cases that drew out their complex implications for women, rather than their remaining, as in so many crime shows in the past, simply a vehicle for a **patriarchal** discourse of sensationalism, **voyeurism** and **paternalism**. This was not achieved without a struggle. Julie D'Acci's (1994) study of the production history of the series tells of the network's discomfort with the show and how its survival depended on the intense loyalty of women viewers. Always marginalized in the schedules, it was only through organized campaigns from women's organizations that it survived at all.

Cagney and Lacey was innovative because it allowed the possibility that the personal and private lives of its central protagonists could be integrated with their professional and public role as policewomen, although not without difficulty. Both women experience the strain of combining a personal life with the demands of a police career. Indeed, the relation between the public and the private formed one of the central issues of the series. In this respect the deployment of gendered spaces was crucial. Not only did we follow the women home after a day spent fighting crime on the streets, and see them tucking up their children in bed or cooking dinner with a new lover, we also followed them into the women's toilets within the police precinct. This was their women's space where most of the really significant conversations in the series took place, where they could talk to each other about the job and their personal lives without fear of interruption from the men they worked and lived with. Instead of disavowing the differences between men and women, this series explored their implications (Clark 1990; Newcombe 2004).

Hybridization with the open-ended, multistranded narratives of serial melodrama created an ideologically ambivalent narrative form that made the identification of 'progressive texts' far more problematic. It affected factual as well as fictional genres during the 1990s with the rise of what has been termed 'docusoap'. Ambivalence arises from the multiple perspectives of ensemble casts and story 'arcs' that, as they stretch over months or years, allow for the exploration of complex motivations and reversals in ways that more closely mirror everyday life. This formal pluralism was found to be well suited to the mass appeal genres of prime time. Increasingly, however, it also affected 'quality' drama in the development of the 'long format' drama series. The emotional tone of these series also became more mixed, with shifts between comedy and melodrama creating an instability in the positioning of the audience in relation to the events depicted. These oscillations, allowing an ironic distancing alongside our emotional engagement with the drama, have been identified as the quintessential ideological attitude of the **postmodern** viewer in consumer culture. The multiple voices and comic ambivalence of these texts have been compared to the ritual symbolism of popular carnival in pre-modern forms of popular culture. The ideological work they do in undoing or reconfirming the disciplinary norms of sexuality and gender is undecidable except as an empirical question in particular local contexts. These questions are pursued further in relation to the melodrama and joking that characterizes the popular response to sex scandals in Chapter 4, and in relation to the ambivalent forms of contemporary television drama in Chapters 7 and 8.

Differentiated identities and hierarchies of taste

During the 1980s, feminism was criticized for privileging white, heterosexual, middle-class women as the subjects of its discourse, while assuming a universal relevance. The 'shared experience' of women or its use as a category of political **identity** is, in these terms, made more problematic by its articulation with other formative identifications – especially sexual orientation, **'race'** and ethnicity, and class. The rise of lesbian and gay identity politics, for example, challenged the heterosexual focus of gender politics. Sexuality was brought centrally on to the agenda, and the politics of sexual representation became more complex as the value of representing transgressive sexualities was argued against the more puritan legacy of feminist debates on pornography and the critique of women's sexual objectification. Campaigns against the cultural invisibility of lesbians and gays arising from the 'heteronormative' narratives that dominated television gathered momentum in the 1980s, given greater urgency by the onset of AIDS and the political backlash against gay lifestyles that it instigated. The emphasis on gay and lesbian sexuality as an 'issue' was supplemented by calls for an 'embodied' sexuality representing homosexual desire. The challenge to heteronormative perspectives in drama is explored in Chapter 7 through a discussion of television drama, which culminates in a discussion of the widely acclaimed *Queer as Folk* (Channel 4 1999/2000; Showtime 2000–), where for the first time all the main characters in a television drama were gay.

At the same time, anti-racist cultural politics drew attention to a very different history of sexual oppression experienced by men and women of colour, in which a hypersexual closeness to 'nature' was attributed to black people or a mysterious eroticism to 'Orientals'. This process of 'othering' , it was argued, secured a belief in the restrained, civilized rationality of white people. Disassociated from the body, this 'anthropological gaze' was accused of racializing the dominant traditions of film. Understood in psychoanalytic terms, this voyeuristic and fetishized gaze incorporated a complex mix of fear and sadism, desire and disavowal in much the same way that the image of the woman's body had been theorized in feminist film theory. This strand of analysis is deployed in Chapter 5 in a discussion of the technoscientific gaze of science documentaries, in Chapter 6 in a discussion of the portrayal of 'foreign' sex workers in documentaries about the sex industry and in Chapter 7 in a discussion of the black and Asian gay protagonists in British 'quality' television drama of the 1980s and 1990s.

The feminist critique of the mainstream media also constructed a damaging gulf between feminists and working-class women whose cultural pleasures were centred on reading romance and watching television melodramas. To denigrate those pleasures as ideologically suspect was to be complicit with a dominant hierarchy of taste in which women's culture is labelled as 'trash' and marginalized as a consequence. This created an ongoing problem for feminist scholars who are caught between the desire to validate and critique these popular pleasures, and to find a way to reconcile the tastes of the majority of women with their own, politically motivated, and class-specific, criteria of value. Doing so, according to Brunsdon's (1997) analysis, involved a contradictory defence and repudiation of **traditional**, domesticated femininity. In the mainstream, the low cultural status of melodrama contributes to fears of trivialization expressed by the cultural elite. The ubiquitous hybridization of all forms of television with the storytelling structures of melodrama fuels widespread concern over the 'feminization' of the public sphere and its lack of serious political engagement. These themes are taken up in Chapter 3, where the development of softcore television pornography is discussed in relation to the marginalization of women's tastes and pleasures, and in Chapter 4, which considers the melodramatic form taken by sex scandals. Meanwhile, the relationship between feminine tastes and cultures of consumption and the address to a 'quality' niche market of affluent women is explored in Chapter 8.

Biological essentialism and performative genders

Traditional conceptions of sexual difference view sex as a biological category dividing men from women on the basis of their chromosomal, anatomical or hormonal characteristics. This biological difference then determines their 'gender identity', and for the majority, their 'sexual orientation' towards the opposite sex. This binary model of the sexes is known as biological essentialism. Chapter 5, 'The Science of Sex', shows how television science programmes reinforce this model. In wildlife programmes, the same assumptions inform the 'sociobiological' discourses that interpret animal behaviour in human terms. The perspective of these high-status, masculine genres rarely acknowledges the feminist emphasis on the social construction of gender as a process that is determined by culture rather than the biological differences between the sexes.

Performative theories of gender, derived from Judith Butler's influential book *Gender Trouble* (1990), are a more extreme form of social constructionism in which fixed categories of biological sex are denied as the grounds for a politics of identity. Instead she argues that the binary division of the sexes is actually an *effect* of cultural discourses of gender rather than their material foundation. This binary, she argues, institutes and maintains heteronormative identities and the resulting hierarchy between men and women, heterosexuals and homosexuals. 'Speech act theory', on which her concept of performativity rests, is based on the way in which the codes of language and other forms of symbolic communication work by repetition to construct the very thing that they name. The 'codes of gender' are learned early and reinforced at every turn until they appear to be natural, but their reliance on 'reiteration' opens the possibility for change. Butler's 'queer' politics, therefore, is based on the transgression and destabilization of these culturally produced categories in order to undermine and refuse their disciplinary effects. Heteronormative practices are subject to deconstruction through drag, masquerade and signifying play. These practices break the normative link between biological sex, gender identity and sexual orientation by drawing attention to the production of gender and sexual identities in the reiteration of bodily gestures and discursive categories. The disruption of discursive regulation is therefore at the centre of Butler's theory and works against a politics founded on sexual identity, whether of women or gays and lesbians.

The growing visibility of 'queer' performances on television, not only on the margins but in advertising and mainstream music videos, comedy, drama and 'reality' television, raises questions about their relation to consumer capitalism. Rosemary Hennessy (1995) argues that the queer emphasis on identity as style and performance is entirely complicit with the aestheticization of everyday life that characterizes consumer culture. 'Lifestyle' becomes a way for the privileged to fashion their identities from commodities that mark their individuality. It is a malleable identity, 'open to more and more consumer choices, rather than shaped by moral codes or rules' (Hennessy 1995: 166). The metropolitan politics of 'queer' is discussed further in Chapter 7's analysis of the drama series *Buddha of Suburbia* and *Queer as Folk*.

This questioning of the foundations of identity politics and a renewed emphasis on 'style' and sexual display has also contributed to the reappraisal of feminism in the 1990s, in what has become characterized as a postfeminist era. For a new generation of women, second-wave feminists are often stereotypically imagined as men-hating, dungaree-clad dykes who didn't shave their legs and had puritanical attitudes to sexual pleasure. Rejection of this image is manifest in a transformed relation to the display of women's bodies, now reappropriated as an assertion of women's sexual power and autonomy and a self-conscious return to the feminine pleasures of body adornment and fashion. This new sensibility, in which femininity as glamour has been rehabilitated as a form of power, is discussed in Chapter 6 in relation to the way in which strippers have been represented in documentaries about the sex industry, and in Chapter 8 in relation to the global success of the comedy series *Sex and the City*. In both these cases, rather than women being seen as victims of male exploitation, their economic independence is presented as a means to reappropriate the objectified body as a source of pride and empowerment.

Summary

In summary, then, the questions that structure this book are focused on the concept of sexual citizenship. I consider the forms of address used by television and how they work to construct and thereby regulate sexual subjectivities. These forms are understood in relation to the discursive politics of a specific time and place as the industry moves into the digital era of multichannel, global distribution, oriented towards a diversity of consumer tastes. Detailed examples are used to identify continuity and change in the embedded conventions of genre and the implications these have for a politics of sexuality informed by the claims for cultural recognition made by the post-war identity movements. The conclusion points to emerging issues of sexual citizenship as television continues to adjust to new regulatory regimes.

2

SEXUAL CITIZENSHIP IN THE DIGITAL AGE

This chapter investigates the ways in which sexual discourse on television is regulated by state intervention and by the operations of the market. I am using 'regulation' here in the Foucauldian sense, which goes beyond the idea of regulation as 'explicit rules' to include the way in which all forms of discourse contribute to the 'regulation of subjectivity' through classification and legitimation (see Chapter 1). A comparison of the state-regulated public service ethos of the UK system with the largely commercial orientation of the US system allows for an assessment of the effects on sexual representation of an increasingly market-led system arising from the current transition to digital television as a global business.

In the first part of the chapter I compare the systems and criteria for regulating 'taste and decency' that arise from relatively long-term, embedded ways of thinking about sexual representations and practices, especially the influence of Puritan religious moralities and liberal political discourses on censorship (Bocock 1997). Subsequent sections consider the address to consumers and the effects this has had on the citizenship claims that have acted as legitimating discourses for television's public service role. Key themes I explore here are the changing relations between the public and the private in liberal democracies, the political challenge to liberalism from the new social movements in making new claims for sexual citizenship, and the rise of consumerism as the dominant ethos of postmodern capitalist cultures. The influence of these changes on programmes is taken up in detail in subsequent chapters. The purpose of this chapter is to explain the broader discursive context in which those programmes are made.

Television regulation in the UK and USA

Underpinning many of the regulatory practices in television are the conceptual boundaries that classify and define what is appropriate to the public and the private spheres. Indeed, television has contributed enormously to the changing boundaries and relations between the public and the private through its central role in the formation of public debate in a mass-mediated, global public sphere. Television is a medium that brings public events and debate into the private world of the home, and, conversely, makes public the private lives of citizens through their representation in a mass medium. Content censorship is designed to protect viewers from harm. The UK obscenity laws demand that nothing be shown that might 'corrupt or deprave'. It is children who are considered most vulnerable in this respect. The definition of 'obscenity' in the USA invokes 'community standards' that would judge the material as appealing to 'prurient interest (arousing lustful feelings)' in a 'patently offensive way'. Should the work have any redeeming literary, artistic, political or scientific value it is categorized as 'indecent' and can be broadcast only between the hours of 10.00 p.m. and 6.00 a.m. (Federal Communications Commission (FCC) Consumer and Government Affairs Bureau: www.fcc.gov/cgb/consumerfacts/obscene/html). These regulations are based on codes of decorum designed to minimize the danger of causing offence using criteria based on socially produced ideals of 'good taste' and 'decency'. They also depend on normative assumptions about the mode of address appropriate to the context of the family living room. Scheduling practices are also differentiated according to time of day, channel and genre in accordance with assumptions about who will be watching. They draw on a whole range of discourses – religious, pedagogic, medical, psychological, political and aesthetic – to determine whether sexual content might be immoral, harmful, tasteless or, conversely, justified by its political, educational or aesthetic value.

The regulation of sexual representation on UK and US television can be understood as an ongoing struggle between traditional religious moral discourses and liberalism. The Christian religion has been an important influence on established regulatory practices (Bocock 1997). The first director-general of the BBC was the strongly religious Lord Reith, who instituted a concept of public service broadcasting that has had a long-term effect on the regulatory framework for commercial as well as publicly funded television in the UK. In his view, television should be a force for social and moral improvement through education and information, as well as entertainment. This agenda was reinforced by the National Viewers and Listeners Association, which was influential during the 1970s and 1980s in promoting 'family values' and the sanctity of marriage in the face of what was perceived as a rising tide of sexual imagery on television and the media in general. Although the UK is an increasingly secular society, the residual effects of these moral codes are still present. The shame attached to sexual pleasure helps to explain a widespread dislike of watching sexually oriented television, especially when viewing in a family context. A question for the future is what effect the many religious faiths of immigrant populations may have on regulatory regimes designed to deliver 'diversity'.

The rise of 'neo-liberal' economics and its promotion of consumer values have joined these religious influences, with contradictory effects. For example, in the UK, the deregulatory aims of the Broadcasting Act of 1990 were tempered by the paternalistic, moralistic conservatism of the ruling Conservative Party. 'Free markets' were encouraged by competitive tendering for broadcasting franchises and the established broadcasters were subject to competition from independent producers, but they also had to pass a public-service-style 'quality' threshold and conform to all kinds of content restrictions on unfettered commercialism. Top-down regulation over content was strengthened in the areas of taste and decency by the formation of the Broadcasting Standards Commission (BSC), which formulated a 'Code on Sexual Conduct' that included strict rules against the portrayal of sexual coercion. This added to the existing framework of Producers' Guidelines overseen by the BBC Board of Governors and the Independent Television Commission's (ITC) Codes of Practice, such as its 'Code on Sex and Nudity'. However, the BSC's extensive audience research during the course of the 1990s had the effect of unearthing a complex array of opinion about what is considered acceptable sexual representation, and what people find pleasurable. This has contributed to the legitimation of a greater diversity in television's sexual address as a consequence.

By contrast, government interference in the mechanisms of free trade has long been regarded in the USA with hostility. It is linked in neo-liberal rhetoric with the protection of the right to free speech guaranteed by the First Amendment. The FCC consists of five people appointed by the Senate who deal with telecom as well as broadcasting regulation. Until 1991 interventions were allowed on the basis of the Fairness Doctrine, which required broadcasters to reflect different shades of opinion on controversial issues (Harvey 1998; Winston 2000: 109). For instance, in 1987 the producers of the crime drama series *Cagney and Lacey* were required to ensure that balance was achieved within an episode concerning abortion, always a controversial issue in the USA, and the focus of lobbying by the Christian 'Pro-Life' and feminist 'Right to Choose' campaigns (Shaw 1999: 88). But now the FCC has very limited powers in relation to content regulation, especially since the deregulatory impact of the Reagan administration in the 1980s (Shaw 1999: xii). However, an exception is anything that is deemed to be obscene or indecent. In the USA, Christian fundamentalism is still a major political influence and acts as counter-discourse to the *laissez-faire* ethics of liberalism and consumerism. At its most fundamentalist it denies the sexual agency or pleasure of women, regarding sex as something that they endure in order to bear children. Puritanism is suspicious of all sensual pleasures rooted in the body, seeing them as an evil distraction from the spiritual life located in the rational mind and the soul (Bocock 1997). Only where sexuality is framed within a pedagogic discourse designed to teach children and teenagers about the dangers of AIDS or the avoidance of teenage pregnancy, for example, is it above suspicion. The fear is that knowledge about sexuality will encourage children to 'experiment' with sex prematurely.

Unlike the British system, the US television industry is an almost entirely market-based, commercial enterprise (except for a very marginal and low-cost public broadcasting channel). For entertainment programmes on the networks (ABC, NBC, CBS, Fox, WBN) the standards and practices department for each company regulates output. It monitors each programme from its inception, basing its judgements on audience research, just as the advertisers do. The effect of this system of regulation is to make US network television far more restrictive in sexual content than the seemingly 'authoritarian' system of state control. The drive to make profits as the sole aim of the networks means that they cannot afford to alienate their audience or, more accurately, the advertisers on whom their profits depend. They are nervous of ratings being adversely affected by controversial content. Unlike the FCC or the ITC or BSC they make judgements about programmes before transmission (Shaw 1999: 51–2). Puritanism exerts a powerful restraint on sexual expression given the much higher proportion of religious believers in the USA compared to the UK and the powerful lobby they represent in support of 'family values'. This internal regulation is considered a matter of commercial judgement and is thus acceptable, and quite unlike the external imposition of regulations by the government (Shaw 1999: 85; Winston 2000: 110). Quite different market imperatives apply to the cable system, which are explored later in the chapter.

Each system of regulation is an outcome of deeply held beliefs about the processes of regulating culture. While the USA feels uneasy about restrictions imposed by state regulation, many people in the UK are worried by the unfettered power of markets to determine what we watch (Winston 2000: 11). However, despite differences in the philosophy and mechanisms of public service and commercial systems, they share the desire not to offend the audience. In both systems institutionalized conceptions of the audience have an important influence on how they are addressed by television. Equally, the expectations that viewers have of television exert a constraint on the choice of topics and the manner in which they are treated. Viewers want to know what to expect so that they can adapt their own behaviour accordingly. This relationship, based as it is on a set of institutionalized assumptions, operates as a key factor in the regulation of television production (Ang 1991, 1996). Avoiding offence can be regarded as a matter of decorum, of manners, the rules for which vary according to context. In deciding on an appropriate mode of address, then, broadcasters must take into account the time and the place of the encounter as well as the assumed characteristics of the imagined audience, with different national systems taking account of prevailing cultural attitudes within the boundaries of their jurisdiction.

As I have already emphasized, television's distribution into the home has had a strong influence on its modes of address. The protection of children from 'unsuitable influences' and their parents from embarrassment in the context of a private, but family, context of viewing has been a paramount concern, even though this kind of household is, increasingly, in the minority. In addressing a household the patterns of scheduling are built on assumptions about who will be watching at particular times of day and what mood they will be in (Gitlin 1994: 56–62; Ellis 2000: 130–47). The time of day, the day of the week, the season, all have an impact on what is deemed appropriate. In the UK, for instance, 9.00 p.m. is known as the watershed. Before that time it is assumed that children will be watching and this limits what sexual portrayal is allowed. For example, no simulated sexual intercourse can appear before that time. More controversial sexual portrayals are scheduled even later. For instance, adverts for gay chat lines are only allowed to appear after 11.00 p.m. and soft pornography channels are restricted to the hours between 10.00 p.m. and 6.00 a.m. These patterns of scheduling are supplemented by verbal warnings at the start of programmes to warn viewers to switch off if they might be offended.

Of course, this also has the effect of advertising sexual content to those people who might actively choose to watch. Research has shown that viewers dislike being surprised by sexual content, as it can make them feel embarrassed, especially if they are watching with other people (Millwood Hargrave 1992). In the USA a new ratings system that combined age and content advice on a sliding scale of intensity was instituted in 1997, at the behest of the FCC but in the control of the television companies. It was designed to work alongside the 'V-chip' technology installed in new sets to enable parents to block out reception of programmes rated as having unsuitable content for children (Gunter 2002: 272–5). These are ways to accommodate a greater diversity in audience address alongside the multiplication of channels and television sets and the time-shift possibilities of video, TiVo and DVD.

A key regulatory influence, in my view, is the ways in which diverse genres and channels, addressed to different segments of the audience, are structured by institutionalized distinctions in taste. The conventions of genre regulate the topics they deal with and the manner in which they are treated. These in turn are based on an assumed relation with an audience: genres addressed to high-status audiences are allowed to be more explicit and controversial (this is discussed in more depth in Chapter 3). The schedule is also divided across a grid of channels, each with its own distinctive 'brand identity' designed to establish expectations among viewers of the type of programmes it will offer and the manner in which they will be addressed. An advertising campaign for UKG2, for instance, a new digital channel based on recycled mainstream programming launched in 2003, shows how significant sexuality is to this branding. UKG2 explicitly distances itself from 'sleazy' sex with the slogan 'Not on our channel' stamped across the middle of a TV screen showing a woman with large breasts in skin-tight rubber flanked by two 'gay' men in skimpy outfits. A sexually explicit 'art film', on the other hand, that could be shown uncut on BBC2 would be cut for BBC1, according to the channel controller Alan Yentob (Shaw 1999: 53). The kind of people who watch BBC2, it is implied, have the cultural capital to appreciation 'art' and this legitimates the sex as culturally worthwhile. Subsequent chapters explore the ways in

Figure 1 Not on our channel. Advertisement for a new digital channel, UKG2 (in *Guardian TV Guide* November 2003).

which these distinctions in taste affect the forms of sexual representation across a range of channels and genres.

Taste cultures change over time, however, as moral attitudes and codes of social interaction change. The growing tolerance among the audience of a wider range of sexual identities on television was noted, for example, in a report published by the BSC in 1992, *Sex and Sexuality in Broadcasting*. It found that while homosexuality still caused the most offence to television viewers, there was a widening gap between younger people and the over 55s. The same trends are noticeable in the USA, where network programmes featuring gay men, such as *Will and Grace* (NBC 1998–) or *Queer Eye for a Straight Guy* (Bravo and NBC 2003–), have achieved popular success.

Concerns over sexually explicit images and language are still central to regulatory regimes but even this is subject to cultural change. A growing informality in language use has become the norm as deference to authority and religious taboos have diminished, although the impact of the new social movements, such as feminist campaigns against sexist language, has meant that new sensitivities and restrictions have emerged. How this plays out in practice requires negotiations between writers and producers over, for example, how many uses of the word 'fuck' can be tolerated in any half hour. While this previously 'obscene' word is now allowed on British television after 9.00 p.m., 'cunt' still lies on the other side of acceptability because of its sexism (Shaw 1999: 109–10). However, in 2004 when John Lydon called the voters 'fucking cunts' on the reality game show *I'm a Celebrity, Get Me Out of Here* and it went out live and therefore uncensored, only a handful of people complained. This led to a prolonged discussion in the press as to whether this indicated that it was now an acceptable word to use on television.

The biggest impact on the degree of explicitness now tolerated on television was the AIDS crisis in the mid-1980s. It made detailed discussion and advice about people's sexual behaviour, including the sexual practices of gay men, a necessary part of television's public service role to prevent the epidemic escalating. Condom advertising was allowed for the first time and advice on how to use condoms was included in the daytime and primetime schedules (Watney 1997). Even so, the display of an erect penis is still a taboo. Various substitute penis-shaped objects were used instead for these demonstrations. This and the ban on showing real rather than simulated penetrative sexual intercourse is still the key boundary marker between 'soft core' and 'hard core' sexual representation (see Chapter 3).

The sexual citizen

The role of television in bridging the public and the private spheres highlights questions of sexual citizenship. This concept overcomes the relegation of sexuality to a private sphere whose eruption into the public sphere is perceived as an aberration or a threat. It also draws attention to the legitimate 'public interest' in regulating sexual behaviour and representations – that people do have rights and responsibilities that, in my view, a *laissez-faire* market cannot guarantee. For instance, what cultural rights do minority sexual cultures have to be represented, to have a voice in the factual and fictional output of television? How much control should they have over precisely how they are represented in a culture where historically they have been subject to stigmatization? Can this lead to a stultifying 'political correctness'? How should television institutions negotiate their responsibilities to these groups in a context where large segments of the audience object strongly to seeing homosexual or other 'deviant' sexual practices portrayed in a positive light? And what right should people have to keep their sexual lives private when public exposure threatens their reputation and livelihood? Should privacy laws protect celebrity and ordinary citizens from the prying gaze of the television cameras or is this a threat to the democratic freedoms of the media to investigate corruption and criminal behaviour?

All these questions arise from an application of the concept of citizenship to a sphere of intimate behaviour that in historical terms was excluded from the public sphere of political debate. As citizens of modern nation states we have certain rights and obligations that in liberal democracies are meant to guarantee equality, justice and freedom. To defend the citizen from subjugation by a powerful state, an ideal model of a 'public sphere' has developed in which the actions of the state are subject to critical debate and reform (Habermas 1991). Television is an important component of this public sphere and, as a consequence, in both the USA and the UK is largely free from *direct* state control. But television companies, in the USA especially, are often part of much larger global media organizations whose power is feared to be a potential threat to the hard-won rights of citizenship. The power of the state is considered by many to be a necessary counter-balance and the source of protection for the public sphere through the financing and regulation of public service broadcasting (Curran 1996). This institutionalized middle-class paternalism has been the subject of much subsequent critical commentary but has remained surprisingly robust as a measure of 'quality' television (Brunsdon 1990; Mulgan 1990; Curren and Seaton 1997).

However, recognizing and valuing diversity challenges the hierarchy of values embedded in the established ideals of a 'rational' public sphere. The new social movements have criticized the way in which this concept has worked to promote the unequal power relations of patriarchy. This works in contradictory ways. First, the public/private boundary excludes certain sexual and emotional issues to a private realm of intimacy beyond the reach of 'rational' political debate. Then this public/private split is subject to a hierarchy in which the issues and people that are associated with the private sphere are regarded as less important than the issues and people associated with the public sphere. In the past, this has legitimized the denial of full citizenship rights for women and sexual minorities, thereby denying them equality in a democratic society. It has also worked against their having an equal access to the public sphere where these decisions are debated and so are denied justice. Conversely, there is concern over the ways in which the private lives of these powerless groups are exposed to public scrutiny in ways that the powerful can resist (Fraser 1995). The concept of 'sexual citizenship' counteracts the inequalities that this liberal conception of citizenship maintained. This denial of rights and these exclusions and invasions of privacy all have a bearing on the politics of television representation, as I hope this book will demonstrate.

In traditional formulations, citizenship is about our political rights as conventionally understood, while identity is about our personal sense of self. The identity politics of the new social movements has linked these two spheres of experience, to insist on the political significance of the personal sphere. Jim McGuigan explains the relevance this has to questions of cultural citizenship:

> citizenship is the key concept for connecting politics with a small 'p', the micro-politics of the self and social interaction, to politics with a large 'P', the official terrain upon which rights are, or are not, recognised in ways that frequently seem very remote from day to day existence yet, none the less, have determinate consequences for the lives of individuals and groups. The relationship between identity and citizenship, then, is at the heart of the matter whether we are talking about the cultural constructions of the self or the rights to cultural resources that contribute to the politics of changing material conditions. Cultural rights should also, however, and much less instrumentally, be about our sense of human dignity, or meaning, the pleasures and knowledges that make life tolerable.
>
> (McGuigan 1996: 147)

This approach to cultural citizenship also challenges the liberal conception of individual rights and instead bases political demands on collective identities – as women or gays or ethnic minority groups, for example.

The emergence of programmes addressed to gay and lesbian audiences on Channel 4 in the UK can be understood as the product of the changing political discourses instituted by the new social movements. Channel 4 was a hybrid institution in terms of the discursive practices that produced it, combining free market economics with left-wing cultural ideals. What emerged was a very different conception of public service broadcasting from the original Reithian ideal. Channel 4's public service remit was to cater for tastes and concerns not dealt with by mainstream channels, to have a suitable proportion of educational programmes, to encourage innovation and experimentation and to allow wider access to programme making for underrepresented groups. There was a conscious policy to commission from people who had never made programmes before. This helped to break the stranglehold of middle-aged, middle-class men who had entered the television industry in the big expansion years of the 1960s and enabled access by groups of gay and lesbian film makers who were determined to find new ways to represent their communities on television. Television's family address had limited the representation of homosexuality in particular. It was considered unsuitable for family viewing except in the occasional sitcom as an object of ridicule, or in a serious current affairs programme discussing changes in government legislation. Channel 4 enabled a shift in the democratic ideal of representation to one based on speaking 'from' a community instead of being spoken for. An early example was a documentary made in 1983 by a gay and lesbian youth group called *Framed Youth: Revenge of the Teenage Perverts*, shown on Channel 4 in 1986 in the *Eleventh Hour* slot, which showcased work made in the independent workshop sector.

Since their rise in the 1970s and 1980s, citizenship demands for equality and justice have themselves, in the 1990s, been subject to challenge from a resurgent **individualism** from a variety of directions, which has been linked by political theorists to the increasing power of global capitalism. One effect, it has been argued, has been to weaken the link between citizen rights and the state in a context where national cultures are fragmenting and the influence of transnational economic forces in the shape of global conglomerates is increasing. Attempts to rethink 'cosmopolitan citizenship' in global terms, based on internationally agreed 'human rights', are not yet anywhere near to being realized. At the same time, market fragmentation has diminished television's democratic role in national politics.

> The proliferation of channels, the fragmentation of audiences and the increased orientation towards fiction and entertainment in total output and viewer's diets have reduced the role of television in that part of the public sphere we attach to democratic functions, such as participation in public debate.
>
> (Siune and Hulten 1998: 31)

It is feared that the public sphere is lost as a place for compromise and consensus building as we split into multiple audiences pursuing our idiosyncratic desires. For example, John Caughie (2000) points to the way that in the UK the *Wednesday Play* in the 1960s and 1970s was a significant exploration of 'the permissive society' that spoke to the whole nation, whereas now, controversial 'quality' dramas are marginalized to subscription or minority channels or schedule slots to be seen by self-selecting audiences, thus reducing their political impact (see Chapter 7). Programming policies based on emancipatory demand for citizenship that brought, for example, the guarantee of an address to minority audiences on Channel 4 are vulnerable to destruction in the face of global competition, to be replaced by consumer versions of identity based on marketing categories. These trends are summarized in Table 2.1.

Table 2.1 Trends in media structure

	Old Media Structure	New Media Structure
Broadcasting	Monopoly	Competition
Goals	Democracy	Survival, success, profit
Means	Programme production, selection of material	Selection of material, programme mix
Logic	Responsibility	Market, economic
Criteria for selection	Political relevance	Sale
Reference group	Citizens	Consumers
Focus on	Decisions taken, power structures	Processes of policy-making, new conflict dimension
Perspective	Nation, system	Individual and global

Source: Siune and Hulten (1998: 36).

The sexual consumer

The structure of the industry in Europe is changing in order to maximize competitive economic pressures and to reduce state regulation of content. At the same time, ratings and market research have become the legitimizing technologies through which to evaluate the 'quality' of programming, just as they have been in the USA from the start. If public ownership is a diminishing component in the face of the expansion of wholly privatized, commercial services, will the fears expressed by the defenders of public service broadcasting be realized? What impact will these trends have on television's contribution to sexual citizenship? Will the increasing emphasis on pleasurable entertainment undermine or enhance the democratic functions of television as a public sphere? The wider debates over the purposes of television as a public service and global business, which I introduced in Chapter 1, include those who see increasing sexualization as a dubious outcome of companies seeking to make profits from titillating entertainment, and a threat to the public service remit to inform and educate (Herman and McChesney 1997; Winston 2000). On the other side are those who see it as a vindication of the democracy of the market, in its ability to overcome paternalistic controls in the service of popular tastes and pleasures to produce a 'democracy of desire' (Hartley 1999; McNair 2002). A less polarized understanding emerges, in my view, with a more careful look at the regulatory effects that each of these systems produces.

Debates over the relative advantages of each system have intensified in the run up to planned regulatory changes for a converged digital media environment and in the context of European initiatives to harmonize the regulatory structures of the member states (Harvey 1998; McQuail and Siune 1998; Steemers 1999; Jones 2001). Free trade agreements designed to promote a global television market overseen by the World Trade Organization and by European legislation on transfrontier television (in 1989 and 1997) are potentially in conflict with the protection of public service broadcasting. Regulation in this context is moving from being based on the social functions of the media towards addressing technical and economic policy issues (Ostergaard 1998: 93). Technical convergence, although in practice this has been slower to emerge than was predicted (Kelly 2003), means that media-specific content regulation becomes problematic. Where the same content may be delivered via a computer or a television set, the distinction in regulation between the Internet and broadcasting becomes harder to sustain. This is certainly true of OfCom, the new regulatory body in the UK from the end of 2003, which covers all of the digital media. This was conceived as a 'light touch' regulator whose primary concern is with facilitating the British industry's place in the global market by adapting the rules on foreign and cross-media ownership. It has been designed 'as a framework for a period of free market consolidation, with an emphasis on commercial robustness rather than cultural protectionism' (Bell 2003). The government claims, however, that it will 'ensure access to a choice of diverse services of the highest quality and that the interests of citizens and consumers are safeguarded' (Hewett and Jowell 2002).

It is important, I think, to understand that the development of digital means of distribution and the fragmentation of the market as channels proliferate are not simply the product of technological advances. There is a deliberate attempt to adapt television to the emergent conditions of postmodern culture in order to make more profits. That is to say, digital media are a means to develop new markets in conditions of rising affluence in a consumer society. The abundance of television channels made possible by digital technology has been legitimized through rhetoric of choice in which the mass audience is reconceived as an aggregate of selective individual consumers.

> In postmodern culture the discourse of choice has expanded exponentially – it is a discourse in which the rhetoric of the liberatory benefits of personal autonomy and individual self-determination has become hegemonic. No longer tied to 'tradition' or the restrictions of class, gender or race, subjects in the postmodern world are now impelled to constantly reconstruct and reinvent themselves; in pursuit of happiness, life is defined as the ability to make an ever-increasing number of choices. The concept of 'lifestyle' articulates this particular post-modern predicament. Lifestyles are the fluid and changeable popular aesthetic formations of identity produced through self-reflexive consumption and disembedded from stable social networks.
>
> (Ang 1996: 13)

A central question for this book is whether the digital era has allowed television to contribute to this process of self-realization through consumption as a result of its increasing diversity. In his book *Seeing Things: Television in an Age of Uncertainty*, John Ellis (2000: 63) argues that 'Commodity production is increasingly aimed at providing people with the means of establishing their distinctiveness from each other rather than their communality with each other.' Its role is no longer to provide a definitive way of understanding the world, in Ellis's view, but to provide a range of materials for audiences to work through in the process of reaching an understanding for themselves (*ibid*.: 78–81). In so doing it both contributes to 'the divisions that come with differences' (*ibid*.: 72) and it works to ameliorate them by offering us programmes that act as a 'witness' to life-worlds for which we are only ever spectators. 'This process never comes to a definitive conclusion because none are available' (*ibid*.: 85). In this context, Ellis argues, public service broadcasting is redefined as providing a space to explore diversity, replacing older agendas of social improvement or rituals of national unity as in the Reithian ideal. Nor is it implicated in the ideological processes of defining the typical and marginalizing minorities, as it was criticized for doing by the new social movements (*ibid*.: 87). In Ellis's view, the fragmenting effects of this diversity are compensated for by television's potential to be a cohesive force, creating better understanding between different social groups. If this is, indeed, the case then it could be a positive influence in gaining legitimacy for previously marginalized sexualities.

This faith in the commercial media to deliver a form of democratic pluralism is subject to challenge from **Marxist** writers who are sceptical of the equation between media 'visibility' and political emancipation. As Ellis (2000: 66) acknowledges, market-ing is 'interested in social movements only to the extent that they will influence consumer choices and create new market opportunities'. In Rosemary Hennessy's (1995) view the emancipatory effect of sexual consumerism is illusory because it is disconnected from the social movements that were essential to the political success of the sexual liberation movements of the 1960s and 1970s. In 'lifestyle' politics sexual liberation has become a 'style' or 'performance' rather than a set of political demands for sexual equality and citizenship rights. Emphasis on the politics of representation has allowed social and economic issues to be marginalized. However, as David Bell and Jon Binnie (2000) point out, this sets up a false dichotomy between social and cultural citizenship. Citizenship includes the right to representation as a form of 'recognition'. These representations can also contribute to the efficacy of campaigns for rights claims in the social, political and economic spheres, although it will always require other forms of political organization beyond the media sphere, as the campaigns for legal reform for gays and lesbians exemplify.

The more convincing aspect of Hennessy's critique derives from Theodor Adorno's analysis of 'the culture industry', which highlights the gap between the market's rhetoric of choice and diversity and the countervailing pressures towards ideological conformity and homogeneity in a market system. The main point of his argument is that the cultural industry pretends to be answering people's needs and therefore people welcome rather than resist it, whereas in fact it functions in the interests of the owners, not the consumers. It is dedicated to making profits above all else, and to ideological support for the capitalist system of which it is a part. The public is made to fit into predetermined categories devised by marketeers; market differentiation is just a tech-nique to make sure no one escapes from consuming products. Whatever the superficial differences between these products, capitalist ideology is the unifying content. For-mulaic genres offer consumers 'recognition' of their everyday lives, merely reproducing life as it is or appears to be on the surface, rather than exposing the real suffering that 'truth-telling' involves. This requires, in Adorno's view, the forging of new shapes out of conventional forms, the true individuation of 'style', instead of conformity to a pre-existing genre that produces a unified culture obedient to the social hierarchy of the status quo. Nor does it offer the satisfactions it promises: its pleasures are those of distraction from the sufferings produced by an exploitative society. Real satisfaction would require the 'austere delights' of truth-telling that could bring about social and political change (Adorno 1993).

From a contemporary perspective Adorno's analysis operates at too general a level of analysis to be directly applicable. He was writing in a different historical era, the 1940s, when the mass production of culture was less differentiated. There isn't a singular 'cultural industry' nowadays, indeed there never was, but multiple cultural industries that operate according to quite different economic, technological and political logics and in response to varying historical circumstances (McGuigan 1996: 74–94). To assess the impact of current changes in the television industries on their ability to deliver ideological diversity requires looking at the characteristics of television markets in relation to historically specific cultural and political conditions. But I think that Adorno's perspective is valuable in prompting us to think beyond the democratic rhetoric of market consumerism to examine its ideological functions in a class-divided, capitalist economy. It invites attention to the impact of industrialized production on the forms of culture. What kind of commodity is a television programme and how does this limit and enable particular kinds of meanings and audience pleasures? It also raises the question of what we mean by 'pleasure' and whether some forms of pleasure are more 'emancipatory' than others. Are the forms of pleasure that are proliferating in consumer culture a realization of the 'good life' sought by the various new social movements in their campaigns on media representation? And even if they are, at whose expense are these pleasures enjoyed? In consumer utopias which social groups remain excluded?

I examine these questions in detail in subsequent chapters, in relation to specific programmes and genres. This next section provides a more general analysis of how the discursive practices of television are shaped by the rhetoric of the market.

Market regulation

Their ability and willingness to buy the goods on offer in a market define viewers as consumers rather than citizens. This allows us to conceive of the market itself as a form of regulation, in the Foucauldian sense, as companies adapt their production output in response to the values and tastes of its potential viewers in order to make profits. This approach counteracts the assumption that the so-called 'free market' offers freedom from control. The processes of commodification and the characteristics of capitalist markets are an important determinant of consumers' access to television (Garnham 1990, 2000). Television companies want to identify and measure the preferences of a 'consuming' viewer who can deliver profits for the advertisers who fund commercial television. This marketing data is gathered by specialist companies, **Nielsen** in the USA and **BARB** in the UK, that sell the information to the television companies. The schedules are subject to the ratings information gathered and the ability of the company to make money. The influence of ratings has increased as competitive pressures have intensified as the number of channels increases (Bell 2003).

As an example of a Foucauldian technology of regulation the ratings system is exemplary, in that it produces power/knowledge through surveillance and categorization. The system of gathering this information affects what knowledge about the audience is produced. The sample is designed to provide commercially useful information, rather than being an 'objective' measure of who is watching. As John Hartley (2002: 61) comments, 'The industry relies on an agreed construction of the viewer, not a true one. But this figment of the imagination is worth billions.' When the system of data collection changes, as it has recently to accommodate the need to count the audiences for a greatly expanded number of channels, the statistics also change dramatically. In order to 'count' as a commodity audience viewers have to be measurable so that they can be profitable (Meehan 1990). This shows the degree to which audience segments are produced rather than described through these technologies, such as 'Housewife with children', 'ABC1 men', '16–34 youths'. The degree to which these constructs match the real viewers watching these programmes, or the adverts in between, cannot be known, although the 'truth' value of what is counted is rarely questioned (Ang 1991). What we *can* study is how these constructs are used to regulate the schedules and how they classify and normalize particular groups of viewers.

Not all viewers have an equal power to influence these decisions because they are only as influential as their buying power. Only those who can afford to pay for subscription services or are rich enough, despite their few numbers, to be attractive to advertisers will influence the provision of minority television. 'Women', for example, became commercially interesting as a commodity audience when they moved into professional jobs during the 1970s and became attractive as 'upscale' consumers. Research by Eileen Meehan (2001: 113–14) indicates that previously advertisers had been primarily concerned to attract men in the 18–34 age bracket in the evening prime time, where most of the advertising spend is concentrated. However, by the end of the 1970s new genres of programming were being developed on the main networks to appeal to this market that had a greater focus on women's lives and interests. By the mid-1980s cable TV included a channel for women called Lifetime. 'Lifetime built its schedule to attract housewives from morning to early afternoon, to attract the household as it reassembled, and finally to target heterosexual couples during prime time via programming that was both "male and female friendly"' (Meehan 2001: 115). But in both these cases, Meehan points out, women are still imagined in relation to their role as members of a family unit or one of a couple, not as individuals. It is only during the day when men are assumed to be absent that they constitute a target group. In contrast, sports channels such as ESPN are more single-minded in their address to male audiences.

Generalizations about men's and women's preferences are in themselves a construction that masks differences *within* these groupings. In this way categories of measurement and analysis normalize and stereotype the complex viewing behaviour of actual viewers, who remain essentially unknowable (Ang 1991). Their importance, though, and why this is of interest here, is the way in which these constructions influence what television producers include in their programmes and how they are scheduled. For example, when it comes to sexual content explicit sexual discussions on talk shows are considered to be of interest to women and are scheduled in daytime slots. Explicit visual images on cable porn channels, on the other hand, are assumed to be addressed to men, or in some cases heterosexual couples, and are restricted in access. For example, slogans advertising Playboy Channel in the UK during 2002 ('£5 can now keep you up all night' or 'Forget thinking about it every 30 seconds. Try a whole hour') address a male consumer despite reports that *Playboy* has widened its target audience to include the couples market (Juffer 1998). These two examples draw attention to the way that sexual content is not only addressed to different categories of viewers but is also assumed to have different purposes. Talk shows and porn assume a very different kind of engagement by the viewer; it is one of the distinctions that separate them as genres.

The homogenizing effects of the market on the television schedules are a matter of debate. Compaine and Gomery's (2000) assessment, based on extensive empirical evidence, accentuates the diversity of the schedules. The tradition of aiming at the whole population with each and every programme is gone. Nor will the limitless potential of proliferating outlets, they argue, destroy quality.

> If the proliferation of television, books and web sites reveals anything, it is that greater diversity means just that: more low brow shows, trash journalism, pandering politics to go along with opportunities for finding more thoughtful and quality outlets for analysis, entertainment and information. Diversity cuts all ways.
>
> (Compaine and Gomery 2000: 578)

Against this view is the evidence from the US free market system, until now, that the pursuit of profit has meant the networks catering to mainstream tastes and ideologies where the maximum demand is found for their products, thus excluding radical or unpopular views (Curran 1996; Jones 2001). 'Progressive' ideologies are pushed to the margins in elite forms of culture, such as 'quality' drama, which are instead offered by commercial subscription television on digital channels such as HBO.

Certainly for those who can pay, in the digital era choice will be assured, but widening extremes of poverty and riches in a neo-liberal political context mean there is a sizeable proportion of the potential audience who will not be able to afford these services. The individualized model of the television consumer depends on households having the disposable income to pay the subscriptions to their digital provider, whether this is cable or satellite. It costs the same to make a programme for ten million viewers as for ten thousand. Niche markets therefore have to be financed by expensive subscriptions or by charging advertisers higher rates. A two-tier market develops, the mass and the marginal, but only well-off consumers will have access to both of them (Garnham 1990: 160–163). It also creates a continuing incentive to find cheaper forms of television, especially if they can also find a large audience. This affects the kind of 'quality' that depends on resources, such as the amount of time spent on researching a programme to make sure it is fair and offers a diversity of viewpoints. 'Infotainment' (talk shows, reality shows) is designed to save money as well as attract new audiences. These economic pressures fuel fears of 'tabloidization' and a decline in television's contribution to an informed political democracy (see discussion in Chapters 4 and 6).

Ideological conformity is promoted by the pressure from sponsors and advertisers for a programming environment that does not undermine the message of their adverts, namely consumption. James Curran and Jean Seaton (1997), echoing Adorno, argue that this means 'feel-good' light entertainment rather than documentaries investigating the dark side of capitalism such as poverty or pollution that might make consumers feel guilty. Low-level anxiety, on the other hand, can work to promote consumption. In postfeminist drama, for example, anxiety about the difficulty of finding a man to marry delivers women to the beauty product advertisements. Similar arguments have been offered to explain the ubiquity of tabloid-style reality television, with its sensationalized diet of disasters and crime that offers simplistic solutions to complex social and political problems. Anxiety is provoked in order to be assuaged through the reassuring structures of the commodity form (Mellencamp 1992; Langer 1998; Dovey 2000).

But the system is far from monolithic. The contradictory nature of television and its multiple possible uses makes ideological analysis a complex affair. Ideological diversity is enabled through the difference between the **exchange value** of a programme for its producers and distributors and its **use value** for audiences. In order for a programme to be popular it may well need to offer meanings and pleasure that are contrary to the long-term interests of capitalism. The incentive for individual companies to make short-term profits outweighs the long-term incentive of the survival of the system as a whole (Frith 1996). This allows for the expression of controversial or potentially subversive ideas if they can sell products. The unpredictability of success that is a feature of cultural production also means that companies have to innovate in the hope of striking lucky. Although successes are then copied and a new standardized format is established, as the case of 'reality television' demonstrates, this works against the incentive always to play safe despite the pressure on television executives to deliver predictable audiences that can be sold to advertisers or sponsors in advance.

Hybridization of genre formats is one consequence of these contradictory pressures. It allows innovation at the same time as retaining familiarity and predictability. Only rarely does an entirely new genre of television emerge that in the process constitutes a new 'public' to whom it is addressed (Lara 1998). These hybridized genres continue to embody conventions from a previous era, acting as a form of cultural inertia. This is very significant for the sexual politics of television, given the marginal position that women and sexual minorities have occupied in its institutionalized genres. The cultural authority of heterosexual, middle-class masculinity has held an assured place long after it was subject to political challenges in the wider social sphere. Nevertheless, genres *do* undergo incremental changes to adapt to changing social and cultural circumstances to stay plausible and relevant. Feminist interventions into television have consciously sought ways to adapt mainstream genres to carry new, more emancipated meanings, for example. But this is uneven in its effects, with some of the more high-status genres remaining relatively unaffected. The potential for women's pleasure in popular entertainment is, however, being given the weight that their central role in consumption dictates now that the politics of the living room during prime time isn't assumed to result in deference to men's viewing preferences (Gauntlett and Hill 1999).

Although the ubiquitous hybridization of factual and fictional genres with the melodramatic conventions of the soap opera is indicative of television adapting to a more *feminized* aesthetic, and therefore its responsiveness to a previously marginalized group, this cannot be assumed to be synonymous with a *feminist* cultural politics. Indeed, this conundrum is at the heart of some of the more intractable questions about taste and cultural value in feminist cultural studies. A similar lack of fit troubles the public sphere debates, where concern to protect the spaces for democratic debate often runs counter to the trajectory of popular pleasures. The decline in the cultural authority of an elite is one of the effects of the hegemonic discourses of the market. These debates are taken up in subsequent chapters as questions about diversity and emancipation are explored in relation to the changing forms of sexual representation in a global consumer market.

Recommended reading

Ang, I. (1996) *Living Room Wars: Rethinking Media Audiences for a Postmodern World*. London and New York: Routledge.

Bell, D. and Binnie, J. (2000) *The Sexual Citizen*. Cambridge: Polity Press.

Bocock, R. (1997) Choice and regulation; sexual moralities, in K. Thompson (ed.) *Media and Cultural Regulation*. London: Sage and Open University.

McGuigan, J. (1996) *Culture and the Public Sphere*. London and New York: Routledge.

Stevenson, N. (2003) *Cultural Citizenship: Cosmopolitan Questions*. Maidenhead: Open University Press.

3 | PORNOGRAPHY AND THE REGULATION OF TASTE

Pornography is central to the regulation of all forms of sexual representation on television because it is their distinction from pornography, as it has been historically defined, that legitimizes the circulation and consumption of erotic texts in the mainstream media. In this way pornography acts as a boundary marker arising from its cultural status as an illicit genre defined though legal prohibitions and restrictions. As a consequence, on television it remains entirely marginal. The marketing of 'adult' cable channels, a term that marks the concern to protect children from exposure, is excluded from mainstream listing magazines and access is controlled by subscription and encryption. These channels are also marginal to the study of television, as is indicated by the overview provided in *The Television Genre Book*, which doesn't mention them at all (Creeber 2001c). Nevertheless, television, alongside video and the Internet, has allowed for the wider distribution of visual pornography and expanded the range of consumers to whom it is addressed, which now, crucially, includes women. This availability is approached here in relation to changing cultures of taste in post-war consumer culture rather than in relation to the anti-porn/anti-censorship debates that have, until recently, dominated discussions on this genre. Through a discussion of four studies that have taken this approach (Juffer 1998; Jankovich 2001; Kertz 2002; McNair 2002), I provide the groundwork for this book's analysis of the discourses of taste that differentiate and legitimate all forms of sexual discourse on television.

First, I want to establish the emergence of pornography as a genre of sexually explicit discourse that was defined through restrictions limiting its circulation. This was premised on the following:

- The differentiation between pornography and legitimate art and literature on the one hand or science and education on the other.

- The assumption that adult men are the primary consumers of pornography, and that women and children should be protected from unwanted exposure.
- Fears that its sexually arousing effects will have harmful consequences. Puritans frame this as moral corruption, whereas anti-porn feminists are concerned that it objectifies and devalues women.

This means that pornography as a genre has developed as a form of 'low' culture for men that lacks cultural legitimacy and is hedged by legal restrictions. This marginal and stigmatized status has meant that on television its circulation has been restricted to late night and subscription cable channels. The more widespread incursion of sexually arousing imagery into mainstream programming has depended on the development of hybridized documentary formats and 'quality' drama series that are legitimized through their educational and aesthetic value. Transformations in genres and their positioning in a hierarchy of taste cultures differentiated by class and gender can therefore be seen as central to the circulation and legitimation of erotic texts for new groups of consumers. This chapter looks in particular at the hybrid 'infotainment' formats that combine documentary with pornographic conventions in an appeal to a new generation of less puritan consumers as well as at new forms of soft core pornography addressed to women.

One of the features of bourgeois (upper-class) taste, in Bourdieu's (1984) analysis, is the belief that art is detached from everyday life, and doesn't have any utilitarian purpose. Bourdieu refers to it as the 'aesthetic disposition'. One objection to pornography then becomes its singular intention to produce sexual arousal. If this effect is offset by other aesthetic 'intentions' that put it in the category of 'art', the same degree of sexual explicitness becomes legitimate, such as the tradition of painting 'nudes' that are on open display in bourgeois homes and in art galleries (Ross 1993). Linda Williams (1990) points to the emergence of pornography as a genre category in the nineteenth century as a consequence of the development of the mass media:

> pornography as we know it emerges at that moment when the diffusion of new kinds of mass media – novels and magazines in the Victorian era, films and videos today – exacerbates a dominant group's worry about the availability of these media to persons less responsible than themselves.
>
> (Williams 1990: 12)

A second problem, then, is the concern that pornography will have a bad effect on 'the masses' who have not developed this aesthetic disposition in relation to erotic imagery; that they will in fact be corrupted into lascivious thoughts and deeds without the protection of this intellectual distancing.

The first piece of anti-obscenity legislation in the UK was the British Obscene Publications Act, in 1857, which defined pornography as material that is likely to corrupt and deprave. That is, it was defined not by any specific textual characteristics but by its presumed effects. In the nineteenth century any type of explicit sexual writing could be liable to censorship. It is through recurring obscenity trials in the twentieth century, most famously the *Lady Chatterley's Lover* trial in 1960, that pornography has progressively been distinguished from anything that could be seen as having any artistic value (Ross 1993). A similar set of legal distinctions developed in the USA, with legislation in 1957 allowing for the circulation of sexual materials that had 'redeeming social importance' (Williams 1990: 96–8) (see Chapters 7 and 8 for how this affects sexual portrayal in television drama).

Another feature of bourgeois culture is the high status of science as a privileged domain of knowledge. In the late nineteenth and early twentieth centuries sexology came to operate as a new 'regime of truth'. While in polite bourgeois society it wasn't respectable to speak about sex, especially in front of women and children, it became something that could be legitimately talked and written about within this scientific framework (Foucault 1990). Thus scientists were able to define the framework for thinking about sexual behaviour, based around classificatory notions of the normal and abnormal, as well as having the power to define what is true and what is false. Because sex had become so hidden in everyday life, in contrast to the pre-modern period (Elias 1994), it became a secret that had to be discovered through techniques of observation, confession, investigation, classification and labelling. Through these tech-nologies of the self that emerged in the new social and medical sciences of sociology, psychiatry and sexology we would gain an insight into who we truly were. Freudian psychoanalysis emerged from this context at the turn of the twentieth century, as did Kinsey, an influential sexologist in the post-war period, who sought to discover an objectively determined body of fact about sex to counteract the 'myths' of popularly held beliefs (Kinsey *et al.* 1948; Kinsey 1953). So it is that, nowadays, in contrast to the prosecution of Annie Besant for obscenity in 1877 for publishing a pamphlet on contraception, any sexually explicit discourse that has a legitimate scientific or educational purpose backed up by 'expert' knowledge is exempt from being defined as 'pornography'. This has had an important influence on the kind of pedagogic address adopted in many of the television documentaries that engage directly with sexual issues (see Chapters 5 and 6).

The disciplinary effects of these legal distinctions between legitimate and illegitimate sexual discourse are realized through 'subjectification'; that is to say, the ways in which people internalize the normative values these distinctions embody. It is a form of self-disciplining in which people adjust their own reactions to sexually explicit imagery in ways that conform to pre-existing cultural distinctions (Juffer 1998: 39). In this way social regulation becomes naturalized as individual 'taste' through what Foucault has called a 'technique of the self'. The bodily effects of disgust and embarrassment that people can experience as a reaction to the arousing effects of sexually explicit imagery and talk are the result of this process. This bodily 'disposition' (Bourdieu 1984) appears to be a 'natural' reaction beyond conscious control, thereby reproducing the socially constructed boundaries between legitimate and illegitimate forms of sexual representation without any conscious awareness of its cultural production. Numerous techniques are used by television producers to establish the cultural worth of programmes that include explicit sexual imagery to help viewers to avoid being disturbed in this way (these are elaborated in subsequent chapters).

Postmodern pornography

It has been argued that these distinctions in taste between high and low culture are no longer relevant as a result of the democratizing effects of the mass media. Brian McNair, for example, in his book *Striptease Culture: Sex, Media and the Democratisation of Desire* (2002), has argued that in postmodern consumer culture the distinctions in taste that structured modern societies no longer operate, thereby drawing pornography into the mainstream, including on to television. This proliferation of explicit sexual discourse fuels political fears that television as a rational public sphere is being debased by 'tabloidization'; that is, the replacement of public service values by commercial profit seeking and the pandering to 'low' sensationalism. McNair, on the contrary, regards these fears as a symptom of the patriarchal authoritarianism that regulated the Anglo-American media in the twentieth century and constrained sexual expression. The power to determine what people can consume is being swept away by the democratizing effects of capitalist markets in which progressive sexual representations are contributing to a more liberated, democratic future. Instead of legitimizing the tastes of the powerful, the market caters for a diversified range of consumers. Crucially, this now includes women as potential consumers of sexually explicit texts, whereas in the past they had been restricted to men.

One of the effects of the blurred boundaries between high and low culture in postmodern culture, McNair argues, is that it allows the margins to exert an influence on the mainstream, with pornography being a particular case in point. 'Pornochic' is the term he uses to describe the effects of this process:

> Pornochic is the representation of porn in non-pornographic art and culture; the pastiche and parody of, the homage to and investigation of porn; the postmodern transformation of porn into mainstream cultural artefacts for a variety of purposes including, as we shall see, advertising, art, comedy and education.
>
> (McNair 2002: 61)

The iconography of pornography thus becomes stylish as it is taken up in fashion and advertising. No longer embarrassing, this 'trash' culture is incorporated into postmodern irony and camp innuendo. McNair also identifies the way in which the proliferation and control of pornography has become a topic for serious discussion in the public sphere of print journalism and factual television. Matter-of-fact explication and academic intellectualism have, he argues, replaced moralistic condemnation as the dominant mode of discourse in these debates. Pornography, he deduces, has lost its low-class social stigma and people now can admit to enjoying it without shame (*ibid.*: 84–6).

There is some truth in this argument, which rightly draws attention to the wider availability of pornography in consumer culture, and the way in which its iconography has been more widely disseminated and its social significance more openly debated. But McNair also oversimplifies the situation. The examples he uses are decontextualized, drawn from across all media forms with scarcely any consideration of their distinctive institutional histories and the regulatory contexts that shape their production and consumption. Pornography as a genre is certainly not universally regarded as 'chic' even if its iconography has been more widely used in this way. It is only through constructing a very selective account that his optimistic progressivism can be justified. There may be more diversity, but moralistic and patriarchal discourses still abound in the discourses of taste that regulate television production and consumption in both commercial and public service contexts. The continuing low cultural status of pornography can be seen, for example, in the history of the first five years of Channel 5, the most recent of the UK's terrestrial networks.

Dawn Airey, the controller of Channel 5 in the first period following its launch in 1997, audaciously declared that her schedule was organized around 'films, fucking and football' or 'beer, balls and bosoms'. The channel quickly became notorious for including late night, low-budget 'erotic dramas' in the schedules. These were typically evaluated in the *Guardian* (a left-wing 'quality' broadsheet) in aesthetic terms as dull, pathetic, sad and unconvincing, and condemned by the *Daily Mail* (a mid-market, traditional paper with a large female readership) in moral terms as 'filth'. But Airey consciously refused to be cowed by the adverse critical commentary and talked the channel up as less straight-laced than other channels, ready to have a bit of fun with sex. Apart from the late night erotic dramas there were also numerous documentaries about the sex industry. These were epitomized by the *Sex and Shopping* series, which 'investigated' the sex industry with programmes on lap dancers, porn, stripping and prostitution in which lingering camera shots of naked female flesh were a key feature (this series is discussed in some detail later in the chapter). It provoked many complaints to the BSC, whose condemnations of the channel's output worked to publicize the channel 'brand' and differentiate it from the existing terrestrials.

This strategy changed, however, when after five years Channel 5 announced a repositioning of its brand. 'The 'football, films and fucking' image could only go so far – a 5 per cent share to be precise. The audience profile was also skewed more heavily than the other minority channels towards the lower end of the economic spectrum, making it unattractive to niche advertisers. In 2002, a new channel controller decided to shed that image, and establish Channel 5 as a serious competitor to BBC2 and Channel 4. To do that it needed 'respectable shows that don't scare anyone away' (Wells 2002). By 2003 a headline in the *Guardian* announced 'Channel Five programming stripped bare of pornography', reporting that the channel had decided to scrap the remaining 'erotic drama' output directed at a post-pub male audience on Friday nights. It had already reduced the number of 'sleazy factual programmes about strippers and alternative sexual practices' in a move to rebrand 'Five' by bringing 'arts documentaries' and 'classic US dramas' into peak time slots. The channel was finding it difficult to shed its 'tacky' image while any of these shows remained, and this prevented it being taken seriously as a mainstream terrestrial broadcaster (Wells 2003b).

This rebranding exercise was timed to be effective before new regulatory rules brought in by the Communications Act (2003) allowed Five to be acquired by a foreign company. The same process has been noted in the trajectory of the US cable channel Showtime, whose logo 'No Limits' was closely tied to the promise of soft porn as a well-publicized component of its schedules, signposted as *The Erotic Zone*. Now part of Viacom, a huge media conglomerate that includes CBS and MTV, it has dropped this publicity and moved instead to promote its showing of sexually controversial 'quality' drama, such as the US version of *Queer as Folk* and the adaptation of Armistead Maupin's *Tales of the City* or films such as Adrian Lyne's *Lolita* (Backstein 2001). We can see, therefore, that it isn't just public service authoritarianism that sustains the distinctions that keep pornography marginal. It indicates that a 'quality' brand, based on well-established aesthetic and moral distinctions, might be considered more valuable than a 'tacky' one on the international market. Local, low budget 'access' channels in the USA are at the other end of the media hierarchy and this is where pornography thrives most freely (Backstein 2001).

The second objection I have to McNair's argument is that, although it is true that popular genres are open to transformation and influence from the vanguard margins, their established conventions don't simply disappear. They act as a residue of past social and aesthetic norms, which are relatively resistant to change. This is especially true of pornography. The exclusive address to men in the formation of the genre, with its iconography of old-fashioned underwear, for example, seems to persist as if nothing has changed, either in fashion or in the relations between the sexes, since Victorian times. The use of this as generic iconography is demonstrated in the cultural references evoked in 'pornochic'. This generic 'time-lag' also contributes to the difficulty in finding an erotic vocabulary for pornography addressed to women, an issue that is taken up in later sections in the chapter. The development of 'infotainment' in which pornographic imagery is hybridized with a range of documentary forms does encourage border crossings between the respectable and the disreputable, the legitimate and the illicit. But this hybridization is produced by the continuing lack of legitimacy of pornography on television. The traffic is between respectable mainstream television at the centre and a highly constrained and conventional soft core pornography on the margins, rather than a more obviously transgressive hard core. However, as *Sex and Shopping* makes evident, television does also function as a kind of marketing outlet for hard core through documentary investigation of the pornography industry that promotes consumer awareness.

A third problem with McNair's free-floating textual examples is that they don't take into account the way in which genre as a system legitimizes certain 'uses' and 'pleasures' for an imagined community of taste (Altman 1999). He makes the mistake of treating the 'people' as an undifferentiated 'mass' with equal access to pornographic texts once they are available in the media. In fact, very fine distinctions in taste separate what is deemed appropriate sexual discourse for particular social groups across the multiple channels and specific spaces of the schedules. Mark Jankovich (2001: 5), in contrast, characterizes the mainstream as a 'construct that is continually defined and redefined through the struggles for distinction between different social groups'. He draws on Bourdieu's analysis of the distinctions in taste that characterize the 'new petit bourgeoise' to explain the emergence of a 'middle-brow' form of pornography in the post-war period, exemplified by *Playboy* magazine. This analysis can help to locate more precisely the different kinds of pornography on television in relation to historically formed taste cultures and to see how class-based distinctions legitimize television's sexually explicit genres.

'Middle-brow' pornography

Mark Jankovich (2001) locates the emergence of *Playboy* in the 1950s in relation to a middle-brow culture of a new post-war **petit bourgeoisie**, which is defined against the transgressive excesses of an elite **avant-garde** on the one hand, and the puritanism of traditional forms of middle-brow culture on the other. In doing so, he emphasizes, as did Bourdieu, the ways in which taste operates as a means to establish and maintain distinctions in class status, which themselves work to legitimize other forms of class inequality. Class distinctions operate not simply as a binary division between bourgeois (upper-class) and popular (working-class) tastes in the well-known categories of 'high' and 'low' culture, but also between different fractions of the middle classes, where the struggles over taste are often most acute. The artists and intellectuals in this class are rich in 'cultural capital', if not in economic power, and have the confidence to challenge established aesthetic and ethical codes through avant-garde experimentation or appropriations of low culture. The traditional petit bourgeoisie (lower middle class) meanwhile have neither the economic nor the cultural capital to give authority to their tastes and a strong incentive to aspire to 'respectability' to differentiate themselves from the lower classes in their quest for social status. Their cultural anxiety is also manifest in their relationship to their bodies, which has none of the 'ease' that characterizes the upper and lower classes.

However, in Bourdieu's analysis, one of the most significant changes of the post-war period has been the rise of a 'new' petit bourgeoisie who are employed in media-related jobs such as fashion, advertising, public relations and, of course, television. They seek to establish their cultural credibility by defining themselves against this 'old-fashioned' lower middle-class respectability and instead embracing 'an ethic of fun' in an attempt to appear modern and sophisticated (Jankovich 2001: 6). This involves not 'wild abandon', but the 'calculated hedonism' identified by Mike Featherstone (1991a: 171) as characteristic of the 'cultural intermediaries' of contemporary consumer culture. Mark Jankovich, drawing on Bourdieu and Featherstone, explains how this affects their approach to sexuality.

> The new petit bourgeoisie displays its distinction from the old through its 'liberated sexuality', but it is a 'liberation' that is only ever achieved through education, discipline and intense self-surveillance. The 'liberation' of the body from its 'repression' is therefore experienced simultaneously as the rediscovery of a natural self and as the enactment of a carefully controlled performance. It is both a liberation from alienation and a whole new mode of alienation.
>
> (Jankovich 2001: 6)

This new class formation is responsible for the rise of the therapeutic society and its plethora of 'expert' guides on lifestyle and how to educate the self and discipline the body. It is also responsible, in its effort to distinguish itself from the 'old' petit bourgeoisie through negation, for 'a whole series of political movements and practices which are defined as alternative (health, environment) or oppositional (non-sexist, anti-racist)' (Jankovich 2001: 7).

Television can be understood as middle-brow culture *par excellence*. In its short history its approach to sexual representation can be seen to have moved from being defined entirely by the puritan restraint of the traditional petit bourgeoisie to a mixed schedule that also offers a range of more sexually explicit genres. The extremes of avant-garde sexual transgression or the low pornographic 'grotesque' of hard core are, largely, excluded except as heavily censored topics for documentary investigation. Soft-core pornography and **carnivalesque** celebrations of sexual excess are relegated to the low status margins of the schedules. The programmes that have taken up a central place are those that offer 'lifestyle' guidance in the factual and fictional genres, which simultaneously offer 'fun' entertainment while educating the audience in the appropriate 'performance' of the sexualized self. Examples from fiction include soap opera 'issues' as sex education, nineteenth-century literary adaptations that focus on the social etiquette and erotic appeal of their characters, or contemporary 'quality' drama, such as *Six Feet Under* (HBO 2001–) or *Queer as Folk* (Channel 4 1999), that explore transgressive sexual identities of various kinds. In factual genres, ordinary people have become subject to voyeuristic, sexualized display in the new popular docusoap formats of the 1990s: the investigations of sexual lifestyles such as *Adult Lives* (BBC2 1999), *Sex Life* (Channel 5 1998) or *Sex Bomb* (Channel 4 1998), all series about changing attitudes to sex, or the series *Real Sex* (HBO), in which people reveal what turns them on. In reality game shows, such as *Wife Swap* (Channel 4 2003–) or *Temptation Island* (Sky One 2001–), people are subject to intense ethical scrutiny of how they conduct their relationships. More explicitly pedagogic expert guidance is provided by sex education formats, such as *Sex Tips for Girls* (Channel 4 2002) or *The Truth about Gay Sex* (Channel 4 2002). The mixture of purposes is balanced in different ways for different spaces in the schedule. The educational purpose comes to the fore on terrestrial prime-time, while sexual pleasure is prioritized in more marginal spaces late at night or on cable.

Where 'fun' is to the fore the programmes are more likely to be addressed to a commercially defined 'youth' audience. We might call them the 'new, new petit bourgeoisie', the children of the generation studied by Bourdieu in the 1970s. Having grown up in a culture saturated with sexualized display and with an experience of television less dominated by the public service emphasis on 'improvement', they are at ease with the exhibitionist potential of 'infotainment'. This market has been developed most fully by the Murdoch-owned satellite company BSkyB on Sky One, in such series as the holiday resort *Uncovered* series that began with *Ibiza Uncovered* (1997). The 'uncut' video version cover blurb says: 'From the series that shocked the nation, *Ibiza Uncut* strips naked the island that offers sun, fun, sex and much more. Re-live the exploits of Jay and his 18–30s crew, the wild and raunchy "Manumission" night club.' Both this series and the equally popular terrestrial copy of the format, *Club Reps* (ITV 2002–), target the 16–34 audience with the carnivalesque excesses of their peer group on holiday. In the face of competition for this audience it was reported in the industry press that 'Channel chiefs have called for more, longer running "tits and bums" style programming to appeal to younger, post-pub viewers' (Robertson 2001). *Temptation Island* (Sky One 2001), a six-part series bought from the Murdoch-owned US network company Fox, aired on Sky One in the UK but was subsequently shown on late night Channel 4 as well. It used the same 'holiday' formula as the docusoaps but this time run as a *Big Brother* (Channel 4 2000–) style game. Three couples are taken to live on a tropical island, then separated and tempted into infidelity over a period of weeks by 26 single contestants. It has the same 'will they, won' t they' narrative drive of *Big Brother* but with the added frisson of betrayal, and flesh, revealed. Both these programmes dramatize the recurring sexual anxieties of the young but in the marginal, satellite version it is mixed with a more pornographic appeal.

This voyeuristic relation to ordinary people's sexual relationships gives some indication of the degree to which sexualized performance and display for the camera have ceased to be the preserve of a class of women who were quite other to 'respectable' people. Nor is there such a clear divide between the respectable audience for documentary and the despised 'dirty mac' brigade of sad misfit men that formed the stereotyped consumers of commercial pornography until relatively recently. For producers, performers and consumers of what might be termed television 'docuporn' the boundaries between 'us' and 'them' have been transgressed. Yet British (and USA) television is still primarily soft core, even at the margins, despite a court ruling in the US reaffirming the rights of cable companies to show what they want when they want (Backstein 2001: 304).

The continuing relevance of this distinction is examined by Laura Kertz (2002), who argues that the boundary between soft core and hard core needs to be understood not as a moral boundary that will eventually disappear as audiences become more liberated, but as a marketing category. Hard core caters for more specialized tastes.

Soft core is characterized by indirectness, working to reduce the anxiety people feel at watching arousing sexual imagery by wrapping it in extraneous 'noise' and misleading 'headers' whose function is to reassure people who are ambivalent about their reasons for watching (Kertz 2002: 1–9). Hard core is characterized by directness, by explicit appeals to specific desires that consumers have to ask for (over the counter, on a pay-per-view menu, using keywords on the Internet) (*ibid.*: 10–12). But, Kertz argues, both hard core and soft core co-exist within a larger consumer culture (*ibid.*: 19). Just as many consumers move across these divisions, so does the displayed content. In Kertz's view, the division between soft and hard core is a function not of the social regulation of taste or legality or normalization but of the regulative power of markets. Although hard core is 'considered the province of artists, academics and the truly depraved – those generally perceived as above or below morality' (*ibid.*: 20), in fact hard core is defined by its specialist appeal. It uses the soft core mainstream to advertise. In my view, however, this sets up a false dichotomy. Markets for pornography are based on distinctions in taste that have developed as a *result* of moral discourses and the political power to establish them as norms.

The way that television now functions to advertise hard core pornography is well illustrated by a series on the pornography business, *Sex and Shopping* (Channel 5 1998–2001). The series was structured around the boundary between soft and hard core, offering British audiences glimpses of sexual material they had been unable to view on television before. Its production values and style were noticeably 'trashy'; that is, low budget and oriented to pleasure rather than education. A handful of interviews with sex shop entrepreneurs, edited into brief sound bites, were intercut with location shots of sex shops and their merchandise from inside and out, and images from porn magazines and videos that exemplify the topic under discussion. These provide the 'sexually explicit scenes' that viewers were warned of (or promised) in the introduction to the programme. Its first graphic extols us to 'Turn off or turn on' to 'Sex sex sex' in bright neon letters, over a montage of sexual imagery and accompanied by brassy stripper-type music. It was clear from the start that this 'frank look at the global pornography business' was intended to arouse sexually as well as to inform. For a British audience it provides tantalizing glimpses of the hard core porn available legally in Europe or illegally in Soho. 'What do you get for your money?', asks a breezy voice-over from Davina McCall (now famous for hosting the *Big Brother* shows). 'Seventy-two minutes of tape. 15 blow jobs, 14 scenes of vaginal sex, 13 anal, 12 come shots and an orgy from the eight performers involved. Not bad for £20 even if the quality left something to be desired.'

Its documentary format distinguished it from straight pornography, however. A legitimating journalistic intention motivated the investigation: the programme contested British laws censoring hard core. Two academic experts, both anti-censorship (Tom Dewes Matthews and Bill Thompson), made brief appearances decrying the effects of censorship on the British porn business. The 'noise' of journalistic purpose, calling into question the domestic laws on pornography, and the cheeky 'header' warning/enticing viewers to 'turn off or turn on' failed, however, to assuage viewer anxiety. Despite its late night slot *Sex and Shopping* attracted numerous complaints to the ITC and BSC in its first season, several of which were upheld, forcing them to be re-edited for the repeats. The BSC declared that six of the programmes included scenes that were 'unacceptable for broadcast at any time' because they showed the female sex organs in detail and the reality of what was taking place, including sexual intercourse (BSC 1999). The way that regulatory boundaries help to promote sexually explicit material to new audiences is demonstrated several times over in this example. The programme used censorship laws as an excuse to show hard core material to a mass-market audience so they would know what was available if they asked for it. Channel 5 used the announcement of the BSC's censure to launch the next series, thereby promoting not only the programme but also its own brand identity as a channel. As a new channel with low viewing figures, it deliberately stepped over the soft core line as a strategy to innovate in a crowded market place and thereby attract audiences. *Sex and Shopping* did a lot to establish Channel 5 in the minds of its potential viewers as a broadcaster of sleaze, which it is now so keen to leave behind, despite its non-judgemental, 'journalistic' gloss.

Presenting their anti-censorship campaign as a feminist goal provided further legitimation for *Sex and Shopping*. The series included a hagiography of a German woman entrepreneur, Beatte Uhse, who is dubbed the 'Queen Mother of Porn'. Her status as a feminist heroine is secured in several ways. As a pilot in the war, she is pictured in her flying helmet, evoking memories of those other female heroines of early aviation. Her business began as an illegal, mail-order contraceptive and advice service for unmarried women, making her a post-war Marie Stopes counteracting the suffering women experienced as a result of their ignorance about sex. Her £100 million turnover is offered as a role model for younger women entrepreneurs who aspire to her economic success. Women are presented as where the future of the sex industry is heading and now the biggest growth market, with Europe leading the way. As one of the sex shop entrepreneurs interviewed for the programme says of his business, 'Everything is changing at a pace unknown before. We have to run to stay up with the market.' The involvement of women in the sex industry and the way in which anti-censorship feminist discourses have been used to legitimize pornography is taken up further in Chapter 6, which looks at documentaries on the sex industry. The next section of this chapter considers the ways in which women's access as consumers of pornography has been enabled by this development and by the availability of soft-core pornography on television.

Women and the gendering of pornography

Jane Juffer's (1998) book *At Home with Pornography: Women, Sex and Everyday Life* considers the democratizing effects of the commodification of sexually explicit materials, especially as it relates to women's access to and engagement with erotic genres. Where she differs from McNair is in the way that she demonstrates the continuing influence of 'quality' and 'trash' distinctions, which, despite their instability as cultural categories, still regulate the circulation of erotic texts. Her method uses textual analysis not to contribute to this process of discrimination but to reveal the conditions of possibility that legitimate a text's circulation and consumption as a product of specific taste cultures, an approach that has influenced the form of this book. She is also concerned to move beyond the moralizing categories of the feminist 'porn wars' (see Segal and Macintosh 1992; Vance 1992 for an overview), and is critical of the tendency in feminist debates about pornography to set up various competing hierarchies of erotic texts in which only certain kinds of 'transgressive' pleasure are legitimated (Juffer 1998: 2).

The kinds of transgressive performance that are cited by feminist writers as exemplary, Juffer explains, are the avant-garde performances of sex positive radical Annie Sprinkle, whose 'Post-Porn-Modernist' pornographic display offers a feminist critique designed to liberate women into a boundary-less world of polymorphous sexuality (Straayer 1993; Williams 1993). This kind of pornography *has* appeared on late night, minority television in the UK, such as the *Renegade TV* series on Channel 4, which included a documentary on Suzie Bright (*Sex Pest*, Channel 4 1998) and included Annie Sprinkle in another (*Sacred Sex*, Channel 4 1999). Other feminist writers, such as Laura Kipnis in *Bound and Gagged* (1999), have celebrated the transgressive potential of hard-core porn in such down-market forms as *Hustler* magazine. Hard core, Kipnis argues, 'contains everything that is excluded from mainstream culture by taboos and prohibitions' (cited by Juffer 1998: 17). In this respect, then, hard core can be seen as a political challenge to a prudish establishment and the stultifying rules that restrain sexual expression. Hard core emphasizes deviant practices and sex for sex's sake in a series of decontextualized sexual encounters that get straight to the action, involving erections, penetration and 'money shots' showing ejaculation. It is the 'real thing' as judged against the ersatz 'second best' of soft core, with its endless fondling of breasts and simulated intercourse, which has been tamed for the 'feminized' mass market (Ross 1993). In its exploration of the open apertures, protuberances and fluids of the sexual body, hard core valorizes the 'grotesque' body of popular culture over the more respectable, closed body of soft core 'glamour'. But the majority of women, argues Juffer, are unlikely to find these high and low forms of pornography pleasurable: not all women want to be transgressive, and to imply that this is the only legitimate form for women's erotic pleasure sets up a hierarchy of desire legislating for correct and incorrect forms of sexual expression. For a popular medium such as television, therefore, these evaluations have little relevance.

Juffer rejects what she sees as the universalizing tendency in which feminist commentators take their own politically or morally motivated values and raise them to the status of 'truth'. She quotes this passage from John Frow's book on *Cultural Values* in support of her position:

Cultural discrimination involves a constant negotiation of position with the aim of naturalising one's own set of values, distinguishing them from the values of others, and attempting more or less forcefully, to impose ones values on others. It is thus not just a matter of self-definition but also a struggle for social legitimation. That is to say, elite tastes masquerading as universal criteria of value.

(Frow 1995: 85 cited in Juffer 1998: 25)

Juffer's argument is part of the wider critique of second wave feminism for promoting the political concerns and cultural tastes of a narrow band of middle-class career women over women's majority culture. This, it is argued, simply reinforces the low status of women's culture in a bourgeois, patriarchal hegemony where middle-class men's tastes provide the standard against which other forms are judged as 'trash'. Popular forms of television have been central to this debate (see discussion in the Introduction).

Juffer also criticizes this approach to cultural analysis for assuming that essentialized meanings are embodied in pornographic texts. Once these meanings have been established by the feminist critic certain effects are then assumed, whether those be a reinforcement or transgression of women's devalued status in patriarchal culture. Juffer's method is to study the material and discursive conditions in which different kinds of pornography are produced, distributed, obtained and consumed and how this shapes their meaning and uses. She asks what factors enable them to acquire this kind of cultural legitimacy and equally what forms of sexual pleasure and identity they make available and culturally 'intelligible'. She draws attention to the importance of textual aesthetics in this process and the significance of *genre* as a means by which texts are made intelligible and legitimate for specific groups of consumers in particular historical and spatial locations. Central to this process, in Juffer's view, is the means by which erotic texts *differentiate* themselves from the regulatory legacy in which pornography has been generically defined by legal prohibitions, secrecy and an exclusively male address. In order to legitimize sexually explicit materials for the main-stream, then, a variety of aesthetic strategies are necessary to make them 'safe' and pleasurable for a wider range of consumers. Soft-core 'erotica' for women counteracts discourses that position women as always the victims of sexually explicit materials. Instead, through a claim to aesthetic complexity in its greater attention to narrative form and characterization, soft core can be justified as expressive of women's desires. As we shall see, she takes up this analysis in relation to erotic dramas on television and how they are made palatable for distribution into the home.

The domestic nature of television viewing is a significant factor. The transgressive consumption of erotic television by women in the home cannot therefore be reduced to a progressive *historical* process in which embedded textual conventions, such as passive roles for women, are broken. Transgressive identities also involve 'going beyond' the *spatial* boundaries that constrain women's sexual agency (Juffer 1998: 112). Crucial to this is the Victorian legacy of the gendering of public and private space in which 'respectable' women were confined to the home, and 'street walker' was another term for prostitution. This was reinforced in the 1950s by liberal legislation in which the home was conceived as a haven free from 'pollution by pornography', which was 'zoned' into specially designated spaces in the city. It ensured women's exclusion from access and defined them as asexual suburban 'housewives'. Television has played a major role in reinforcing this construction throughout the 1950s, and beyond (Thumim 2001). New possibilities were opened up, however, from the 1980s by the development of new technologies – the video recorder, cable television and now the Internet – that have changed the material conditions of domestic space and its temporal rhythms, carving out new possibilities for women as consumers of pornography. It has enabled the provision of 'adult' videos and subscription channels addressed to heterosexual couples as well as to men, and late night erotic programming on more mainstream channels, albeit hedged around with warnings of their sexual content. These new material conditions have not eradicated previous assumptions but have allowed some renegotiation of the aesthetic and social practices regulating women's access to erotica in the home, although in uneven and contradictory ways.

In her analysis of cable porn channels, for instance, Juffer (1998) asks what texts are available to enhance women's mundane everyday sexual practices in the home. In her view, the fact that they offer pleasurable fantasy should not be subject to judgements from intellectuals about what counts as 'good' porn (*ibid.*: 14–21). Their textual features are politically contradictory. They are inclined to reinforce conventional heterosexual relationships and a narrow range of identities but they do offer a greater focus on women's sexual pleasure. Rather than the placeless utopia that is characteristic of most pornography, their sexual fantasies are located in relation to everyday life, a feature that Juffer regards as enabling their integration into women's lives. Their use of legitimizing narratives, which motivate the sexual encounters, might be 'noise', in Laura Kertz's terms, designed to reduce the residual cultural anxiety that still attaches to watching arousing images. But it is these aesthetic features that make them available to ordinary women. She compares them to the new genres of erotic novels for women, such as the *Black Lace* series, which try to distance themselves from pornography by emphasizing their literary qualities. This provides the legitimacy that enables more widespread distribution in mainstream outlets such as respectable bookstores. The involvement of women as writers also helps in this respect, a factor that is illustrated in the Playboy cable example discussed below.

Television pornography is much less diversified than the market for erotic novels, in part because of the much stricter regulations governing the medium. Soft core for women on the premium channels such as Showtime is addressed to the affluent women who can pay the subscription charges. There are strict limits to the identities shown. For instance, women in soft porn are never shown as mothers, and rarely as lesbians or ethnic minorities. An exception is a series called *Women: Stories of Passion*, produced by Playboy Enterprises and written and directed entirely by women. Although the Playboy cable channel is almost exclusively addressed to men, Hugh Heffner's daughter, who now runs the business, has a strategy to diversify into 'couples' pornography in order to regain legitimacy for a business whose profits were damaged by the feminist anti-pornography campaigns of the 1970s and 1980s. This example is an intimate confessional narrative format structured around a woman writer who is collecting women's sexual fantasies. These include lesbian encounters, older women with younger men, guiltless promiscuity and a critique of racial stereotyping. Moreover, it shows men's bodies as much as women's (Juffer 1998: 224; Backstein 2001: 312–13). This is very rare. Even where soft core narratives emphasize female pleasure the visual focus usually remains on the (conventionally attractive) female body, not on men's bodies, and especially not their penises, which are still subject to censorship (Juffer 1998: 203). The long history of pornography's exclusively male address means that there is an underdeveloped visual aesthetic for eroticizing the heterosexual male body.

Showtime's long-running *Red Shoe Diaries* (shown on late night Channel 5 in the UK) is a series that has attracted substantial critical attention because of its explicit address to women and its relatively high production values (Juffer 1998; Backstein 2001). It employs a number of contradictory textual strategies which indicate, in Backstein's (2001: 308) view, an attempt 'to net a mixed gender audience while remaining for the most part, unable to disengage fully from the male viewing position'. A male narrator frames each week's episode. The pretext is that these stories arose out of his discovery of his dead fiancée's journal, in which he found out for the first time about her sexual betrayal. This provokes him to advertise for other women's sexual confessions (*ibid*. 2001: 309). (In a parallel move, the Showtime website invites viewers to write their own diary entries.) Although bracketed by a man's judgemental perspective on her revelations, it also reverses the gendering of romance conventions in that it 'emphasizes the male quest for romance and the female quest for independence within romance'. Here it is the man who 'needs the reassurance of a secure relationship' (Juffer 1998: 220). The 'confessions' allow for a series of erotic short stories told from a woman's perspective, which give women the sexual agency to make their fantasies come true. The 'private' confessional as narrative form, originating in Richardson's novel *Clarissa*, has many parallels in other women's genres, such as Nancy Friday's collections of women's sexual fantasies (1976, 1991) or the letters on Oprah Winfrey's talk shows, which supplement the participants' performances (Wilson 2003).

In 'You have the right to remain silent', for example, a woman's fantasy about one of the men in the gym where she is exercising is pursued in 'real life'. She uses her position as a traffic cop to pull his car over, handcuff him and put him behind bars while she seduces him. Juffer (1998: 221–4) comments on the mobility of the female protagonist who moves across the boundary between public and private spaces, which, she argues, is essential to sexual agency. She is also in control of the desiring gaze, when, for example, watching him exercising in the gym. This scene uses the convention of showing the active male body as a way to avoid the potential feminization of objec-tification, whereas the handcuffing and cage scenes draw on the iconography of sadomasochism, with the woman as uniformed dominatrix. However, as soon as the narrative nears its sexual climax, the woman's body is moved centre frame in order to obscure the man's penis and we return to the conventional language of soft porn in a sequence of arched backs and undulating torsos to suggest pelvic thrusts (Backstein 2001: 313–14). The narrative resolution also emphasizes the return to convention, with the man declaring 'we are going to be like normal people' (Juffer 1998: 223).

We can see, therefore, that although still extremely marginal, soft-core television for women has 'progressive' elements, in, for instance, its inclusion of women as central protagonists whose actions drive the narrative, the visual structuring of a desiring female gaze, the assertion of women's sexual power and autonomy. On the other hand these innovations are grafted on to more traditional romance and soft-core conventions in which a focus on the display of women's bodies and a 'respectable' – that is, heterosexual, white, middle-class, suburban – lifestyle provides the narrative frame. Juffer's argument is that, rather than denigrating these texts (and by implication the women who consume them) for reinforcing women's objectification, it is possible, instead, to recognize the way their aesthetic strategies legitimate pleasurable con-sumption of pornography for women within the home. As with soaps, the importance of soft-core television pornography is that it can be integrated into the spatial and temporal rhythms of women's everyday lives. This approach avoids the problem of colluding with paternalistic censorship regimes, as the anti-porn feminists are accused of doing. It also avoids universalizing the tastes of an elite minority of urban sophisticates, a problem that has bedevilled feminist cultural politics from the start, while recognizing the ways in which cultural tastes are socially produced and regulated. It also recognizes the feminist case for equal sexual citizenship in the cultural sphere; women's access to a diversity of sexual representations is assumed as a right.

Conclusion

The historical formation of taste means that generic conventions constrain the pro-duction and consumption of sexual representations in ways that cannot quickly be undone. Nevertheless, I would argue that we do need to recognize, and challenge, the limitations in what is currently legitimate for circulating on television. 'Soft core' restrictions such as the exclusion of erect penises or 'real' intercourse are actually doing women a great disservice by limiting the focus to the display of women's bodies. This works to perpetuate a construction of female sexuality that exists only to the extent that she arouses the passions of the male viewer (or lesbian viewers reading against the grain). Soft core also works to limit the availability of erotic entertainment for marginal sexualities that fall outside the heterosexual norm. The day has yet to come when cable television carries gay male pornography (as far as I am aware). The vanguard has its uses in this respect. As McNair and Kertz have pointed out, the mainstream raids the margins for new forms that often connect to emerging social forces and identities. It is in this way that an aesthetics of transgression can have a wider influence.

But these new social forces are not inevitably benign or 'progressive' in the sense understood by the campaigns for sexual citizenship mounted by the democratic new social movements of the post-war era. It is important, therefore, not to represent access to pornography as an inevitable progress towards 'liberation'. The risks as well as the pleasures of sexual relations still apply. The widespread mediation of sexuality via visual forms of pornography will have social effects, contributing to the techniques of the self that regulate our sexual practices. While these may not be as straightforward as the copycat theses of the discredited 'effects' tradition, that doesn't absolve us from thinking through what they may be. In an increasingly 'liquid modernity' the future pattern of sexual relations is uncertain but seemingly oriented towards greater transience and individuality (Bauman 2003). At the same time, projections of the potential for virtual sex made possible by the interactive television of the future are imbued with male fantasies of control over women's bodies (*Pornography: The Secret History of Civilisation*, Channel 4 1999). Can cyber-technologies linked in with television enhance the democracy of desire and pleasure? If machine-sex replaces people-sex what happens to intimacy?

Recommended reading

Bourdieu, P. (1994) *Distinction: A Social Critique of the Judgement of Taste*. London: Routledge (originally published 1984).

Juffer, J. (1998) *At Home with Pornography: Women, Sex and Everyday Life*. New York: New York University Press.

McNair, B. (2002) *Striptease Culture: Sex, Media and the Democratisation of Desire*. London: Routledge.

Segal, L. and Mackintosh, M. (eds) (1992) *Sex Exposed: Sexuality and the Pornography Debate*. London: Virago.

Williams, L. (1990) *Hard Core: Power, Pleasure, and the 'Frenzy of the Visible'*. London: Pandora.

4 | SEX SCANDALS

In 1998 the 'hottest' story on prime time television news was the scandal of US President Bill Clinton's sexual exploits with a young intern in the White House, Monica Lewinsky. Commentary on the scandal appeared on the network news at the family dinner hour, provoking concerns about how parents should handle the ensuing questions from their children. *Newsweek* gave advice on 'How to handle your children's questions about the Clinton scandal', headlined with the query 'Mom, what's oral sex?' *Newsweek*'s advice was to refuse to discuss the details but instead to reinforce the moral point that Clinton had behaved very badly (Merck 2000: 7). This example illustrates the fact that one of the consequences of high-profile, political sex scandals in the 1990s was to bring discussion of 'deviant' sexual activities into the very centre of the network television schedules. Scandals on television and scandalous television seemingly conflict with the institutionalized address of television to the 'family', with its reliance on ideologies of childhood innocence, and contributes to moral panics about the effects of the media. Yet scandal is the dominant form through which 'deviant' sexual practices are circulated in the mainstream media. This is because of its double structure, nurtured by Puritanism, of exposing sexual trans-gression in order to condemn it. Therefore scandal, and the news media that circulate it, function as a significant regulatory discourse through which the boundaries of acceptable sexual behaviour are continually renegotiated.

This chapter explores this symbolic process and its political implications through a discussion of the characteristics of scandals as media events, and the role played by television in their circulation. It engages with the debates over the effects of scandals and whether they do, as some commentators believe, reinforce the social, sexual and political order, or, as others argue, undermine it. Whether the latter is seen as a threat depends on one's own relation to that order. One of the pleasures of scandals is the opportunity they afford to undermine and mock the powerful, although they can just as easily be used against the powerless. A central issue, which develops the arguments introduced in Chapter 2, is the liberal division between the public and private spheres and how it can work to protect the privileges of the powerful and to hide sexual exploitation. The potential for radical uses of scandalous publicity has therefore been recognized in bohemian, feminist and queer critiques of liberal sexual politics. At the psychological level, the chapter explores the dynamics of secrecy, shame and celebrity exposure to explain the intense levels of popular engagement that scandals provoke. Why have scandals become such a staple of the contemporary media? What is it that makes them so popular?

Sex scandals as media events

For the majority of the 1990s the news agenda in the UK and USA was dominated at frequent intervals by politically significant sex scandals that produced widespread media coverage. In the UK, in the first half of the 1990s, a seemingly endless stream of sex scandals buffeted the Conservative Government. Unwisely, the Prime Minister, John Major, in an attempt to unite a divided party around a traditional moral agenda, had called for a return to 'family values' in a speech in 1993 (Epstein and Johnson 1998: 73–98). The resulting contradiction between the normative ideals guiding policy-making and the deviant behaviour of prominent members of the government made them susceptible to accusations of hypocrisy as well as immorality. The government was fatally undermined by these events, not least because the Conservatives became known as the party of 'sleaze'. During the same period, the British Royal Family was subjected to an equally relentless stream of rumour and revelations of sexual misconduct as the marriage of Princess Diana and Prince Charles, the heir to the throne, disintegrated. The election of the New Labour Government in 1997 and the death of the princess in a car crash later in the same year brought this period of intense exposure of the private lives of the British establishment to a (temporary) close. It was soon replaced, however, by the global reporting of the President Clinton/Monica Lewinsky scandal.

There is nothing new about this phenomenon. There has been a long tradition of sex scandals in the political culture of the UK and the USA, nurtured by the popular press and by a lack of privacy laws of the type that protect French politicians from exposure (Thompson 2000: 130). British tabloid newspapers, in particular, are strongly sexualized, while the broadsheet newspapers and television will pick up on these stories once they have broken, often to provide meta-commentary on the events and their potential consequences, especially where political figures are concerned. Never-theless, their intensification through the 1990s has been argued to be symptomatic of a number of related cultural changes in modern societies. John Thompson (2000), for example, has argued that 'mediated visibility' and the accompanying cult of celebrity are making politicians' personal character and reputation the primary foundation of political power, while policy matters are sidelined. Liberal democracies, he argues, are finely balanced between a need for openness and scrutiny to maintain democratic control over political elites and the dangers of pervasive distrust and cynicism. Scandals undermine politicians' reputation and consequently the trust on which the political process is based (*ibid*.: 246–59). The management of scandals is therefore fundamental to the political ecology and explains the emphasis on news management and 'spin' that gives communications directors and press officers a central role in contemporary government.

The development of modern media networks has been one of the factors fuelling the growing importance of scandal in the political arena. The development of visual communication technologies and their use by the media industries has produced a culture in which people's private lives are increasingly open to public scrutiny. Intensified competition, expanded capacity and lighter regulation of the television industry accelerated this trend as new genres of media spectacle were developed to attract larger audiences (Lull and Hinerman 1997; Thompson 2000; Kellner 2003). These 'infotainment' formats, such as confessional talk shows, 24-hour rolling news channels and live coverage of court cases, were all ideally suited to the dissemination of scandalous stories, whether of celebrities, politicians or ordinary people made famous by their 'deviant' behaviour. The watershed was in 1991 when the O. J. Simpson murder trial in the USA gripped the whole nation, showing just how effectively scandals could be used by television to attract large audiences as events unfolded, sometimes live on television, over extended periods of time (Morrison 1997; Kellner 2003). The Clinton/Lewinsky scandal escalated over the course of more than a year, culminating in the televised impeachment proceedings against the President. As each fresh revelation occurred its commodity value as 'news' was renewed, while its existence in recorded form allowed for its retelling. It received extensive coverage throughout the world, facilitated by global news networks such as CNN (Thompson 1997).

Although each has its own particular trajectory, Thompson (2000: 67–75) has proposed a model of the typical unfolding of a mediated scandal in four phases: the pre-scandal phase, the scandal proper, the culmination and the aftermath. A transgression of moral codes is the point of origin, but in the pre-scandal phase this will be known only to the people directly involved. The scandal occurs when those people fail to control the 'leakage' of information from the private areas of their lives into the public domain, where it becomes visible to thousands or millions of others. Yet the scandal proper only begins if the transgression is regarded with disapproval. It is then amplified and disseminated by a proliferation of media reports on the affair, which generate a climate of moral censure. This will extend over a period during which allegations and revelations are publicized and their veracity is investigated until a culmination is reached – when media organizations decide that public interest in the affair has waned or when a 'line is drawn under the affair' in some way, by a confession, a resignation or a court verdict. It may constitute a 'media event'; that is, 'an exceptional occasion which is planned in advance and broadcast live, which interrupts the normal flow of events and which creates an atmosphere of solemnity and high expectation' (Thompson 2000: 75). Television is central to these types of staged intervention, such as happened in the O. J. Simpson trial when the verdict was delayed in order to be broadcast live, or in the televised impeachment trial of President Clinton.

As the people involved in the scandal get caught up in a process that is very difficult to control, the original transgression at the centre of the scandal is often compounded by 'second-order transgressions'. Typically these involve deception, which is later exposed as such, as participants seek to deny the offence, in the hope of avoiding public humiliation and shame, by facing down their accusers. Media evidence is one of the factors that gives a scandal 'legs', with the publication of letters, tape recordings, photographs and video footage. The fact that they have been recorded allows them to be replayed over and over again on television (Thompson 2000: 68). In this process of repetition certain phrases and images become iconic, circulating in popular culture in multiple ways but especially in cartoons and jokes. Even where guilt is established, the effects of a media scandal, its aftermath, are hard to predict in advance. It can result in irrevocable damage to people's reputations, from which they will never recover, or, alternatively, their careers might subsequently prosper from the publicity. Uncertainty contributes to complex negotiations while the scandal unfolds as each of the participants seeks to profit from, rather than be destroyed by, the publicity. This explains the growing importance of press officers and public relations advisors, some of whom have, as a consequence, acquired celebrity status. They use their established media contacts in an attempt to control the flow of information, and give expert advice to their clients on how to present themselves in the best possible light, to gain public sympathy.

Politicians caught up in a sex scandal can berate journalists for ignoring the really important political news, betraying their proper professional role of acting in the public interest, by focusing instead on the 'trivial' matter of politician's private lives. This is an especially effective approach where television is concerned because it chimes with the prevalent concerns over 'dumbing down' as television succumbs to a news agenda set by the tabloid newspapers. Wider concern over the loss of privacy in contemporary media cultures is also invoked when it is argued that the exposure of people's private lives to public scrutiny is a threat to the freedoms guaranteed by a liberal democracy (Thompson 2000: 238–41). Clinton used an appearance on *60 minutes* in 1992, with his wife Hillary, to appeal to traditional liberal sentiments about the 'privacy' of the family and his marriage. In effect he said 'it's none of your business' to underline the point that serious journalism should be about the real political issues, not sexual tittle-tattle (Gronbeck 1997: 127). He chose to say it on a network television news magazine, immediately after the Super Bowl, thereby ensuring a much larger audience than usual. They then drew a line under the affair, consigning it to another time and place of no relevance to the present in a bid to bring the story to a conclusion. 'Thus the affair was safely consigned to the past/private, and of no political relevance to the public/future' (Gronbeck 1997: 128). It was an effective strategy, if only in the short term, because the news media are not interested in history.

A quite different strategy underlies the development of another television genre, the confessional interview as public relations event, in which rather than asserting a right to privacy the interviewee hopes to take control of the media agenda, to reframe the story and to portray a sympathetic image by revealing previously hidden secrets. A famous example of this is the interview with Princess Diana on the flagship BBC current affairs programme *Panorama* in 1995. It set a much-copied precedent as a means for figures at the centre of a scandal to give their side of the story in a highly rehearsed and controlled format. Indeed, Martin Bashir, the interviewer, has built his subsequent career on this role, leading to his being chosen by Michael Jackson in 2003 as the person to rehabilitate his tarnished reputation following accusations of child sexual abuse (Wells 2003a), a strategy that failed to prevent his subsequent arrest. The very high viewing figures and deluge of subsequent media commentary in both these cases indicate the potential these interviews have as 'event' television with global reach. The style of these interviews owes much to the confessional culture of television talk shows. As with the case of Diana's 1995 interview, these have provoked disagreements about their feminist potential for allowing women to tell their side of the story. These debates are discussed further in the next section, followed by a detailed examination of the responses to the *Panorama* interview.

The gendering of publicity

The increasing exposure of private lives to public scrutiny on British television is often regarded as an effect of North American commercialism on an indigenous tradition of public service broadcasting. As Thompson (2000) explains, more generally this cross-Atlantic influence is seen as the consequence of the tradition of greater 'openness to scrutiny' in the USA, which coexists with a puritanical moral traditionalism that is intolerant of marital infidelity. The European tradition, as exemplified by France's privacy laws, is to maintain greater secrecy along with a greater acceptance of men's sexual transgression as a 'normal' expectation in marriage. Debate in the UK often finds itself stretched across these alternatives in contradictory ways. The protection of class elites in the political establishment from too much intrusion has a long history, despite a commitment to the need for accountability. Indeed, the public service tradition was founded on a contract of 'trust' that those in charge of running the institutions of the state, including the BBC, would act in the interests of the wider populace. It is a system hedged about with numerous techniques for maintaining secrecy. On the other hand, the freedom of the popular commercial press to expose sexual transgressions (and marital infidelity in particular) has been facilitated by one of the least restrictive legal and regulatory frameworks in the world (Thompson 2000: 130).

Another contradiction exists between continuing debates in liberal discourses on how to manage the relation between the public and private spheres and the incisive critique arising from an emergent feminist engagement with these issues (Fraser 1995; McLaughlin 1998). This gendering of the analysis has drawn attention to the emancipatory potential of exposing private behaviour to public scrutiny through confessional discourse and radical uses of scandalous publicity. Indeed, the increasing prominence of media scandals may be partly a consequence of this challenging of the established moral codes of patriarchal societies. The Clinton/Lewinsky scandal, for example, arose from accusations of sexual harassment, a sexual crime that arose from feminist campaigning for the reclassification of sexual behaviour in these terms. Scandals do not simply work to reconfirm moral norms, but can also work to expose and challenge the power relations of class, 'race' and gender that structure modern societies (Morrison 1992; Fraser 1995; in relation to Clinton/Lewinsky scandal see Berlant and Duggan 2001).

The dangers of loss of privacy have to be balanced, Nancy Fraser (1995) argues, against its potential political usefulness. Publicity can be a political weapon, an instrument of emancipation and empowerment. The Clarence Thomas/Anita Hill case in 1991 allowed many women in the USA to speak out about sexual harassment for the first time, instead of suffering it as a private humiliation. Jenny Kitzinger's research in the UK also provides an example of the transforming power of media publicity:

> The media discovery of sexual abuse fundamentally transformed private and public discourse about this issue: opening it up for both personal reflection and community discussion. [In the past] the isolation, stigma and taboo around abuse were such that it was a difficult subject to raise.
>
> (Kitzinger 2001: 99)

The media's attention transformed it from a shameful, individual secret to a public, social issue. Drawing on the work of Hannah Arendt, Maria Pia Lara (1998: 7) argues that power inheres in the ability to draw boundaries between the public and the private, and to redraw them, thereby creating a new meaning of the 'public'. In this respect, disclosure is an instrument to draw attention to the narrowness of previous conceptions of justice. To rectify past exclusions, she argues, there has to be a struggle to reconceive normative conceptions of the 'we' through symbolic intervention in the public sphere. Narratives of emancipation are a demand for recognition. They are also capable of envisioning utopian futures, what 'ought to be' rather than what 'is' (*ibid.*: 1–3).

Women have less power than men do to draw boundaries between the public and the private. This is highlighted in Nancy Fraser's analysis of the high-profile Clarence Thomas/Anita Hill case (a black male judge nominated for the Supreme Court was accused by a black woman law professor of sexual harassment when she had worked for him years earlier at the Equal Employment Opportunities Commission). Women, and this is even more so for black women, Fraser argues, are vulnerable to intrusive publicity. African-Americans' history as slaves denied them domestic privacy and the ability to protect themselves from invasions of their space, including, for women, unwanted sexual attention. Although 'privacy' and 'publicity' are gendered categories,

> It is not the case now, and never was, that women are simply excluded from public life; nor that men are public and women are private; nor that the private sphere is women's sphere and the public sphere is men's; nor that the feminist project is to collapse the boundaries between public and private. Rather feminist analysis shows the political ideological nature of these categories. And the feminist project aims to overcome the gender hierarchy that gives men more power than women to draw the line between public and private.
>
> (Fraser 1995: 305)

To have any effect, disclosure in the public sphere requires 'illocutionary force' (Lara 1998: 3). It isn't simply a case of rational argument, as emphasized by Habermas, but depends on the rhetorical and emotional power of storytelling. Emancipatory narratives, in Lara's analysis, connect two forms of validity, the moral *and* the aesthetic. Of particular significance for women has been the emergence of autobiography and biography as a powerful means by which women's private experience is transformed into public knowledge. The widespread influence of the emotional and visceral power of certain forms of storytelling and visual rhetoric challenges the previous norms of ostensibly rational debate in the public sphere, and is held in deep suspicion by dominant, masculine elites, both academic and political. Kitzinger (2001: 100) also warns against a narrow conception of the political that 'emphasises what people "know" without looking at the constitution of imagination and feeling'.

This gendered critique of the *forms* of public discourse contributes not only to an understanding of the reaction to Diana's interview, but also more generally to the suspicion of 'subjective' narrative in the factual genres of television, as is discussed in Chapters 5 and 6.

The effects of publicity cannot be assumed in advance. Rather than thinking of disclosure and publicity as inevitably a force for progressive transformation, Fraser (1995: 306–7) suggests that we should conceive of the public sphere as an arena for staging conflicts. Once in the public domain there will be a discursive struggle over interpretation. In the case of the Hill/Thomas hearings, Fraser argues, this involved the meaning and moral status of sexual harassment in a context where the law naming it as an offence had failed to win popular support. Indeed, it became part of the backlash against 'political correctness' as an affront to men's right to free speech. Hill also lacked support because some black women saw her as aligned with middle-class white feminism because of her relatively privileged job. Gender solidarity cannot be assumed across boundaries of 'race' and class, or, for that matter, political loyalties. A very different range of political alignments were in play in response to President Clinton's impeachment proceedings in 1998, when his affair with Monica Lewinsky was taken up by right-wing moralists as an affront to family values. For some feminists this was an unforgivable case of sexual exploitation of a younger woman by an older, more power-ful man; not for the first time, feminist opinion was uneasily aligned with right-wing moralism. But opinion among feminists was divided, with many well-known feminist commentators, including Betty Friedan, rallying to his support.

Scandals can be seen as a means of articulating the hegemonic struggle to establish or maintain the legitimacy of certain kinds of sexual ideologies at the expense of others. Debbie Epstein and Richard Johnson (1998) identify a dominant version of the sexual in scandal discourses as constructed around a belief in an uncontrollable sex drive in men, a drive generally agreed to be heightened by power. This is often explained in hormonal terms as the consequence of high levels of testosterone, from which men derive their impetus for both sex and power and the daring to take the associated risks. This explanation acts as a counterweight to the moral frameworks within which scandals are structured, allowing for commentary that excuses men's transgressive behaviour by naturalizing it as an effect of biology, and therefore beyond men's conscious control. It coexists with an assumption that it is women's role as their wives to control these drives within the context of a 'healthy' – that is, sexually fulfilled – marriage. How the wife reacts to betrayal is one of the sources of narrative suspense and therefore a focus for public discussion. The loyal wife is one of the staples of the scandal narrative, ready to stand by her man through the ordeal of his exposure. Beyond this, the 'other woman' is variously presented as whore or victim, often depending on her relationship to the media. 'Kissing and telling and getting paid for it is taken as the decisive comment on their morals' (Epstein and Johnson 1998: 82).

Joshua Gamson (2001) has explored the dynamic of this link between sexual promiscuity and media publicity. In particular, he shows how the 'age old' division of women into virgin and whore has been integrated with contemporary discourses of feminism and celebrity. He is struck by how limited women's roles in sex scandals remain.

> Confronting the dichotomy with a liberal-feminist-derived woman-as-public-agent frame does not necessarily make much of a dent in the virgin–whore narrative. As long as women's publicity itself is narrated by analogy to sex – the virtuous woman protects her chastity from predatory media, the woman who seeks out media attention is a harlot – the independent woman, even when she is of the out-of-my-way-mister, I'm-my-own-commodity variety, is easily absorbed back into the role of the prostitute.
>
> (Gamson 2001: 170)

This is apparent in the way Monica Lewinsky was portrayed by the media. Mandy Merck (2000) draws attention to the way her mouth came to figure in the scandal. For women, long silenced by the masculinization of speech in the public sphere, she argues, the mouth is a site of erotic meaning – a symbol of desire rather than its capacity for speech and language. As the scandal worked through the victim or whore scenarios intrinsic to the genre, Monica's big lips became the signifier of her sexual availability.

> The specifically oral nature of the pleasures promised *per se*, the blowjob, was endlessly caricatured in representations as the pneumatic fellatrix of the sex shop. But unlike her conveniently deflatable counterpart, 'Monica the Mouth Organ' proved, in the words of one columnist, a walking, talking . . . blow-up doll.
>
> (Merck 2000: 191–2)

In the aftermath, Monica turned to the confessional television interview (in the UK on Channel 4 1999), as well as to writing a book, to escape this reductive image of her role in the affair by telling her side of the story.

Affairs of the state on confessional television

The contribution of the confessional television interview can be seen as an important corrective for women caught up in sex scandals. It is a place where they can exercise some control over the presentation of the story as it circulates in the public sphere. Certainly, this appears to have been the case in recent scandals where the television interview as 'media event' has assumed a significant role. The interview can potentially draw attention away from the body of the woman and its sexualized meanings, the scandalized woman as whore, by giving primacy to the woman' s voice, and her point of view in the scandal narrative. The use of 'survivor narratives' is reminiscent of the confessional talk show in which women's ability to recover from adverse life events is used as a feminist signifier of women's strength in community, regaining their sense of self-esteem in the process (Wilson 2003). Initiated and controlled by the woman and her PR advisors, a heavily scripted and rehearsed event counteracts the 'victim' stereotype, even if it leaves her open to accusations of being manipulative. But women can only intervene with the hope, rather than a guarantee, that their version of events will prevail. The interview enters into a discursive struggle with competing versions and interpretative commentary. In assessing their wider significance, at best this exposure can subject the sexual politics of a still predominantly patriarchal political establishment to public critique. At worst it simply reconfirms women's capacity for suffering in a therapeutic context where recovery is an entirely personal matter of overcoming adversity.

The different strands in this debate can be traced in the responses to Diana's confessional interview on the British current affairs programme *Panorama* (BBC 1995). It was seen by 23.2 million people in the UK alone, and broadcast in 112 countries around the world (Thompson 1997). The response was diverse, with commentators filling the studios and front pages of the newspapers with interpretations of its significance. For example, the *Guardian*, a 'quality' daily newspaper in the UK, filled six pages with commentary on the following day. At its most hostile, this commentary included various establishment figures (such as Prince Charles's close friend Nicholas Soames) attempting to smear her with the imputation of madness, of being an unreliable witness owing to her emotional and psychological instability.

The extent of Diana's courting of media publicity was used in the case against her, and accentuated the suspicion that she was using this interview to influence public opinion as ammunition in her marital battle with her husband. She was condemned for being manipulative as a consequence of her obviously rehearsed answers and carefully vetted questions, asked by an interviewer whose deferential and gentle manner helped to create an atmosphere of hallowed reverence. 'It had a Sunday evening feel', as one commentator said, with the Princess's sober demeanour echoed by the formal surroundings and dim lighting. She was accused of using her feminine appeal to manipulate the situation to her advantage, presenting herself as a victim rather than being an authentic case. The television critic Mark Lawson described it as 'Southern European widow' (the dark suit, the heavy eye-liner, the subdued demeanour, the bowed head). It was a persona calculated to elicit respectful sympathy for her suffering, while allowing for the full play of melodramatic emotions that the deployment of a

Figure 2 Princess Diana being interviewed by Martin Bashir on *Panorama* (broadcast on BBC1, 1995)

well-known visual stereotype allows. Its theatricality lent it to sceptical mockery and subsequent parody (most notably on Channel 4 by the political satirist Rory Bremner).

Several well-known feminist commentators interpreted the interview as the culmination in a biographical narrative of emancipation from the forces of class and patriarchal oppression, enabled by the therapeutic intervention of Diana's feminist counsellor, Suzy Orbach, to cure her bulimia. The journalist Beatrix Campbell 'claimed it to be one of the most important social documents of its time' (Hinds and Stacey 2001: 162). Elaine Showalter called Diana 'a feminist heroine of epic stature' (Holt 1998: 188). It is in the verbal narrative, rather than her visual image, that perhaps the strongest claim to feminist meaning resides. It was a story of a traumatized identity through which new claims for emancipation were articulated. But several writers have subsequently questioned this assessment and seen it instead as a symptom of the decline of rational political feminism in which the display of feelings and the cult of celebrity have become a substitute for political analysis. 'Mixing the language of traditional romance with the cliches of psychotherapy and popular feminism . . . it replicated the intimacy and therapeutic promise of women's talk shows', argues Linda Holt (1998: 193). She considers the interview:

> an archetypally feminine act – disclosure of romantic hurt and pain, presented with doe eyes, flirtatious eyes and downtrodden demeanour . . . Notably absent from her *Panorama* interview was any *political* questioning of the ideologies and social structures underlying her role and treatment as a woman . . . By laying claim to feeling, nurturing, loving, she appealed to the age-old association of femininity with emotion.
>
> (Holt 1998: 193, 194–5)

It thereby contributed, in her view, to the trend in which the personal has become a substitute for the political.

Rather than seeing these differing feminist interpretations as alternatives to choose from, Hilary Hinds and Jackie Stacey (2001: 163) take up a recurring theme in postfeminist theory to argue that the interview offered 'a fantasy reconciliation of feminism and femininity hitherto unimaginable to the British media'.

> The interview condenses a critique of the objectification of women by the media, a challenge to the gendered inequalities of the institution of marriage, a plea against male infidelity and duplicity, a thorough refusal of the myths that suggest that being a wife and mother is necessarily satisfying for today's woman, and that the family is a safe place for her to be. Diana combines head tilting and wide eyed gestures of traditional middle-class feminine innocence with a more knowing deployment of pauses and half smiles to indicate the extent of the violations to which she was subjected, and to underscore her restraint from detailing them further in this public forum.
>
> (Hinds and Stacey 2001: 162–3)

The feminist meanings this embodied were perceived at the time as potentially threatening to the institutions of patriarchy as epitomized in the hierarchical traditions of the royal family. More recent sexual scandals in the royal household during 2003, fuelled by secret tape recordings made by Diana and kept after her death by her butler Paul Burrell, contributed further to this potential.

Raka Shome (2001) also points out the significance of racial identity in the transgressive meanings this television event produced, thereby disturbing the boundaries of 'Englishness'. Diana chose to make her critique to a hitherto little-known British-Asian television journalist, Martin Bashir, whom she chose as her interviewer. Given her ideological role as the epitome of white femininity, this intensified the scandal.

> [White femininity] is an ideological construction through which meanings about white women and their place in the social order are naturalized. As symbols of motherhood, as markers of feminine beauty (a marker denied to other women), as translators (and hence preservers) of bloodlines, as signifiers of national domesticity, as sites for the reproduction of heterosexuality, as causes in the name of which narratives of national defence and protection are launched, as symbols of national unity, and as sites through which 'otherness' – racial, sexual, classed, gendered and nationalized – is negotiated, white femininity constitutes the locus through which borders of race, gender, sexuality and nationality are guarded and secured.
>
> (Shome 2001: 323)

Moreover, Shome (2001) argues, her later romantic association with the Egyptian Dodi El Fayad, and the Pakistani doctor Hasnat Kahn, provoked racist fears of miscegenation at the heart of the establishment, thus confirming the 'transgressive' nature of her desires. Nevertheless, after her death, the ceremonial role of television at her funeral and in commemorating her memory worked to restore her to her 'rightful' place in the iconography of the nation. Hoping her death would bring 'closure' to the scandal proved optimistic, however, as continuing revelations underline.

In her glamourized image, Diana represented the epitome of feminine allure, overlaid by our knowledge of her emotional suffering expressed hysterically through its enactment on her body through self-harm and bulimia, and by her persecution at the hands of the press photographers. The *Panorama* interview signifies her attempt to take back control of her image in the public sphere, as the culmination of a struggle to regain control of her body in the private context of her therapy (Coles 1998: 165). Stretched across the traditional and the modern woman, a princess in a fairy tale and a media celebrity, Diana's image was forged by the modern media of photography and television. But as Gamson (2001) has pointed out, in contradiction to the kind of 'power feminism' advocated by Naomi Wolf (1993), the process of self-commodification has contradictory effects. The degree to which women have control over this 'self-fashioning' is illusory in a context where men still overwhelmingly own and produce the media in which they are circulated. Reading practices also draw on old-style, sexist interpretations whatever the intentions of the performer: 'her femininity was not a masquerade she was in control of' (Holt 1998: 196), a fact that the manner of her subsequent death underlines.

Sensationalism, shame and the cult of celebrity

The reason why scandals generate such intense audience interest is because of their ambivalent symbolic form. That is to say, they allow for the expression of transgressive impulses as well as a reassertion of normative ideals in a ritual process that occurs over time. In this respect they can be compared to the traditional popular festivities of carnival, in which a temporary burst of sexual licentiousness and inversion of the social hierarchy is followed by a reinstatement of disciplinary social norms in the mock trial of the figure of Carnival that draws it to a close (Bakhtin 1984). The political effects are unpredictable. The communal effects of the public expression of trans-gressive behaviour can, in some historical circumstances, produce a longer-term change in the normative social order. More often, it simply allows for some temporary psychological relief from everyday disciplines. The aesthetic forms deployed, and modes of participation invited by scandal, enable these psychological pleasures. In particular, I want to look in this section at how the structure of sensationalism allows for the expression of fantasy and the displacement of personal shame on to celebrity transgressors, and, in the next section, at how melodrama, joking and parody are used in the telling of these stories. What becomes clear is the ambivalent politics of these pleasures.

All forms of scandal depend on 'the closet', although it is a term more closely associated with the legal restrictions put on the public expression of homosexuality. 'The unveiling of sexual identities and practices is intrinsic to the scandal genre whether the subjects are heterosexual or homosexual' (Epstein and Johnson 1998: 88). Although 'coming out' of the closet was encouraged by the gay liberation movement, and coming out stories are now an established narrative genre in both fictional and documentary forms (Plummer 1995), the use of the media for involuntary 'outing' was a surprising development in radical politics in the 1990s and the product of a more confrontational 'queer' politics. It has been used in the UK, for example, by the gay activist organization Outrage! and its leading figure Peter Tatchell. As a radical politics it was justified by the argument that citizenship rights for gays and lesbians are pro-moted by their visibility, their presence in the public sphere. It challenged the liberal approach that tolerates, and legalizes, homosexual behaviour only if it is kept private and invisible. While 'outing' had previously been a hostile tactic used by the tabloid media to generate a scandal whose effects would punish people involved in 'deviant' sexual behaviour, as used by Outrage! the intention was to force prominent people into the open about their sexuality so that the closet, and the hypocrisy it sustained, was no longer an option (Epstein and Johnson 1998: 88–9).

'Outing' and 'coming out' have a different relation to the psychology and politics of shame. 'Coming out' is an attempt to redefine the significance attached to a stigmatized sexual identity by a self-declaration: 'I am not ashamed of my sexuality and therefore have no reason to hide it.' It is a defiant act in which the intent is to convert the shame attached to an identity to something that can be owned with pride through a performative act of naming. 'Outing', on the other hand, is a coercive act that could be argued to intensify shame, in that the person named is forced into a public humiliation where the real scandal is their hypocrisy. Where 'coming out' has been the province of television talk shows and drama, where the narrative is told from the point of view of the person involved, 'outing' is an exclamatory form, the stuff of newspaper headlines and live television interviews, where the exposure is brief but dramatic.

Scandals often feature powerful men in the public arena, whether in the world of politics or entertainment, having heterosexual relationships outside their marriages. In a minority of cases, the sex is seen as abnormal, involving such 'perversions' as homosexuality, prostitution, group sex, auto-eroticism or (most stigmatized of all) paedophilia. The key factor is that they reveal sexual behaviour that carries a moral stigma even if the particular activity involved is not illegal. The telling of these stories is 'sensationalist' to the extent that they seek to have an impact on the senses and to provoke an emotional response. In sexual terms this means they may have the potential to excite the viewer sexually. However, the moral discourse in which they are framed means that the behaviour that provokes this reaction is simultaneously condemned. The condemnation allows for the 'return of the repressed'; that is, all those potentially pleasurable aspects of sexual experience that are excluded from the sexual codes of a traditionalist, and patriarchal, moral discourse. The norm is heterosexual monogamy in a sexual union designed for the reproduction and care of children rather than for sensual pleasure *per se*. These reports therefore allow for the vicarious enjoyment of the thrill and excitement of doing something 'bad' in a structure that, in Freudian terms, placates the internalized prohibitions of the superego (Epstein and Johnson 1998).

It is similar to the double structure Freud found in smutty jokes, where the structure of the joke licenses the temporary evasion of the superego and the pleasure of indulging in transgressive sexual wishes (Freud 1991). In both cases, as well as imaginatively enjoying an image of sexual transgression, the teller and the listener are positioned as superior, while the victim of the scandal or the butt of the joke are subjected to humiliation and shame. It is a psychologically and culturally sanctioned technique, known as 'projection', in which bad parts of the self are disavowed and positioned in the world beyond the self, where they can be condemned and punished. It is a way to avoid the acknowledgement that one might harbour these prohibited desires oneself. In this way, Freud argues, we are able to evade the discomfort produced by feelings of shame while publicly reconfirming our social standing as respectable members of the community. In Freud's early writing, shame, disgust and morality are the forces that organize and repress infantile desires – the shame of incest is an extreme instance. It is one of the ways we try to forget a part of ourselves, curb our unruly desires. As Jacqueline Rose (2003: 1) points out, 'I would rather die' is the phrase that conjures up the appalling nature of shame. It has a visceral quality:

> People turn red with shame, are flooded by shame, as though shame – rather like the sexuality it can cow into submission – brings the body too close to the surface, inner organs and liquids bursting through the dams of the mind.

To confess to shame is a most intimate act. 'And yet shame is also an action, a transitive verb – to shame – with a very public face . . . Shame therefore shunts back and forth, crossing the boundary between our inner and outer worlds' (Rose 2003: 1–2). This psychodynamic can be traced in the interrelations of public scandals.

Rose (2003: 201–15) uses psychoanalysis to explain what it is that people – both celebrities and their watchers – really want from the glare of publicity. She speculates that the cult of celebrity in the contemporary media is an expression of a guilty secret, 'a veiled way of putting into public circulation certain things which do not easily admit to public acknowledgement. Hence the pull and the paradox, why it is so exciting and demeaning at the same time' (*ibid*.: 203). In this way she teases out the ambivalent desires involved in our voyeuristic enjoyment of the exhibitionism of celebrity in a Judaeo-Christian culture that, historically, has valued humility and modesty over **narcissism**. Celebrities disavow their desire to court publicity – they publicly declare how much they value their privacy and how ordinary they really are (despite the attention they are receiving). In doing so they embody and carry for us the shame at our own narcissistic and exhibitionist desires. We want to put them on a pedestal as an ego ideal, while at the same time punishing them for their narcissism.

So the idealization of celebrities, in Rose's view, is a consequence of the same psychic processes as the pleasure we take in their humiliation when they are shamed by scandal. Celebrities inspire awe but also dread and an 'excited gasp at the fall' (*ibid*.: 4). These ambivalent feelings emerge in the frenzy of curiosity that creates celebrity and the relentless investigative uncovering of the scandalous news story. Rose points to the strongly violent component driving this curiosity. 'It feels shameful in direct proportion to the murderous frenzy with which it is pursued (the death of Diana would simply be the most glaring instance of the trend) . . . we create celebrities so that our curiosity, or rather curiosity at its most ruthless, can be licensed and maintained' (*ibid*.: 214). Curiosity does violence to its object; there is no such thing as a pure and virtuous curiosity. But, she argues, we have an interest in hiding this fact in order to maintain an idealized image of ourselves. Media attention is 'sadistic in direct proportion to its vaunting of its own virtue' (*ibid*.: 211).

Melodrama and the carnivalesque

Sensationalist moral discourses dominate the tabloids' approach to celebrity scandals and emerge on television in the more popular styles of factual programming, such as daytime talk shows or primetime news and current affairs programmes, in which the intermittent potential for scandal afforded by celebrities is supplemented by the exposure of ordinary people's deviant behaviour. The story convention through which they are told is melodrama, a popular form of culture that has, in modern societies, largely remained on the unrespectable side of the division between high and low culture (though it can cross over this boundary in its more excessive, parodic forms). Characteristically, melodrama embodies morality tales of good versus evil in which stereotypical characters enact excessive, unrestrained behaviour that elicits a strong emotional reaction from the audience. The melodramatic potential of scandal is enhanced by the graphic visual evidence of wrongdoing gathered by secret cameras in investigative reports, or the staged encounters between wronged parties on talk shows, and studio audiences' noisy involvement in the process of passing moral judgement.

As argued above, these morality tales are not simply normative but are also an outlet for fantasy and wish fulfilment, and a way of coming to terms with our own fears and anxieties. Elizabeth Bird (1997: 108) emphasizes the way in which the scandalous forms of melodrama are embedded in oral culture, and involve the audience in speculation about how such shocking things could have come about. 'The narrative must speak to issues or emotions that engage readers and viewers in speculation, fascination, and downright relish in the melodramatic excess of it all' (ibid.: 117). The openness of scandal narratives – no one knows quite how each will end – encourages audience involvement. It is often not clear who is the real victim in the affair and whether guilt will be proven. 'As people speculate they tend to look for answers from within their own experience' (ibid.: 110). It is the degree to which scandals connect with that experience that determines the level of audience interest.

But the nature of our engagement with scandal also depends on the tone and the point of view from which the story is told. Melodrama is potentially both serious and comic and particular instances or phases of the drama will have different emphases in this respect. 'Once something becomes an over the top melodrama the people caught up in it begin to seem less like real human beings and more like cartoons or symbols' (ibid.: 116). Excessive displays of shocking behaviour inviting harsh moral judgements can equally provoke ribald laughter and joking. As the joking increases so does the distancing effect, enabling us to withdraw our empathy with the suffering of the victims. Jokes also allow those who tell or share them to feel superior, thereby adding a further layer of enjoyment for those who partake in this ritual humiliation. Patricia Mellencamp (1992), in her study of scandal and comedy, regards this 'doubling', in which seemingly contradictory responses are simultaneously evoked, as the defining characteristic of contemporary television. 'Television embodies contradictions rather than an "either/or logic", one of "both/and", an *inclusive* logic of creation/ cancellation' (ibid.: 5). Morally, this enables us to enjoy indulgent consumption of dubious pleasures without sacrificing a sense of our own, superior respectability. As viewers we are typically positioned as respectable, middle-class conformists who jeer and humiliate those below or above us in the social hierarchy, who enact the sexual transgressions denied to us by our normative codes of behaviour.

The most notorious example of this tendency is the globally syndicated *Jerry Springer* talk show (1991–), which is based on a gladiatorial, confrontational structure culminating in a moral judgement meted out by the show's host in a piece to camera at the end. It is designed to heighten the melodramatic division between the victims and the villains, and between our condemnatory position as viewers and the transgressors on display. For many commentators the programme works to reinstate cultural norms as a result of its moralistic tone and closed narrative structure, and the low social status of the participants. These features, and the frequently violent encounters it displays, encourage condemnation of the show, and the people who appear on it, as 'trash'. Jane Shattuc (1997) argues, however, that it also provides a spectacular display of polymorphous perversity in a carnivalesque array of sexual transgressions among the least powerful in our society. As a consequence, younger viewers especially have read it through a trash aesthetic, as a subversive display of excess and bad taste.

The radical potential of carnival in Bakhtin's (1984) analysis is only realized where everyone participates: the high and the low, the indigenous and the foreign. Irreverent parody is used to subject dominant norms and conventions to subversive laughter, a process in which the boundaries that categorize our everyday experiences, and the social hierarchies they maintain, are thrown into question. Carnival holds the utopian potential to imagine a world not yet in existence. It is this version of carnival that informs the staging of scandalous events in queer activism, where the struggle to gain respect is pursued through a refusal to accede to dominant notions of respectability. Television has participated by exposing this transgressive sexual behaviour to view. On mainstream networks this is as likely to be in 'respected' genres (arts programmes, quality drama) as in 'trash' genres (daytime talk shows, late night docuporn). But, as Kathleen Rowe (1995) has pointed out, there is a difference between the inclusive, participative rituals of carnival and the spectacle of modern media. On television the unequal power relations of voyeurism and its sexist and racist visual conventions mediate these performances. This works to position the audience as outside and superior to the spectacle they are witnessing unless great care is taken to destabilize these ways of looking.

The use of satiric parody to challenge dominant sexual norms in ways that genuinely disturb everyday ways of categorizing the social world would need to implicate us all in its critique. This was achieved, I would argue, in the comedy series *Brass Eye* (Channel 4 2001), which included an episode on paedophilia. It caused hundreds of complaints to the BSC, who subsequently reprimanded Channel 4 for causing offence (BSC 2002). The programme satirized the media's portrayal of paedophilia using a parody of the sensationalist style of populist journalism that had dominated reporting in the 1990s. The moral panic surrounding paedophilia is sufficient to make it risky to joke about these scandals without causing offence, but celebrities such as Michael Jackson have been subject to running gags over several years (see Hinerman 1997). Catholic priests are a similar target, with knowing references recurring in newspaper cartoons and television sitcoms. What made the *Brass Eye* case different? Why did it cause such a strong negative reaction?

I would argue that it was because it was the media coverage itself and the public reaction to it that was subject to condemnation, not the actions of the demonized paedophiles themselves. This implicates the television audience for its complicity in a consumer culture in which ever-younger children are being targeted in advertising, drama and music videos as a market for beauty products, fashion, toys and pop star imagery, in which a sexualized image is promoted as an ideal (Jenkins 1998). Further, as avid consumers of the paedophile sex scandals, whose sensationalist structure is exposed by the satire, we are complicit in the processes by which our culture promotes, then disavows, the child as sexualized image (Kinkaid 1998). In Valerie Walkerdine's (1998) view the ideological commitment to childhood innocence and purity requires a repression of any conscious acknowledgement of this process although an increasing number of newspaper articles now make this point (see Walters 2003, for example). It is this hypocrisy that was being exposed by the satire. The scandalized reaction also returns us to the psychoanalytic discussion of shame at the start of this section. The figure of the demon paedophile, which dominated the news media in the 1990s, successfully displaced the widespread evidence of family incest that emerged as a public issue in the media during the 1980s (Kitzinger 2001; Critcher 2003). It is far more comfortable to project our shame on to these notorious perverts than to admit to the possibility within our own homes.

Conclusion

The 'epistemology of the closet' has been identified by Eve K. Sedgwick (1990) as a binary structure organizing sexual discourses in Anglo-American societies, a legacy of Puritanism rather than, as Freud believed, an inevitable feature of the processes of repression involved in achieving adulthood. In this binary structure one side of the dichotomy lacks sexual legitimacy and is therefore subject to concealment and the threat of scandalous disclosure. Women and homosexuals are particularly vulnerable in this respect, as when their sexual activities are exposed in the public sphere they are subject to moral condemnation and in some cases criminal prosecution. When it comes to children, the binaries are based around a belief in childhood innocence and abstention, which makes sexual knowledge dangerous and a possible catalyst for sexual initiation (Epstein and Johnson 1998: 92).

Debbie Epstein and Richard Johnson (1998) offer a critique of this legacy in the belief that we need to undermine the power that scandals exert on the popular imagination. The closet, they argue, 'implies a kind of knowledge that is never fully conscious or critical, a suspicion, a half spoken assumption, a nudge, a wink, a leer' (*ibid.*: 92). It is the opposite of the explicit knowledge promoted by education. They advocate a more general 'coming out' in the culture at large, thereby making the censorious morality and prurient curiosities promoted by scandal less potent as the primary means by which children come to learn about sexual relations in the public sphere. Where one of the main sources of knowledge about sexuality is news reporting of sexual scandals, they argue, prurience and ignorance are two sides of the same coin. Sexual discourse on television might usefully be evaluated in these terms, and in relation to adults as well as children. If this were the case, the educative, public service role of television in bringing sexuality 'out of the closet' would be recognized and welcomed, so that certain forms of sexual explicitness would be a positive recommendation for family viewing, rather than the reverse.

Recommended reading

Carter, C., Branston, G. and Allan, S. (eds) (1999) *News, Gender and Power*. London: Routledge.

Fraser, N. (1995) Politics, culture and the public sphere: towards a postmodern conception, in L. Nicholson and S. Seidman (eds) *Social Postmodernism: Beyond Identity Politics*. Cambridge: Cambridge University Press.

Lull, J. and Hinerman, S. (eds) (1997) *Media Scandals: Morality and Desire in the Popular Culture Marketplace*. Cambridge: Polity Press.

Rose, J. (2003) The cult of celebrity, in *On Not Being Able to Sleep: Psychoanalysis and the Modern World*. London: Chatto and Windus.

Thompson, J. (2000) *Political Scandals: Power and Visibility in the Media Age*. Cambridge: Polity Press.

THE SCIENCE OF SEX

Science and wildlife documentaries occupy a pinnacle of respect in the rhetoric of public service broadcasting. They exemplify the epitome of 'quality' factual television in contrast to the docusoaps that dominated the schedules in the latter half of the 1990s. Although associated in the UK with the public service ethos of the BBC and the long-standing 'blue chip' wildlife films of the Natural History Unit, the global success of series such as *The Human Body* (1998), *Walking with Dinosaurs* (1999), *The Blue Planet* (2001) and *The Life of Mammals* (2002) has also depended on a joint venture agreed in 1996 between BBC Worldwide, the commercial arm of the BBC, and the Discovery Channel, a highly successful global cable company based in the USA specializing in factual programming (Chris 2002: 18). These blockbuster series help to reinforce the reputations of both companies as prestige global brands. Heavily marketed in advance, they attract large audiences as well as winning industry prizes. Their brand value is then exploited further through subsequent product spin-offs such as books, videos, DVDs, computer games, music CDs, educational toys, inter-active CD-ROMS and websites, which are promoted on-air and sold direct on the Internet to schools as well as the general public (Chris 2002: 20).

The prestige of these documentaries owes a great deal to their use of the legitimating discourses of science and of the latest imaging technologies. Production personnel have close links with scientific institutions; indeed, many achieved a doctorate in science before they became television producers. The cultural assumptions that are inscribed into science as an institution and method of enquiry pervade this generic form. Yet their address to a mass audience means that they are also structured as entertainment. Their popularity rests on their ability to provide education in ways that appeal across the generations to a family audience. The pleasures of narrative and of visual spectacle are important here as a means to engage audiences. Discovery has 'strategically cultivated the entertainment value of non-fiction' (Chris 2002: 12). This has been achieved through a focus on topics with global appeal, such as natural disasters or human and animal mating practices, which are presented to emphasize dramatic story lines. Since its inception in 1985, Discovery has now expanded to eight channels that address very precisely targeted niche markets. For example, Discovery Health is oriented to a feminized 'lifestyle' niche, while Animal Planet, a channel devoted to wildlife programming, is oriented towards a younger market and is explicitly educational in its address.

Given these developments, the focus of this chapter is on the interrelation between the demands for 'quality' in the deployment of 'technoscientific' discourses in science and wildlife programming and generic innovations that have enhanced their popular appeal. It also considers the implications of this interrelation for the sexual politics of these genres, which traditionally were structured around a gendered binary between the detached observer, coded as masculine, and an embodied 'nature', coded as feminine. My analysis derives from feminist challenges to these hegemonic discourses and the gendered hierarchy they sustain. The second half of the chapter takes up this analysis in relation to the series *The Human Body* and its construction of sexual difference. The focus here is on how the programme's use of digital imaging, metaphor and narrative work to produce 'intelligible bodies' that conform to normative conceptions of sex and gender. This is compared to alternative 'feminist' or 'queer' explanations of the relation between sexed bodies and cultural genders that emerge on the margins of the schedules. The chapter concludes with a discussion of the potential, in a global market, for discursive innovation in these genres and the implications for their sexual politics.

The technoscientific gaze: a critique

There is a perceived tension between the detached, objective pursuit of knowledge about the world in 'quality' science programmes and the popular appeal of emotion, drama and storytelling. Yet this dichotomy is not as clear-cut as it might at first appear to be. I will be arguing here that science is not as '**disinterested**' or 'objective' as it is often believed to be, and that this is especially the case with science documentaries. In the shift towards more popular forms the use of rhetorical techniques has merely become more immediately transparent as the spectacular and emotional appeal of the genre has been intensified.

The mode of address traditionally associated with science documentaries has been characterized by Bill Nicholls (1994) as a 'discourse of sobriety'; that is, serious in tone with an emphasis on the cerebral and the rational rather than the sensual and the emotional. Authoritative (male) voice-overs or respected presenters whose credibility is assured by age and experience embody this elite, institutionalized mode of address – men such as David Attenborough, whose long career presenting wildlife films has made him emblematic of the genre, or Professor Robert Winston, whose reputation as a fertility consultant was pre-eminent even before he became the presenter for *The Human Body*. When they speak to the audience they offer not personal opinion but scientifically proven fact. Knowledge is produced through observation and reasoning, knowledge that is presented as quite independent of the subjective bias of the film-maker. This is guaranteed either by the use of interviews with academic experts in the field of enquiry, or by generic strategies that work to deny the embodied, situated production of knowledge in favour of a disembodied, objective form of 'knowing' embedded in the scientific method. The only legitimate role for emotion is in the passionate curiosity that drives the enquiring mind. Through these means the genre promises to capture on film 'nature as it really is' for the education of the television audience. It is an ideal that depends, in Nicholl's view, on a naive photographic realism and a disavowal of the degree to which images are open to subjective interpretation.

To meet the professional criteria of 'quality' expected of the genre, blockbuster science documentaries enjoy generous budgets for global travel and state of the art technology that can provide images of the nature that otherwise would be hidden in faraway places or be invisible to the naked eye. This helps to guarantee the scientific discourse of 'discovery', a discourse that works to deny the degree of mediation of nature involved in this process of visualization and that foregrounds the use of technology to see what had been previously hidden. These are the qualities that are valued by their fellow professionals; for example, *The Human Body* (BBC 1999) received three BAFTA awards in 1999 for Best Factual Series, Best Graphic Design and Originality for its display of the inner workings of the body. In an accompanying documentary on the making of *The Human Body* the emphasis is almost exclusively on the imaging technologies used and the way they were used to bring 'entirely new ways' of seeing the body to the television screen. These included an electron microscope, an endoscope, magnetic scanning machines, motion capture techniques linked to computer modelling, underwater cameras, time lapse and time slice photography. Similar technical ingenuity is used in wildlife documentaries, relying on studio shots, chromakey overlays and digital enhancement to edit with the raw footage gathered in the wilds of Africa or Antarctica or deep in the ocean. These techniques appeal to the desire to know, but they also provide a sumptuous visual spectacle that appeals to the senses as well as to the intellect. Imaging technologies therefore also draw on the techniques developed in entertainment film, television and computer games to create excitement and visual pleasure, and to create the illusion of 'being there'.

As a consequence, these genres reproduce the ways of looking instituted in a number of film traditions as well as those developed in medical and scientific imaging. A substantial body of work has developed which argues that these cohere to produce sexist and racist relations of looking that have been used as an instrument of domination over the bodies of women, people of colour and animals. In Nicholls's (1994) view, the potential for the body and its sensuous desires to disrupt the detached and cerebral mode of address of 'science' is largely repressed or disavowed by the rhetorical techniques of the documentary form. This disavowal depends on the creation of embodied 'others' who are the objects of science's disembodied gaze. It has its roots in the ethnographic film and its racist structures of looking at 'primitive' peoples in their exotic, natural habitats. It is also structured by the dichotomy of a male scientist or film-maker extracting the 'secrets' of a 'female' nature (Crowther 1995; Lindahl-Elliot 2001: 297). This conceptualization has been traced back to the very beginning of the emergence of science in the Enlightenment of the eighteenth century (Merchant 1989).

The repressed body disavowed by scientific rationality returns in science documentaries in their focus on the physical behaviours that constitute the boundaries of taste and decency on television. Getting good close-up shots of the three Fs ('feeding, fighting and fucking') is regarded as a basic requirement of the wildlife genre, a challenge that has to be met through great ingenuity on the part of the film-makers (according to four female TV producers, whom I interviewed at the BBC Natural History Unit in 1996). Indeed, science documentaries are one of the few genres where embodied sex is acceptable for family viewing. This is confirmed by audience research undertaken by the Broadcasting Standards Commission, which used a clip from *The Human Body* to test people's reactions to depictions of sex and nudity. In approving its suitability as 'family television', respondents referred both to the fact that the programme 'looked good' and the fact that it was associated with the respectable educational output of the BBC. Even though it showed ejaculation (for the first time on British television according to the pre-publicity for the programme), it was done 'tastefully' in their view and wouldn't cause embarrassment to those watching it with children (Millwood Hargreave 1999: 58–62). Although it was broadcast at 10.00 p.m. all of the respondents thought it suitable for pre-watershed scheduling.

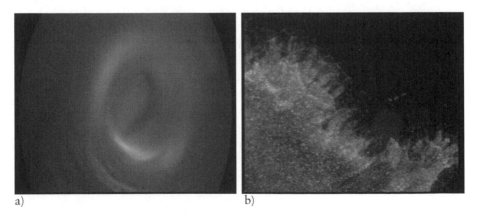

a) b)

Figure 3 a) Ejaculation. b) Sperm travelling along the vagina (From *The Human Body*, BBC 1998, filmed by Dr David Barlow).

Discovery Channel

A market governed by co-productions and by the competitive pressure to capture large and diverse audiences to justify high budgets has led to generic innovation in wildlife programmes during the latter part of the 1990s. In the same way as the rest of television's documentary output, the discourses of sobriety that have dominated wildlife programming in the past have been joined by a full-blown exploitation of the genre's dramatic possibilities. The fully fictionalized *Walking with Dinosaurs* (BBC/Discovery 1999) was both a critical and a popular success (Donnelly 2001). Its use of digital imaging to create a primeval nature inhabited by dinosaur characters owes as much to imagination as to scientific evidence; the standards of realism are set by Hollywood film rather than 'nature as it is'. Here, advanced technology is used to create an entertaining story of a mythical past. The individuation of the 'characters' in this drama and our emotional engagement with their struggle for survival is foregrounded in ways that speak to a cross-gender and cross-generation family audience oriented to computer game animations and soap opera drama, thus justifying its place in network prime time.

The success of Discovery has also depended on the development of popular and cheap infotainment formats. Small independent production companies produce much of the low-budget content. Animal Planet, for instance, offers *The Planet's Funniest Animals*, *Animal Cops*, *Amazing Animal Videos* and *Growing Up Grizzly*, in which sitcom star Jennifer Anniston invites us to 'get to know a unique grizzly bear family, and join a live chat with its patriarch' (Animal Planet 2004). The drama of animal lives performed in front of the camera or constructed through the editing process creates anthropomorphic stories that engage the audience's emotions (Crowther 1995; Lindahl-Elliot 2001). Heightened emotions are a necessary, if disruptive, presence because these films are addressed to a mass audience for whom animals are a matter of emotional connection rather than the object of scientific study. Yet Nils Lindahl-Elliot (2001) points to the way in which the professional legitimacy guaranteed by science has in the past required a disavowal of this aspect of the genre's appeal. He cites a producer in the 1970s who declared, 'I had laid it down as one of the tenets of *Survival* that we would always avoid sentimentality and that we would never allow ourselves to be accused of anthropomorphism' (*ibid.*: 289). Yet, he argues, this is an impossible ideal. Even in the most scientific of approaches 'humans cannot but be anthropomorphic when speaking about nature' (*ibid.*: 290–1). The conventions of the genre have obscured this process, he explains, by working to naturalize the degree to which the programmes privilege a particular perspective. This is true both in the choice of shots and in the narrative conventions deployed. A recurring example is their use of masculinist, quest narratives that originated with the 'big male hunter' scenarios of imperial adventures in Africa.

In an advertisement for Discovery Channel (Channel 4 1998) we can see a different mode of address in operation, one in which the anthropomorphic and dramatic

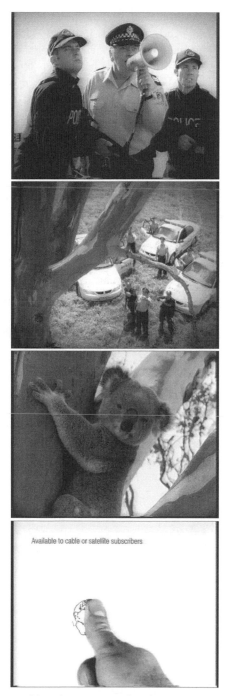

Figure 4 Discover our World. Advertisement for the Discovery Channel (broadcast Channel 4, 1998)

pleasures of the genre are explicit and the origins of the genre in the big game hunter adventures of the colonials lightly satirized. It begins with lots of fast cut shots of police cars, sirens wailing and police marksmen leaping out with guns at the ready. One shouts into a megaphone, in an Australian accent, 'Come on mate, give yourself up. You're surrounded.' The next shot is from up in a tree, looking down at the police below, with a voice-over saying, 'There is an animal who has fingerprints almost identical to our own.' It then cuts to a shot looking up to a koala bear hugging the tree trunk. On the sound track the police are now gently coaxing, 'That's it – come on, come on.' It cuts to a human thumb printing on to a white screen that turns into a globe forming part of the Discovery Channel logo, with the caption 'Discovery Channel. Explore Your World.'

This references the origins of the genre in a world where men use guns to hunt down wild animals, exerting their control over nature. But instead of presenting this to us straight, the advert gently makes fun of this demonstration of masculine prowess. It starts with police-series narrative conventions that lead us to expect a dangerous criminal fugitive. When we see the cuddly koala, therefore, we laugh. From this point, there is a softening, a feminization of the narrative in which our biological closeness to this creature is asserted in our shared fingerprints, and our relationship to it domesticated by its equation with coaxing a pet cat out of a tree. Although we are invited by the camera to see the world from the koala's point of view, it is structured so that at first we assume it is a human point of view. We are also reassured that that is 'your world', on which you can imprint your identity. It is a different kind of domination that works by an assimilation of the wild into the domesticated context of our living room, a world in which we relate to wild animals as if they were our pets or our children.

Infotainment formats also draw heavily on the fictional narratives of heterosexual romance. The Discovery website (www.discovery.com), for instance, in the week before St Valentine's Day, included an account of animal mating behaviour introduced by the headline 'Dancing and Romancing':

> Katherine Hepburn and Spencer Tracey, Humphrey Bogart and Lauren Bacall, Anthony and Cleopatra. Their passion is legendary. But can it compare to the male alligator, which blows bubbles on his sweetie's cheeks? Or the banana slug, which presents a blanket of slime? The ritual of finned, feathered and furred courtship, designed to stimulate and tantalize a female, may not involve flowers and chocolates, but their flirtations are just as sweet.

This accentuates a narrative that has been intrinsic to the wildlife genre from the start. Critical accounts have shown the ways in which wildlife narratives have been structured around reproduction (Crowther 1995), while any animal behaviour that disrupts a conventional heterosexual account is routinely ignored (*The Truth about Gay Animals*, Channel 4 2002).

Discovery's mode of address is unashamedly designed to appeal to a mass market for whom sobriety is displaced by humour, fact is interchangeable with fiction, and the gap between humans and animals is dissolved. The website continues:

> Sex is on our minds. So it is with animals. Like humans, all mammals, birds, reptiles, amphibians and fish spend a better part of their lives flirting, fighting, dancing and romancing so they can mate and reproduce to pass their genes on to the next generation. Those we've included here have developed wild ways of wooing their partners.

The comparisons between human and 'wild ways of wooing' that can be found in animals, which gestures towards the potentially disruptive nature of our 'animal desires', is foreclosed by the assertion that sex has only one purpose, the reproduction of our species.

This 'sociobiological' account of animal reproduction, in which animal and human sexual behaviour are both understood through the same socially constructed narratives derived from evolutionary biology, is characteristic of the wildlife genre and is fundamental to the genre's sexual politics. The next section examines this aspect of the genre in more detail through a discussion of a science documentary that examined the sexual politics of 'primatology', the study of apes, and its interrelation with the politics of wildlife film-making. Indeed, according to the introduction to a book on women and science, 'Primatology may be viewed as the soap opera of contemporary sociobiological narratives of sexual evolution' (Jacobus *et al*. 1990: 1).

Beauty and the beast

The feminist scientist Donna Haraway has argued that science evolves through complex, historically specific storytelling practices rather than through a detached analysis of the 'facts'. She has drawn attention to the political and economic interests that are reproduced by the narratives of science (Haraway 1991). The most powerful of these in relation to the wildlife genre is the evolutionary myth of 'sociobiology' that dramatizes scientific accounts of sexual difference. Sociobiology rose to prominence in the 1970s following the discovery of DNA in the 1950s, which brought genetic explanations of human life into the foreground. It is used in wildlife commentaries to tell us how to understand the animal behaviour we are watching. By drawing parallels between human and animal behaviour it also offers us an explanation of human behaviour grounded in our evolutionary past. In this narrative we are the products of an evolutionary process of selective adaptation designed to maximize the reproductive fitness of individuals so that they may pass on their genes. It constructs an explanation of sexual behaviour and sexual identity that emphasizes sexual difference. Male behaviour is thus oriented towards competition with other males for dominance in order to give them priority access to females for mating. Female animals ensure optimum conditions for the reproduction of their genes by mating with the dominant males and so producing offspring more fit for survival. It is an ideological discourse that has been criticized for naturalizing male promiscuity, aggression and dominance over women. It is also consistent with a capitalist perspective that imagines society as based on the survival of the fittest, an individualized, competitive environment in which sexual relations are governed by an investment strategy designed to ensure the continuation of the 'self' as embodied in a set of genes (Haraway 1990).

Given the proximity of apes to humans in this evolutionary history, they have played a central role in establishing the validity of these discourses. Yet it is through primatology, a field that has attracted many women scientists, that a feminist challenge to the patriarchal narratives of sociobiology emerged in the 1970s and 1980s. These women told a different story, reporting, for example, patterns of behaviour among some animals in which female apes took the initiative in their social organization. However, Haraway (1990) points out that this deconstruction of masculinist discourses is still contained within a sociobiological framework, with female apes defined through a construction of altruistic motherhood. The more radical challenge posed by their work, she argues, is in the methods that they used. They developed close relationships with the primates they studied, thus calling into question the model of the disinterested scientist. This 'close encounter' proved scandalous to more than just the scientific community. The films of these studies, made and distributed by National Geographic, provided the finance for the research but also enabled it to reach a wider audience. They were therefore breaking not only scientific conventions but also the power relations of the male gaze embedded in the established conventions of the documentary film. Images of young blond women in the arms of large brown apes were imbued with racist meanings, meanings that drew on established racist myths of the dangers of miscegenation. Dianne Fosse, one of the most notorious of these women, was accused of having 'unnatural relations' with the gorillas she studied.

This history is recounted in *Beauty and the Beast*, the second programme in a trilogy called *Sex and the Scientist* (Channel 4 1996). Donna Haraway's analysis of feminist primatologists' storytelling practices, which opens the programme, is then balanced against an interview with Steven Pinker, a well-known sociobiologist, who provides further critical comment on the significance of the women primatologists' research methods and findings. In Pinker's view, the fact that they found female animals to be at the centre of the social group while the males were on the margins was simply the product of the feminist ideologies of the time and incompatible with value-free science. To him the women scientists exemplify the dangers inherent in crossing the boundaries between the observer and the observed, the human and the animal, culture and nature, the boundaries that, in his view, secure the scientist's detachment. His perspective is then legitimized and prioritized over Haraway's account by the framing provided in the (female) voice-over. This works to undermine the more general case made by Haraway that *all* scientific interpretations, and not just feminist science, arise from their sociohistorical context, with sociobiology being a case in point.

This programme provides an interesting example of how science documentary-makers are caught between their use of the cultural power of storytelling and a reluctance to let go of a belief, which they share with the scientists, in detached observation. This is embedded in the conventions they use. The programme follows the classic expository form of 'expert' interviews from a variety of viewpoints edited with archive footage. These provide the evidence that legitimizes the explicit claims made in a reasoned argument presented in the voice-over. In this case the overall argument offers a critique of the anthropomorphism displayed by the women primatologists. This puts the case that our desire for close encounters with wild animals is incompatible with the scientific study of an uncontaminated nature. This trend is criticized as the product of the financial entanglement between research into animal behaviour and the commercial exploitation of filming rights, which 'changed scientists into film stars and changed primatology into the study of individual animals with personalities', as the voice-over comments. The sexual allure of the women primatologists who appeared in the films and the domestication of the apes they studied, treating them as if they were human, are blamed for undermining the scientific study of apes in the wild and endangering the habitat they depend on. It turned science into entertainment.

This is an audacious argument to put in a documentary film about nature designed as television entertainment. Indeed, it requires a complete disavowal by the film-makers of their own part in the processes they describe and condemn. The film promotes an environmentalist perspective that is concerned to protect nature from despoliation by human intervention and they use science to legitimize their argument. But they use the emotive power of visual images of animals to support their case. Close-up images of cuddly pictures of human-like apes at the start of the film, as we watch the women primatologists at work in the African jungle, are replaced by disturbing images of ape skulls, deforestation and hoards of tourists with cameras as the destructive effects of their studies are explained. These techniques appeal to the desire to know, but they also provide an engaging visual spectacle that works unnoticed on the emotions alongside the explicit argument. The film's perspective can also be shown to be a product of the emergent stories characteristic of the historical period and of the commercial conditions in which it has been made, rather than as the product of disinterested science. That this programme should use an environmentalist discourse to critique feminist primatology is consistent with the relative decline of feminist politics and the rise during the 1990s of environmentalism as a new social movement. For an independent production company (Diverse Productions) with a history of making anti-establishment documentary, environmentalism offers a more contemporary form of oppositional discourse with an appeal to the youthful viewers sought by Channel 4. Feminist critique is now often seen as old-fashioned.

Feminist critiques of the genre have never had more than a marginal influence. The group of women producers in the BBC's Natural History Unit whom I interviewed were inspired to try by a lecture they had attended by Barbara Crowther, a cultural studies academic. She had suggested paying more attention to 'the behaviour and role of infertile or post-reproductive females, sex as a pleasurable activity not necessarily dominated by the need to reproduce, or whether females ever express a preference for less bullish males' as an alternative to the narratives of sociobiology (Crowther 1995). Their subsequent attempts to innovate in this way included trying to change the use of standard vocabulary, such as resisting the practice of describing groups of female animals as a 'harem'. Or they looked for alternative narrative forms that could accommodate a varied understanding of animal social relationships and our relation to them. One producer, in a programme called *Watch Out*, had introduced a magazine format that allowed for multiple perspectives, and based the series nearer to home by looking at the wildlife in urban neighbourhoods. But they felt that these initiatives remained marginal in a context where the prestige of the 'blue chip' wildlife documentary inhibited change. They also drew on the pervasive sociobiological frameworks of the genre to explain their lack of influence. They felt themselves disadvantaged in a competitive male hierarchy where 'displays of dominance' are integral to the way in which the power relations of the field are worked through. Their inability to inhabit the masculine, heroic role of the risk-taking, naturalist adventurer had limited their status and career development.

The intelligible body: machines and cartographies

In the opening of 'An Everyday Miracle', part 2 of *The Human Body*, a voice-over tells us, 'Professor Winston continues his remarkable journey inside the human body.' Then we are told, over a pulsating red fleshy wall in a white circle:

> You're looking at a baby's heart. It's beating 120 times a minute. But that's not the only thing keeping this baby alive. That's done by the most sophisticated life support machine on earth. To find that machine we have to leave the heart and travel through an artery the thickness of a drinking straw.

A zoom takes us through a dark inner and red outer circle until we hear swooshing noises, and we are told: 'Through a wall comes the sound of the engine room. It's a mother's heart and we've just made the journey from the inside of an unborn baby.' In less than thirty seconds, the spatial and functional relations governing our viewing of the pregnant woman's body have been established in a combination of visual imaging techniques with verbal analogies using metaphors of a journey. This offers us an imagined geography of the body that is reminiscent of the 'ethnographic gaze' of the wildlife documentary but in which the body of the other has been metaphorically transformed to a machine.

It locates the professor as the organizing point of view: it is *his* journey that we are being invited to share (and admire as 'remarkable'), and it is *his* words that will interpret the shifting kaleidoscope of colour we see along the way. The journey metaphor also applies to sperm in what is introduced as the 'drama of conception'. In a purposeful, but dangerous, journey the sperm race against time to be the first to break through the walls of the egg, while facing 'many mortal dangers' in the hostile terrain of the vagina. The egg isn't simply passively waiting. 'As they get near the sperm are lured towards their goal by a chemical signal sent out by the egg.' As Deborah Lupton (1994: 10) argues, 'Once it is recognised that the ovum plays an active role in fertilization, metaphors of entrapment and aggression, the representation of the ovum as a femme fatale replaced the passive metaphors of the medical texts.' Thus a heroic masculinity is established, from the single sperm to the eminent professor, both engaged in a quest that typically includes discovery and conquest and tests of prowess. It uses a spatial metaphor to construct a here and there with a clear border between – in this case outside and inside the body – that places the body of the observer within the scene of the 'other' who is to be observed. It constructs authenticity – I know, I was there – and thereby underwrites the truth claims of the documentary, especially when the person who knows is already positioned as an expert in the field.

Nicholls (1994) argues that this form is a vehicle of domination, an exercise in knowledge/power that disavows the acute contradiction between impersonal scientific knowledge and the personal experience on which it is based. It is a tradition that works to legitimize scientific discourse over experiential knowledge. This involves disavowing whiteness and maleness in the body of the observer that constitutes their subjective experience. So too it disavows the representational conventions that construct the knowledge as meaningful, including the conventions of heroic western narrative, the emotional impact of the image and the erotics of the gaze. Instead it references the institutions of science and technology that legitimize knowledge (*ibid.*: 66–70). Nicholls concludes that in this way of looking, 'Rather than seeking to make strangeness known, "we" seek to *know* strangeness. By being beheld at a distance strangeness eludes full comprehension but supports an imaginary coherence . . . what we might more generally call the self that constitutes itself through an imaginary geography' (*ibid.*: 74).

Imaging the body as a machine, rather than, for example, a house or a temple, emerged in the wake of the Industrial Revolution. The nature of this machine has changed alongside technological developments. It has been imagined as clockwork, a combustion engine, a chemical factory and, most recently, as a computerized cybernetic system. It was the discovery of DNA and the genetic code in 1953 that enabled the body to be imagined as a chemical factory, with DNA as the blueprint for manufacturing chemical building blocks. These blueprints were in turn imagined as 'maps' to an undiscovered and unchartered territory, a new frontier for the scientist to explore and document. The metaphorical language used is imbued with meanings that work to naturalize gender differences. These metaphors operate within male-dominated scientific and medical institutions that emphasize competition in the race to be the first to make a discovery. The body thus becomes positioned as the focus in a battle for male supremacy in which technology confers an advantage (Lupton 1994: 60–4).

These technologies allow for the unveiling of the body such that its feminine mystique is 'rendered open to the masculine gaze' and to exploration (*ibid.*: 69). 'A biotechnical gaze restructures space to see the invisible and makes the body intelligible, and controllable on an infinitely small scale as a mosaic of detachable parts' (Harding 1998: 31). Technical intervention by a male medical profession gradually displaced the midwives' role in childbirth during the course of the nineteenth century (Lupton 1994: 147). As a consequence, scientific knowledge that emphasizes looking rather than listening became valorized over experiential knowledge. Technological developments in digital imaging have refined this process, allowing for an increasingly mediated visual knowledge of the inside of bodies and their workings (Treichler *et al.* 1998).

In *The Making of the Human Body* (BBC Worldwide 2001) we are told that the producer's intention was 'to link the outside world with the inside world' using the imaging techniques made available by medical technology. Imaging technologies offer a simulation of bodily processes through visual analogy. The images on the computer screen depend on existing conceptual models of the body both in the programming of the computer software and in their interpretation (Treichler *et al.* 1998: 10). Analogy is used in order to restabilize our sense of self, just as in the ethnographer's film when any strange scene is 'domesticated by being naively explained as analogous to something in our culture' (Nicholls 1994: 78). The journey inside of the body can be imagined as analogous to space exploration. The 'landscape of the interior' is imagined as a science fiction space adventure, Haraway (1992: 320) argues, where we journey through 'blasted scenes, sumptuous textures, evocative colours, and ET monsters'. In *The Human Body*, the producer wants to use the 'aesthetic charm and style of television graphics' to simulate the sensation of 'flying through the body'. Winston's commentary also draws on this space imagery: 'We're inside one of the fallopian tubes – heading towards the ovary – and at the end of the tube there it is – that huge white moon'. In Haraway's view these strange, alienating scenes destabilize our sense of perspective about our bodies as a self-contained, knowable part of self and 'we seem invaded . . . by our own strange parts' (*ibid.*).

The use of existing cultural imagery to interpret these medical images is one of the many ways in which film and television cultures cross over with medical imaging (Treichler *et al.* 1998). The image of the foetus provided by foetal ultrascans has been compared to the already circulated image of astronauts floating in space, joined to the space ship by the umbilical cord. It has given impetus to the notion that the foetus is a fully constituted human being, distinct from the mother (Lupton 1994: 151–5; Harding 1998: 31–3; Stabile 1998). This ultrascan image has been incorporated into diverse social relations and practices, from anti-abortion campaigns to its inclusion in the family album as the first picture of the new baby. In *The Human Body*, the emphasis is on its facilitating the inclusion of the father in the experience of pregnancy: 'I feel like I'm only looking on from the outside – there are times when I wish I could feel the physical side of things so I could understand more.' In fact it is only when he sees the ultrascan image that he realizes there *is* something in there. Imaging technologies can help men to overcome their sense of exclusion from women's embodied experience of pregnancy, allowing them to establish a relationship with the foetus that exists independently from their relation to the pregnant woman.

The appropriation and control of pregnancy and childbirth by a technologically oriented medical profession is argued to have been accompanied by a down-grading of embodied knowledge. As a consequence, women's own experience of pregnancy as a source of knowledge is considered inadequate (Lupton 1994: 147–60). 'An Everyday Miracle' is consistent with this tendency. The programme is entirely motivated by the possibilities created by visual technologies to create a spectacle of pregnancy, rather than to explore how it feels. Although it chooses to focus on a couple, who are interviewed about their experience of the pregnancy, they are completely subordinate to the computer graphics and to Professor Winston's commentary. Winston assures us that, 'Even when we live through it, experiencing the months of pregnancy first hand, our bodies still conceal the marvel of what's going on within.' While we might overlook this use of 'we' as simply the product of a desire to be inclusive of the audience's experience, it is also an example of Nicholl's complaint against the universalizing tendencies of the scientific mode of address in documentaries. By including himself in this 'we' who will experience the months of pregnancy first hand, Winston evades the gender-specific nature of this knowledge and his own embodied subjectivity. Although his own role as an infertility consultant who creates life outside the womb might give him more excuse for thinking he can share in this experience, the truth is he can only *see* what is going on. The 'real' of the woman's body, the secrets of its interior, remain in experiential terms forever beyond the panoptican ambitions of 'the deeply predatory nature of the photographic consciousness' (Haraway 1991).

The feminist critique of the medical control over childbirth emerged in the 1970s from the belief that women's experiential knowledge, grounded in the female body, offered a way to counteract male dominance. Women's supposed closer relation to the body and to nature was appropriated as offering a source of resistance to technoscience as a system of domination. Since then, the development of technofeminism, following from Haraway's (1991) publication of *The Manifesto for Cyborgs*, questions any necessary connection between technoscience, the machine metaphor and male domination over nature and, by extension, women's bodies. She argues that feminist politics should refuse the binary distinctions that sustain the hierarchies of **modernity**. In this view, rather than evading technological domination through calls to a return to nature, women should be embracing its possibilities. In a context where technoscience is using the manipulation of genetic binary codes to generate new life and the manipulation of electronic binary codes to create intelligent machines the boundary between humans and machines is, anyway, rendered indistinct. In refusing the equation between women and nature, the connection between women's bodies and reproduction can be broken and more diverse potentials realized. It also opens the scientific method itself to revision, since the separation and distance on which it is founded are thereby undermined (Jacobus *et al.* 1990: 1–10).

Constructions of sexual difference

In addition to the focus on women's reproduction, there has been a preoccupation in the biological and medical sciences with the question of sexual difference. In medical textbooks prior to the nineteenth century, drawings of male and female anatomy, based on the dissection of dead bodies, had emphasized the degree to which women's sexual organs were identical to men's, but inverted and hidden within the body (Laqueur 1990). This was consistent with a gender politics in which women were regarded as an inferior copy of man, and with the Christian myth that Eve was made out of Adam's rib. But as the bourgeois ideal developed of women's separate sphere in the private home, so their biological difference from men was given anatomical grounding and their weakness and vulnerability accentuated. Women were conceived of as at the mercy of their reproductive biology, especially their wombs (Lupton 1994: 137).

The construction of sexual difference through anatomy has been superseded by an increasing emphasis on hormones, which 'have replaced specific organs as the marker and cause of sexual difference' (Harding 1998: 57). Men and women differ only in the relative amounts of their sex hormones; that is, men have some oestrogen as well as testosterone and women have some testosterone as well as oestrogen. Jennifer Harding (1998) points out that this could have led to a break with dualistic assumptions about sex. Instead hormones have been used to naturalize sexual difference through the designation of 'male' and female' hormones that control our bodies and our behaviour in ways that we are powerless to resist (*ibid*.: 59). These definitions and the hormonal technologies developed to 'normalize' and control sexed bodies are the products of male-dominated scientific institutions. These work to 'shape the collective creation of scientific facts about sex hormones, their origins and functions and help to secure authority for some, and not other, knowledge claims' (*ibid*.: 61).

The binary model of sexual difference as produced by our body chemistry can be seen at work in 'Raging Teens', part 4 of *The Human Body*. Instead of being positioned as in control of the technology of exploration, like Professor Winston, teenagers are on a 'roller-coaster ride' and have no control over it because there are 'chemical messages racing through our bloodstream', that 'order our body to change'. But alongside these bodily changes goes a sequence of cultural assumptions about what it means to be a man or a woman – assumptions about behaviour, attitudes and sexual desire. In this the programme reflects the culturally positive evaluation of masculinity as compared to femininity without comment or critique. Beatrice, a teen-age girl interviewed for the programme, is very negative about the changes happening to her body, especially her periods and breast and hip development, but Winston tells us 'like it or not, once the roller coaster ride starts there's no stopping. With hormones pulsing through her day after day, Beatrice's body races ahead, out of control.' It is all happening, we are told, so that Beatrice's body 'can nurture new life', and again, 'A girl's body changes to get ready for bearing children' (over an X-ray of pelvic bones).

This reinforces the equation of women's bodies with their capacity to reproduce and the erasure of women's capacity for sexual pleasure.

In contrast, a group of American boys tell us they like the changes happening to them, 'You feel stuff getting bigger – so you feel kinda manly.' Instead of period pains and uncomfortable bras they discuss their first experiences of sexual arousal, visualized through heat-imaging shots of an erect penis and endoscope images of an ejaculation from inside the penis. 'Once the sperm factory is up and running there's no going back.' Girls' pain and discomfort in preparation for reproduction is contrasted with the boys' growing sense of a powerful masculinity expressed through body size and the ability to ejaculate. In line with evolutionary biology, Winston tells us the changes in a boy's body stem from his need in times gone by to be strong. 'The testosterone in his system has dramatic effects' (over shots of boys playing basketball, cut with internal shots of bone and muscle). The binary construction of masculinity and femininity, the heterosexism, the inability to address female desire and the assumption that boys have little control over their sexual desire – in every way this programme conforms to the stereotypical assumptions about sex and gender that Epstein and Johnston (1998) criticize in their study of the baleful state of sex education in British schools. Not surprisingly, this is one of the markets to which the video and DVD versions are targeted.

The normative influence of science is also apparent in *Anatomy of Desire*, a three-part series on Channel 4 (1998). It doesn't have the high technology of *The Human Body* but its budget was sufficient to construct an interdisciplinary analysis of sexual desire drawing on widespread research across the world, and especially in the USA. The perspective of this programme is entirely, and uncritically, patriarchal, although in a secular, libertarian mode in which evolutionary biology is presented as a liberating discourse in the face of a repressive Christianity. In the second episode our sexual identity, sexual orientation and sexual practices are presented as the product of our genes, hormones, childhood experiences and first sexual experience. A sexologist from Johns Hopkins University describes this as our 'love map', which remains relatively fixed throughout life, as 'a template in the brain'. The programme is structured as a series of case studies in a scientific mode, with a male 'authoritative' voice-over linking a series of interviews with American and Dutch psychologists, sexologists and sex therapists. It uses a normative framework against which to set abnormal sexual development. For example, Violet was 'over-active' sexually as a child as a result of high levels of testosterone, and now enjoys being dominant in sadomasochistic scenarios, while John, an asexual man, had his desire for sexual relationships displaced by his overly intimate relation with his mother. A third case is an intersex person whose genitals were female at birth but whose hormonal influences led to her being reassigned as a boy by the time she was six months old. The evidence that he really is a man is the fact that he had always preferred boys' games and desired women rather than men. In all three cases, we can see how their abnormality is measured against normative, binary assumptions about female and male behaviour and sexual orientation.

In the past decade the binary model of sexual difference has been undermined by subcultures where indeterminate, transsexual bodies and queer sexualities are being recognized. Judith Butler's (1990) influential book *Gender Trouble* provides the philosophical grounding for these cultural developments by questioning whether there is any ontological grounding for a biological differentiation between men and women; the idea of 'plastic sexualities' that are open to transformation is challenging the certainties of heterosexual or homosexual identity (Giddens 1992). But these developments are almost entirely invisible in the world of television science, except for a recurring interest in sex reassignment surgery through which the normative alignment between bodies and binary genders is restored. However, there are some exceptions. Cynthia Chris's (2002) study of the Discovery Channel notes the inclusion of 'cutting edge, risky programming' on sexual issues. *Is It a Boy or a Girl?* (2001), for example, was praised for its sensitive handling of the issues raised by intersex babies both by the Intersex Society of North America and by the Gay and Lesbian Alliance against Defamation (GLAD) (Chris 2002: 11). Another exception is *Sex Acts* (BBC1 1995), which was part of a science series called *QED*. A link introduces it by saying: 'Gender comes under scrutiny now as *QED* questions traditional stereotypes and considers the acceptance of a third sex, the contents of which could upset some viewers.' What was so radical about it that it needed a broadcast warning?

This is a much lower budget production than the previous examples. There are no computer graphics and it only lasts thirty minutes. There are only two expert interviews, both British, plus filming of a gender workshop in London and an interview with its (American) leader, plus interviews with a small group of transsexuals. The overall argument is that sex is a continuum not a binary, and that being forced into a binary model makes some people very unhappy. It also argues that gender is a performance that is learned, although a psychiatrist concedes the influence of anatomy and hormones in directing people in either female or male directions. This process is demonstrated by the drag king workshop in which a group of women learn how to look, move, behave and speak like men before going out in public for the evening, as men. The feminist leader of this workshop explains how the differences between men's and women's gestures and behaviour are the product of men's greater power, which gives them the confidence to take up space and expect to be listened to.

Instead of going inside the body to find out more about sexual difference, this programme provides a different kind of spectacle – the spectacle of transformation through performance and dress. By setting the transsexual interviewees, several of whom had undergone reassignment surgery and hormone treatment, against the drag king workshop, it offers two models of gender transformation. The potentially conservative gender politics of surgical reassignment, in which bodies are realigned with a person's psychological gender, are set against a more malleable understanding of gender in which a mismatch between one's anatomical 'sex' and one's social 'gender' can be employed as a transgressive act (Wilton 1999). Where these include body modifications that use hormones and other technological interventions it is more in the spirit of Haraway's *Cyborg Manifesto*, which looked to technology to destabilize rather than secure gender binaries. The use of hormones to effect bodily changes doesn't have to involve menopausal women taking replacement oestrogen to make them feel feminine again. There are women taking testosterone to enhance their energy and performance to help them compete on the job market, while others, like the drag king photographer Della Grace, are taking it to grow beards and moustaches in a radical gesture to confuse the markers of gender (Kidd 1999).

Conclusion

Sex Acts was produced by Richard Dale, while the series editor was Lorraine Heggessy. What is perhaps surprising is that these are the same people who made *The Human Body*. How could the same two people be responsible for programmes making such widely diverging claims about sexual difference? It seems we cannot look to the political and philosophical beliefs of the individual programme-makers to explain the contrast. Nor can we look to channel branding given that they were both broadcast on BBC1. Nor can we assume that society is gradually becoming more progressive in relation to sex and gender and that television documentaries then reflect this. *Sex Acts* precedes *The Human Body* by several years. Nor can we simply assume that these two examples exemplify the rich diversity of discourses that can be found in science documentaries. I could find no evidence that this is, in fact, the case. It is safe to say that the vast majority draw on normative science and social science for their validating expertise.

What institutional forces are in play that can explain the very different approaches taken to sexual difference in the programmes discussed? In my view co-productions between the BBC and the Discovery Channel are perhaps part of the answer. The use of American scientific 'experts', with a view to marketing the programme more globally, appears to result in an emphasis on evolutionary models of sex and sexuality. The recurrence of sociobiological narratives of gender can be explained by their hegemonic position in American academia as a counterweight to the religious Right and its creationist beliefs. Another characteristic of high-budget co-productions is their use of visual spectacle as a marketing 'hook'. It promises pleasure to a generation with high expectations of the visual image, built up through computer games and Hollywood films. In marketing terms it is important to be able to offer something 'new', that has never been *seen* before. This takes precedence over *saying* something new. In fact the familiarity of the narrative forms used and the metaphorical concepts deployed ensures they are less likely to offend against the expectations and beliefs established by the generic form.

It could very well be that a low budget is what allowed *Sex Acts* to be radical and to risk alienating some sections of the audience. It didn't have to find co-production money, it wasn't made with a view to selling it around the world or to maximize income from educational as well as broadcast markets, it had to rely on people talking about their experiences because it didn't have the budget for expensive graphics. In these circumstances it was able to *say* something new – but it didn't win any industry prizes.

Recommended reading

Haraway, D. (1991) A Cyborg Manifesto: science, technology and socialist feminism in the late twentieth century, in *Simions, Cyborgs and Women: The Reinvention of Nature*. New York: Routledge.

Harding, J. (1998) *Sex Acts: Practices of Femininity and Masculinity*. London: Sage.

Lindahl-Elliot, N. (2001) Signs of anthropomorphism: the case of natural history television documentaries, *Social Semiotics*, 11(3): 289–305.

Nicholls, B. (1994) The ethnographer's tale, in *Blurred Boundaries*. Bloomington: Indiana University Press.

Treichler, P. A., Cartwright, L. and Penley, C. (eds) (1998) *The Visible Woman: Imaging Technologies, Gender and Science*. New York: New York University Press.

6 | DOCUMENTING THE SEX INDUSTRY

Documentary 'investigations' of the commercial sex industry have been a significant presence in the network schedules since the mid-1990s. This has contributed substantially to the increase in explicitly erotic sexual imagery on mainstream television. This was also the case earlier in the twentieth century with cinema, when documentary acted as a stage in the development of film pornography (Williams 1990). The proliferating documentaries whose purpose is entertainment through erotic display and talk have been joined by others that are designed with more 'proper' purposes in mind. Social histories and anthropological studies, current affairs journalism and personal perspectives from celebrity film-makers have added to the quite extraordinary number of documentaries addressing this topic. The blurred boundaries between legitimate investigation and erotic entertainment in these cases have provoked a hostile reaction. The Broadcasting Standards Commission (BSC) reported that 'The increase in documentaries about the sex industry has contributed enormously to the perception of an all-pervading filth on the air waves' (Millwood Hargrave 1999).

Should all these documentaries be dismissed as worthless voyeurism, a symptom of the decline in our public service broadcasting system, as some commentators believe? Or do they overcome a long history of stigmatization of sex workers, as others have argued? What are the ethics involved in the production of these documentaries? How can producers give participants a voice and escape the charge of exploiting them? This chapter compares a range of documentaries on the sex industry, from late night 'docuporn' to prime time journalism and 'auteur' documentary, in order to explore these questions about quality, exploitation and empowerment in the representation of sex workers.

The forms of documentary on television changed during the 1990s to enhance their entertainment value for a wider audience, or they were pushed to the margins of the schedules (Dovey 2000; Winston 2000). This development began in the 1980s when the deregulatory impetus of the Reagan era ensured the disappearance of 'serious' documentaries from the US television networks, to be replaced by 'infotainment' formats of various kinds. On cable, niche audiences watch educational documentaries on the Discovery Channel while other cable channels have been free to develop what I will call 'docuporn'; that is, cheaply produced 'investigations' of sexuality, such as *G-string Divas* or *Real Sex* (HBO). These proved popular with subscribers and then spread to mainstream television (Winston 2000: 45–9). This trend crossed the Atlantic as a result of the increasing commercialism, tight production budgets and reduced regulatory restrictions that have accompanied the rise of multichannel television. Nevertheless, in the UK, public service regulations still require that terrestrial broadcasters include in their schedules a certain proportion of 'serious' factual programmes, despite their minority appeal, thus guaranteeing that some, at least, of these sex industry investigations are made with more than their erotic appeal in mind. The increase in documentaries on the sex industry is part of a more general rise in the number of documentaries about sex in this period. Analysis of the trends[1] shows that on terrestrial television in the UK between 1995 and 2001 the numbers doubled in 1998, peaked in 1999 and then fell back to a midway point in 2000 and 2001 (Appendix, Figure 1).

More extensive analysis of the peak year, 1999, shows that if the statistics for some of the more popular digital channels are also included, there were literally hundreds of documentaries about sex in that year (Appendix, Figure 2). The regulatory effects of the watershed are shown in the fact that 95 per cent of these were scheduled after 9.00 p.m. The effects of the regulated time bands of the schedules are also apparent in the marked variation in generic address at different times of the day. The emphasis during the daytime is on educational programmes, some specifically for schools, with 75 per cent being historical or educational and only 25 per cent categorized as infotainment (Appendix, Figure 3). In the early evening the emphasis is on current affairs (46 per cent) with infotainment staying at around the same level as in the day (Appendix, Figure 4). After the watershed the emphasis shifts heavily to infotainment, constituting almost three-quarters (71 per cent) of the total output (Appendix, Figure 5). After 11.00 p.m. infotainment dominates almost to the exclusion of all else (87 per cent). A very high proportion of these are sex industry 'docuporn'; that is, they are intended to be sexually arousing (Appendix, Figure 6).

The differentiation across channels is also very marked (Appendix, Figure 7), with the mainstream, public service channel BBC1 showing very few sex documentaries of any kind, while the minority BBC2 has mainly current affairs. Both the minority Channel 4 and at a lower frequency the mainstream commercial channel ITV are evenly divided between current affairs and infotainment. Channel 5 is heavily skewed to infotainment, as are the digital channels Living, Bravo and Sky One, which account for the vast majority of the documentaries shown (see Appendix, Figure 8). This pattern reflects the differentiated audience address arising from channel branding within a public service regulatory framework (see Chapter 2).

The legitimacy of documentaries about the sex industry can never be assumed, but has to be achieved. The first hurdle is for the audience to be reassured that they don't need to feel ashamed for watching it. The BSC found that viewers were far less tolerant of explicit sex in what they perceived as a 'tacky' as opposed to a tasteful documentary, a distinction that depends on all kinds of markers of class status (Millwood Hargrave 1999). In current affairs documentary, a genre closely tied to a journalistic agenda originating in news stories, these markers map on to a difference in the mode of address of 'quality' and 'tabloid' journalism. 'Quality' depends on an elite perspective embodied in expert opinion, while 'tabloidization' is characterized by melodramatic forms of storytelling and is widely regarded as 'dumbing down' to an ostensibly depoliticized agenda. But, as already discussed in relation to news scandals in Chapter 4 and science documentaries in Chapter 5, this evaluation is complicated by the gendering of these aesthetic approaches. In the case of current affairs documentaries, the issue is how to give a 'voice' to the political interests of sex workers, who are predominantly women, while avoiding the voyeuristic potential the topic invites and the normalizing effects created by 'official' disapproval and, in some respects, criminalization of their activities. The constraints are rather different in the documentaries of celebrity film-makers, who are able to distance themselves from the generic requirements of journalism. An 'authored' perspective carries more idiosyncratic markers of 'quality' bound up with aesthetic complexity, in terms of its visual and narrative form.

There are also ethical concerns over declining standards of professional conduct in the production of programmes and the exploitation of the participants in documentary. Sensationalized and intrusive treatments of intimate sexual experiences are of particular concern in this respect. In the current conditions of production in the British television industry, Brian Winston (2000) is concerned that these issues are being ignored, with casualization leading to a decline in professional standards of conduct. Reliance on economically insecure, independent production companies and a decline in budgets has led to more 'hit and run' productions that have no budget for proper research, and film-makers who have no proper training or purpose beyond survival in the industry (Winston 2000: 160). Even with the best of intentions, documentaries designed as critical interventions have been subject to criticism. At the height of the feminist campaigns against pornography, *Not a Love Story* (Klein 1982), for example, a film intended to expose pornography to more widespread condemnation, was criticized for its moralism and sensationalism (Rich 1986). There is always a danger that films about exploitation will be exploitative.

Unequal power relations between film-makers and their subjects is a concern in this respect. The *Good Woman of Bangkok* (O'Rourke 1991), a much-debated documentary made by an Australian male film-maker about a Thai female prostitute, is a case in point (Berry *et al.* 1997; Winston 2000: 147–8; Stones 2002). Challenges from feminist and lesbian film-makers to the long history of male dominance in the film and television industries have since the 1970s created a critical practice designed to counteract these inequalities. Since the 1980s in the UK there has been an influx of women into the television industry, enabled by the growth in independent production. Is women's involvement any kind of guarantee against exploitation and, conversely, can male film-makers ever escape the charge? In considering the ethics of making these documentaries, what difference does it make whether the participants are male or female, 'First' or 'Third World', rich or poor? Industry guidelines emphasize 'informed consent' as a guarantee against exploitation, but is this effective? Or is it the case that these documentaries are inevitably voyeuristic and exploitative whatever the relations between the participants?

An emphasis on how sex workers are represented has overshadowed an equally significant issue, namely the limited perception of who is involved in the industry as clients. Documentaries on the provision of sexual services to the mentally and physically disabled (*Forbidden Pleasures*, Channel 4 2000) and to single women (*Under the Sun*, 'What sort of gentleman are you after?, BBC2 1998) have offered interesting interventions in this respect. Nevertheless, given the long history of debate on the progressive representation of sex workers that has emerged out of feminist activism, the focus of this chapter remains with the sex workers themselves.

From prostitution to sex work: a history of feminist intervention

The changing politics of sex work in feminist activism of the past twenty years can be traced across the transformations in Channel 4's approach to documentaries about the sex industry. Although it is Channel 5 that is famous for it, the majority of 'docuporn' on British terrestrial television is shown on Channel 4, as a consequence, it can be argued, of its having shifted to selling its own advertising and the more commercial priorities that ensued. This highlights the enormous changes that have occurred on British terrestrial television, as well as in feminist cultural politics, since the launch of Channel 4. Its minority interest, public service remit led it to become the first channel to use documentary to explore the sex industry as a political issue for women. *Pictures of Women* (Channel 4 1982), an experimental series made by a women's collective, arose out of the women's movement and feminist film-making cultures of the 1970s. It included programmes on prostitution and on pornography in which the dominant perspective was a feminist critique of these industries as forms of patriarchal exploitation. The book accompanying the series gives access to the ideological approach taken, although the programme was also formally innovative in an attempt to disrupt conventional forms of looking at women (Root 1984). Subsequent magazine series, which, among other items, occasionally addressed the sex industry as a political issue, continued through the 1980s and the first half of the 1990s (*Watch the Woman, First Sex, Out on Tuesday*). These series were premised on an address to a politicized constituency of feminist women, or in the case of *Out on Tuesday*, gays and lesbians, an address that narrowed their appeal (Richardson 1995).

These overtly political series disappeared and were replaced in the latter half of the 1990s by commercially successful, voyeuristic documentaries that fit seamlessly into an established culture of soft-core porn reading practices. By this I mean that sexual arousal is stimulated by the display of female bodies in a structure of looking heavily coded as heterosexual. What we have now is a combination of traditional soft-core pornography given new legitimacy by its association with a feminist discourse of empowerment (see further discussion in Chapter 3). The turning point was Channel 4's late night season of documentaries in 1995, the *Red Light Zone*, which offered an exploration of lesbian, gay male, transsexual, as well as straight women's, involvement in the sex industry. It was a diverse range of films, varying in quality, scheduled very late over several Saturday nights. The series attracted wide press coverage. The importance of this television 'event' was in announcing the channel's changing brand identity, distancing itself from the identity politics of the 1970s and 1980s and aligning itself with the more entrepreneurial, individualistic and hedonistic values of consumer culture. It also marked a recognition of the changing politics of sexuality in which the transgressive politics of 'queer' had challenged the feminist antipathy to the sex industry and, alongside the sex workers' own campaigns, questioned the construction of women sex workers as 'victims'. The majority of the films were commissioned from women keen to counteract the male dominance of pornography production and the perceived puritanism of second-wave feminism.

The influence of 'sex-positive' strands of feminist and 'queer' politics and the rise of enterprise culture in the 1980s and 1990s enabled not only the emergence of these women film-makers but also the rise of women as sex industry entrepreneurs. Documentaries about the sex industry often celebrate their economic success and their ability to explore their sexuality free from ignorance and shame (as we also saw in the *Sex and Shopping* report on Beatte Uhse discussed in Chapter 3). The interviews with female sex workers in these types of programmes often tell a story of independence born of economic rewards, and a sense of power in their own sexuality as they perform for their customers. This one-sided perspective, designed not to disrupt the programmes' erotic appeal, cannot accommodate the more ambivalent feelings that are evident in other autobiographical accounts and ethnographic research with sex workers. This appropriation of the sex-positive agenda by television docuporn has been seen as a cynical strategy to bring the sex industry into the mainstream. Television is now heavily involved through its marketing of the services available and in its provision of erotic programming. Women speaking out about their experiences to avoid being positioned as stereotypically helpless victims have merely served to produce (cheap) camera fodder. This is the view of the *Guardian*'s (male) television critic:

Is there a stripper in the entire country who hasn't been followed around by a camera crew intent on 'uncovering the real women' behind the lip gloss and titty tassles? What with high-class erotic performers, private dancers – any old music will do – and lesbian strippers peek-a-booing out from television lately, it's a

miracle that these working women actually manage to fling their G-string anywhere without it landing on a big furry mike. Strippers have replaced animals
and airline employees as the docusoap-makers' subject of choice. The number
of willing subjects comes as no surprise. After all, in what is quite literally
showbusiness, it pays to advertise.

(McLean 2001)

Gareth McLean's review of *Strippers* (E4 2001) pinpoints the problem women face in
trying to produce 'feminist' documentaries about the sex industry, and he makes a
convincing case:

Strippers, implies the narrator, isn't your average exploitative tits'n'ass TV,
designed to titillate its male post-pub audience. *Strippers*, she goes on, has been
made by 'an all-female team'. Well dip me in honey and throw me to the lesbians.
How feminist is that?. . . . What the 'all-female team' fails to realise is that the
audience doesn't care what these women think or say. Just as the customers in the
pubs where the strippers dance treat them like a fruit machine or a juke box – they
pop 50p into a pint glass for a brief distraction – so the camera does the same.

(McLean 2001)

The power of speech is illusory when sandwiched between the erotic appeal of lingering
shots of gyrating bodies on late night television, turning the women's assertion of
empowerment and pride into the familiar power relations of voyeurism. Support for
this assessment is found in the BSC's audience research. Reacting to a clip showing
a stripper dancing and sitting on a man's lap, taken from *Friday Night Fever*, a late
night programme about stripping shown on ITV, a third of the sample of viewers
thought it 'degrading'. Whatever the intent, viewers' responses are regulated by the
embedded cultural codes of pornography (Kuhn 1982). To disrupt these codes and
to transform people's existing attitudes to sex workers takes more than changing the
sex of the person behind the camera. Generic assumptions about what and who these
programmes are *for* tie them into a long history of institutionalized reading practices
for pornography in which sexualized images of women are coded for men's masturba-
tory pleasure. The devaluing of the women involved is also linked to a history of
stigmatization of sex workers that is tied to the power relations of patriarchy. It is to
this history that I now turn.

   The discursive construction of sex workers in the contemporary media has its roots
in nineteenth-century conceptions of gender and sexuality, in which women were
defined as 'other' to men. Women's 'purity' provided the necessary restraint to control
men's sexual desires. The incitement to loss of control, symbolized in the figure of
the prostitute, brought fears of chaos and disorder. Women who transgressed the
feminine ideal of sexual restraint were branded as deviant and immoral. Female virtue
was defined against the figure of the 'fallen woman', whose class or race identity often
served to accentuate her 'otherness'. The binary division between respectable and

disreputable women was also a division based on a spatial boundary between women's place in the privacy of the home and the dangers of the public street. As well as being defined as a threat to the moral order, prostitutes were perceived as carriers of venereal disease. Soldiers were regarded as the most at risk from infection, thus potentially weakening their ability to defend the interests of the British Empire. This exacerbated the sense of threat that prostitutes posed to the health and safety of the nation and justified state intervention to regulate their activities (Walkowitz 1992). Feminist interventions calling for the abolition of sexual 'slavery' originated in campaigns against this policy of imprisoning infected prostitutes. This was reinforced during the suffrage movement in the early 1900s when campaigners were concerned that the existence of prostitutes would undermine the status of all women at a time when they were campaigning for full rights to citizenship.

In the 1970s a split emerged between feminists who opposed prostitution as a form of male exploitation and those who wanted it revalued as a form of work from which women can benefit. Where some emphasized the danger and coercion, for others it was a pleasure and a choice (McLaughlin 1991: 251–2). Although there is agreement between these opposing camps on the overall aims – that is to reduce the harm caused by the industry – there are deep divisions on how this might best be achieved. These disagreements are also reflected in government responses, which vary considerably. Even within the European Union there are diverse policies in place that range from abolition to regulation and even legalization (Kilvington *et al.* 2001). But since the 1980s, the weight of opinion among feminist activists has shifted from condemnation and campaigns that favoured increased regulation and abolition, to an acceptance of commercial sex as a legitimate industry from which women can benefit if they are given more control over how it is run. Key to this transition has been the redefinition of the people involved as 'sex workers'.

> The term 'sex worker' was coined by sex workers themselves to redefine commercial sex, not as a social or psychological characteristic of a class of women, but as an income generating activity or form of employment for women and men . . . Similarly, the use of the term 'sex industry' was aimed at inclusion of exotic dancers, masseurs, telephone sex operators, receptionists (maids) and a whole host of people (including men) who sell sex.
>
> (Rickard 2001: 112)

One important effect of this redefinition is that sex workers now have a voice to fight for their own rights rather than being subject to philanthropy. They have become involved in existing feminist organizations and set up their own International Union for Sex Workers (IUSW). Among their demands in setting the agenda for reform are calls for an end to stereotypical portrayals in the media through recognition of the diversity among sex workers and their clients. These calls for positive representation are part of a more general campaign for legitimization. In particular, they question that women should always be perceived as passive victims rather than women who make choices to maximize their opportunities for economic security. They also want recognition that sex workers can actively enjoy their work. Negative portrayals are seen as the result of media producers projecting their own feelings about sex being dirty and seedy on to the situation. The resulting stigma provokes and permits violence against sex workers (Mistress L 2001: 148–50). It also affects all women by contributing to the psychology of 'shame' that constrains their sexual freedom and prevents women having control over their own sexuality. In seeking to promote pride where once there was shame, the IUSW is using tactics developed by gay rights activists: calling for decriminalization, campaigning against negative media portrayals and organizing celebratory carnivals to turn the secrecy of shame into the public display of pride.

The problems posed by calls for positive representation are in many respects identical to those faced more generally by campaigners seeking to influence the representation of stigmatized social groups. One is the need to recognize diversity within the represented group so that a uniform negative stereotype isn't simply replaced by a uniform positive stereotype that is just as 'unreal'. This implies an acceptance of difficult and potentially damaging portrayals among the mix. Concern has been expressed over the incentive sex workers have to portray a falsely positive image of their work in order to encourage more custom. In portraying sex work as an attractive career option, ignorance of the more negative aspects of the job made it easier for women to make their debut selling sex. In effect, it lowers the entry barrier (Skibre 2001). It should instead be recognized that some aspects of the job are positive while others are negative, and these will vary over time, just as with most jobs (Rickard 2001: 128; Liepe-Levinson 2002). Ambivalence towards the job they do is a recurring feature of sex workers' own writing about their experiences (Johnson 2002). This ambivalence needs to be recognized as existing within individuals rather then being distributed across a class hierarchy in which high-class escorts are glamorized while street workers are portrayed as helpless victims.

In the past few years attention has turned to the global dimension of the sex industry and the flows of people and commodities that thrive on variations in national regulations and economic inequalities. The desire in Britain to seal national borders against foreign 'contagion' from hard-core pornography and foreign prostitutes can be understood as a question of both national identity and the protection of markets. It suits established interests in the sex industry who want to protect their business from potential competition from outsiders. European hard core threatens to undermine the dominance of the market by British soft core producers (Thompson 1994; O'Toole 1998). In prostitution an influx of low-paid workers from abroad threatens to undercut the going rates for everyone. But there are strong countervailing forces that arise from the creation of an expanding European Union, the post-communist economic liberalization of Eastern Europe, and the effects of the globalization of capital on the growing inequalities in the world economy. These developments encourage the movement of economic migrants into Western Europe with high hopes of improving their life chances. The illegality of prostitution combined with the illegality of working without a permit undermines attempts to regulate this trade for the benefit of the women involved. This leaves them prey to exploitation by organized crime on the one hand and criminalization by the authorities on the other.

Feminist organizations are campaigning on behalf of these women. Jo Doezema (2001) warns, however, against the danger of 'Orientalism' in the interventions made by 'First World' feminists to 'save' 'Third World' women from exploitation. She argues that interventions made by Western feminists on behalf of 'Third World' prostitutes deny these women self-representation. It produces 'Third World' women as helpless; their only hope is to be rescued by others in true colonial fashion, bringing the feminist values of a more civilized Western culture to bear on their situation (*ibid*.: 28). This works, she argues, to maintain the superiority of the 'saving Western body', while the most likely outcome of legislation to protect women against trafficking will be to restrict the freedom of movement of the prostitutes themselves (*ibid*.: 24–9).

The debate over sex work is part of a much wider debate about sexuality that has caused deep divisions within feminism. The 'sex wars' of the 1980s, in which approaches to the censorship of pornography were at the centre of the dispute, remain unresolved (Vance 1992). Sex-positive radicals accuse anti-pornography campaigners of allowing feminism to be appropriated by the conservative puritan agenda. They in their turn have been criticized for colluding with the commercial sex industry in a capitulation to the values of entrepreneurial capitalism, and its structurally embedded racism, homophobia and class exploitation (McLaughlin 1991: 267). Thus there is no one feminist approach that can be mobilized as an intervention in the public sphere. Instead the diversity of views and practices that make up the full range of feminist political arguments should be recognized, if the media are to represent fully those constituencies whose interests are most closely affected by this issue.

Current affairs documentary and political debate

There are fears that the competitive pressures on television companies to retain audience share have led to a gradual decline of the kind of current affairs documentary that makes a genuine contribution to political debate in the public sphere. These changes have been termed 'tabloidization' in a comparison with the differences found between 'quality' and 'tabloid' newspapers. Tabloidization in newspapers is characterized by an increasing focus on personalities, sports, fashion, culture and consumer reporting over national and international politics. Even in quality newspapers there has been 'a greater stress on the personal and the private at the expense of the public and the structural' (McLachlan and Golding 2000: 35) in an attempt to attract a new readership, especially women and young people for whom reporting on political elites has had little perceived 'existential utility' (Sparks and Tulloch 2000: 32–5). There are also differences in the style of address, with more concrete language, humour and melodramatic extremes replacing abstract, sober and measured reporting. Several writers in the defence of public service television have identified, and often regretted, the same trends in television as it has become more market-oriented (Langer 1998; Dovey 2000; Sparks and Tulloch 2000; Winston 2000). Jon Dovey (2000), for example, is suspicious that what he terms 'first person narrative' and 'true life melodrama', which are grounded in subjective experience, leave the underlying social and economic reasons for suffering and powerlessness unexamined and responsibility for change devolved to the 'empowered' individual.

These concerns are, however, entangled in questions of taste that have class and gender implications. The forms of rhetoric valued in 'serious' broadcast journalism, with their emphasis on a detached impartiality, the balanced reporting of 'expert' opinion and the use of depersonalized, disembodied voice-over narration that positions the viewer in relation to the people and events portrayed, has been criticized for its construction of an elite and masculine perspective masquerading as 'objectivity' (see Chapters 4 and 5 for further discussion of this critique). Myra Macdonald (2000), however, cautions against drawing too rigid a dichotomy between the kind of analytic journalism that contributes to the public sphere and the entertainment values of popular culture because it works to reinforce a gendered hierarchy of values (mind/ body, rational/emotional, public/private, fact/fiction). She makes a case for the use of personal testimonies to enhance our political understanding of an issue rather than to reinforce existing prejudice, and to mobilize affective involvement rather than simply satisfying our voyeuristic curiosity (Macdonald 2000: 254). This coincides with the emphasis sex workers themselves place on self-representation to overcome the 'othering' effects of media discourse. Even so, she argues, personal testimony cannot substitute for meticulous research that draws on a variety of forms of evidence that go beyond the personal. I will be drawing on this evaluative framework to compare the political utility of the two examples discussed below.

The first is *The Sex Trade*, in the long-running BBC current affairs series *The Money Programme*. The other, called *Vice: The Sex Trade*, is taken from a more populist, short-run, current affairs series on the UK's mainstream commercial network channel, ITV. The comparison between these two examples will be used to consider whether the demands made by feminist activists and sex workers for the recognition of diversity, ambivalence and self-representation are being met by current affairs programmes. Do they work to encourage empathy with the women portrayed or does the generic imperative in current affairs to draw clear boundaries between the 'normal' and the 'deviant' work against this ideal? Moreover, do the rhetorical differences between 'quality' and 'tabloid' journalism affect the contribution each programme makes to political debate on matters of public importance arising from the sex industry?

The Money Programme is a current affairs documentary series that has been on BBC2 for over thirty years. It has a journalistic interest in the speed of getting stories on to the screen, and it claims to be providing straightforward facts in order to contribute to the national debate on issues of concern. The 'long and distinguished history' of the series, as well as the reputation and prestige of the BBC as an organization, legitimizes the claim to be uncovering the truth (BBCi). *The Sex Trade* (1998) demonstrates its impartiality by presenting a range of issues and perspectives without being tendentious. It recognizes a diversity of viewpoints, including those of the sex workers involved. It conveys the complexity of the issues posed by the expansion of the industry, largely without falling into predictable narrative patterns of victims and villains. It has carefully researched the scope and structure of the industry, and the range of political approaches taken to it. It contributes to public debate by setting out alternative perspectives. The (female) voice-over begins by signalling this range, while two sex workers conclude it with contrasting views on the question 'Would you recommend it as a job?' This is a well-researched contribution to the debate.

The first part of *The Money Programme* looks at the sector as a story of business success, detailing the expansion of sexual services in the UK, especially its expansion into 'respectable' city centre and suburban areas. Here the language and agenda match those of the International Union of Sex Workers: 'It's just a job. Nothing more, nothing less. I work to support my family', says one street worker interviewed by the programme. It doesn't glamorize or demonize either the women or the job. The testimony of the sex workers helps to undermine any over-generalized assumptions about the women who work in the industry and their motivations, while offering a map of its hierarchical structure. We encounter escort services in the West End of London that help middle-class girls to pay for their education, and women with few other viable job options working to pay for a drug habit in the streets of Manchester. Moving beyond Britain we are told of the plight of exploited Eastern European economic migrants in Western Europe in contrast to contented women working in legal brothels in Germany.

A diverse range of professionals also offer evidence to provide a wider context for understanding these experiences in economic and political terms, rather than offering moral approval or condemnation of the lives these women lead. Further statistical research evidence was commissioned by the programme to support its analysis in a context where facts are thin on the ground. We learn about how businesses make money, their choice of location, their marketing strategies, their customer base, the career opportunities and working conditions for staff, the regulatory environment and how to stay within the law. An interview with a rich entrepreneur explains how he made the business work. If the programme had finished here it would have resembled a guide to 'how to run a successful sex business', with some caution about the effects it might have on women caught up in the business at street level. It exemplifies the now legitimate view that for respectable, middle-class people the industry is an acceptable way to earn money. It then links the issues raised by all these forms of evidence to the policy initiatives being taken in Europe. It lays out the policy options without any prior assumption that the British way is best. Indeed, it rather suggests that the UK is failing to address the issues at all and this programme's function is to draw attention to them, thereby fulfilling its public service role.

There is, however, a caveat to my offering this documentary as exemplary investigative journalism, and this is the othering process that affects its approach to the 'trafficking of women'. The programme includes an investigation of the suffering caused by 'organized gangs tempted by easy profits' who are accused of the 'trafficking of women' into 'sexual slavery'. This became a news item in the wake of a United Nations report in 1998, followed by further policy initiatives in the European Union. It is significant that where the programme moves most clearly from a business to a news agenda, the generic imperative to draw boundaries between the 'normal' and the 'deviant' comes to the fore. This is a live political issue that the programme views from a dominant ideological perspective. News narratives associate prostitutes with death, disease, drugs and crime. They define prostitutes as victims in need of salvation and as a risk to social order who need to be controlled. They accentuate their difference from other women (McLaughlin 1991). The language expresses moral outrage and comparisons are drawn with the international drugs trade. In this section expansion of trade is a sign of a lack of control over criminal activity, with the programme's role being to set out the options for political intervention.

Only when we move to consider foreign involvement in the business is the criminality of the business emphasized. Up to this point the approach is to show how loopholes in the law enable legitimate business. Concern over the sexual exploitation of women from poor countries becomes entangled in the politics of immigration. Orientalist representations are constructed of the foreign men and women involved (Doezema 2001). In contrast to the first section of the documentary, where everyone is treated with respect, here we are shown men covering their faces in shame as police raid a London massage parlour. The commentary tells us the owner is 'Maltese Charlie', who specializes in providing under-age Thai girls. The voice-over tells us he was imprisoned, while some of the girls were deported as illegal immigrants, but ten days later it is business as usual at the massage parlour. It is implied that there is an unstoppable flood of potential immigrants to replace the ones lost, an implication that feeds into contemporary xenophobic discourses about immigration, the concern to protect British borders from invasion by 'foreign hordes'. Nor are there any direct interviews with any of the traffickers or the women being trafficked, so all the information is provided in the third person. 'These women' are positioned as voiceless victims and the 'extremely resourceful, clever gangs who make lots of money' are faceless and powerful criminals whose desire to make money is no longer a justification in itself as it was in the earlier, British section of the documentary.

This example reveals, in my view, that the boundaries dividing the sexually 'respectable' from the 'disreputable' have been reset. No longer is the sexual respectability of the British structured by a division between the private and the public, between the home and the street, between the bourgeoisie and the working woman. Instead national borders are the spatial markers. It is the ethnic others from whom we must be protected or who are subject to our philanthropic zeal. The fraught political question of maintaining British national identity in the face of European integration and of protecting British business from the effects of global markets is tied up here with issues of sexual regulation. Doezema's Orientalist critique, discussed in the previous section, which challenges the agenda being set by the European Commission and by the Coalition against the Trafficking of Women, lacks the political legitimacy that would enable it to be included in this news agenda.

The normalizing effect of this discourse, returning us to the historical link between prostitution, deviance and crime, can be seen very clearly in another, more populist, current affairs series broadcast on the UK's main commercial channel, *Vice: The Sex Trade* (ITV 1998, repeated in 2001). The series overall attracted complaints from 53 viewers (a relatively large number), who considered it too uncritical of the sex trade. As in *The Money Programme*, critical perspectives were reserved for those foreign 'others' who invade national boundaries. This programme, entitled 'The New Slave Trade', positions prostitution within a discourse of scandal and deviance. It shares a vocabulary with anti-immigration rhetoric, with its emphasis on an uncontrollable increase in numbers. 'Seventy per cent of off-street sex workers are not British.' The women from Eastern Europe who are the focus of the investigation are helpless victims, at the mercy of the villains who are identified as 'the Red Mafia', a more vivid label for the Eastern Europe criminal gangs also referred to in *The Money Programme*. The melodramatic, tabloid style of this programme allows for no ambivalence: this is corruption of innocence by evil. The women, we are told, are dehumanized by their suffering. Sensationalist language invites moral outrage, promising at the outset to 'expose the new slavery at the heart of Britain's sex trade', a rhetorical flourish often repeated with slight variations as the hook leading into each advertising break.

Sensationalism is the product of a fascination with stories of sexual transgression in which the moral righteousness of exposing wrongdoing is entwined with the often unacknowledged pleasure of vicarious participation (see Chapter 4's discussion of the reporting of scandal). The sensationalism is enhanced by lurid details in the voice-over of the women being stripped, gang-raped and imprisoned so that we can imagine the degradation and humiliation of the scene. Undercover, secret reporting adds to this voyeuristic frisson, with grainy hand-held shots secretly capturing the women at work in dark, depressing rooms, which, we are told, they are seldom allowed to leave. None of these women would have been asked by the film-makers for their 'informed consent' to being shown in these humiliating circumstances, often naked but ignorant of the fact they were being filmed. None could complain, knowing that their position as illegal immigrants undermines their ability to do so. A British woman academic speaking for the International Organization for Migration explains the women's plight on their behalf. The Orientalist relation this sets up is slightly offset by several interviews with women sex workers. But these are with a high-class escort service set up in Russia that flies young, educated, beautiful women to Western Europe for up to several nights with rich businessmen. It is not these women who are the problem the programme is exposing. It is the impoverished 'hordes of women' who have 'flooded' the massage parlours of London.

Both of these programmes are engaged in normalization through the demarcation of deviance in ways that are generically driven. The same discursive boundaries dividing the normal from the deviant operate across quality and tabloid modes of address. This raises some doubt, in my view, about the stark difference that is perceived in their relative contribution to public debate. It also shows that, in comparison with an analysis of the US media at the beginning of the 1990s (McLaughlin 1991), discourses about prostitution have changed substantially in response to the growing legitimization of the sex industry in advanced Western economies. It is one effect of the way that enterprise culture and consumerism has become hegemonic during the 1990s, a development that has influenced feminist as well as mainstream political norms. The boundary between respectable and disreputable women is still based on class differences; now, however, globally defined. Women's respectability no longer requires them to be sexually pure as long as they are rich and successful. It is the poverty and therefore the powerlessness of the foreign prostitutes that exposes them to the 'othering' process produced by news 'scandals'. In a context of global economic inequality our ability to empathize takes on an ethnic and nationalist inflection. The following section looks at a documentary located in New York, at the other end of the economic spectrum, and shows how our empathy is elicited with the sex workers there.

'Auteur' documentary and the ethics of production

In *Fetishes* (Nick Broomfield 1996, broadcast on Channel 4 1997) everything works to reassure the audience that they will not be debased by what they are watching. The markers of 'quality' designed to assuage the viewers' anxiety about watching a programme on sadomasochism include the choice of location (just off Fifth Avenue), the high social class of the clients, the use of historical archive footage, the use of literary quotations over a soundtrack of Mozart (labelled as 'a well known **fetishist**') and the leisurely production schedule. In fact, its purpose is established as pedagogic – the point is to share the film-makers' quest to try to understand sadomasochism and what motivates people to be involved. But the truth is not to be found in balancing competing perspectives, as in current affairs documentary: the auteur provides the truth as he sees it. We must trust him to be a reliable guide.

Here what matters is Broomfield's reputation and persona, though as Stella Bruzzi (2000) notes, there is a distinction between Nick Broomfield the film-maker, and 'Nick Broomfield' the persona the film constructs. His presence as the sound recordist, the interviewer, the director and the editor gives his films a personal signature that distances them from the institutional address of television, a distance that provides more freedom in the approach taken. *Fetishes* is introduced as 'Nick Broomfield's controversial and highly personal enquiry into the world of sadomasochism'. It is scheduled in a documentary strand called, with intentional paradox, *True Stories*, a title that signals the constructed nature of 'truth'. Broomfield presents himself as a sexual innocent, who hadn't chosen sadomasochism as a topic but responded to a request to do it. 'I was intrigued but uneasy. It's something I'd heard of over the years but not heard much about', we are told. This allows the audience to share his innocence, his doubts and his curiosity, a position that enables us to feel justified in continuing to watch without feeling bad about our own motives. He wears a bright white T-shirt throughout, speaks in a subdued middle-class accent, and looks sheepish and coy whenever it seems that he might be drawn further into the activities he is investigating. In other words, he does everything in his power to offset any possible imputation of prurient interest or motivation.

Broomfield's reputation as an 'auteur' rests on his use of 'performative documentary'; that is, the events in his films are shown to come into being in the course of the film being made. They are performative in the linguistic sense; that is, they describe and perform an action simultaneously. This is not the same as saying that a film is *about* performance, such as a film about drag artists, although in this case the film *is* also about performance. 'In performative films the fact of the camera and crew is emphasised as an inevitable intrusion that alters the situation they enter' (Bruzzi 2000: 155). This is crucial to the way the film unfolds, and in this case, I would argue, to its ethical exploration of the dynamics of sadomasochism.

The question of power and control is central to this film's subject matter, and more to the point, the pleasure that (mostly) men find in relinquishing power and control in certain tightly defined, constructed scenarios. Mistress Raven, the central figure in the film, gives us a guided tour of the settings provided for this process to take place: 'Your imagination is pushed to the limits here. All kinds of bondage, all kinds of transfer of control and power', she tells us. Fetishistic and sadomasochistic scenarios are played out before us, where the camera concentrates on the clients more than the mistresses. These scenes are interspersed with interviews with the mistresses and some of their clients to explore their motives and how it makes them feel (and how they feel about the film being made), and a sparse, voice-over commentary from Broomfield. The pacing is leisurely, the camera dwelling on a series of scenes in which men gain pleasure from humiliation: a male slave kneeling at his mistress's feet to have a cigarette stubbed out in his mouth; a Wall Street broker during his lunch hour being fully encased in a rubber suit and treated as a dog; a Jewish client being dominated in neo-Nazi scenarios; and finally a man with murderous fantasies in real life being forced to lick a toilet bowl clean with his tongue. These are cut against speeded-up shots captured by a surveillance camera of people passing through the hallway between the rooms. This emulates the rhythms of the women's working environment, with its periods of waiting followed by intense activity.

'Here Mistress Raven, who doesn't like to be called Betty, tries to persuade me to do a session', says Broomfield early in the film. In this short comment the power game the film plays out between Broomfield and Mistress Raven is announced, with the other women in supporting roles. Broomfield's task is to gain sufficient control of the situation to get his film made, while resisting the women's attempts to control him. The progress of that game is revealed to the viewer in a series of understated scenes and comments that reveal the extent to which they all know what game they are playing. They are professionals. As he gradually wins their trust, many of the women gradually concede and let Broomfield have the access he needs to make the film, despite their misgivings about the bad effects it might have on their lives. Broomfield wants Mistress Raven to be filmed doing a session but she will only be filmed doing a session if Broomfield is the client. 'What would you do?' he asks. 'I don't know, we'd have to feel what its like – go with the flow', just as Broomfield must do as a documentarist. She jokes about his resistance to being dominated, his need to stay in control. 'A lot of restraint – total constraint for you', as a wide shot shows Broomfield being surrounded and touched by the women (he chews gum and looks pleased but non-committal). 'And it's all mind games. We can take you down without even touching you. You can break a grown man just by your will', comments one of the other women.

Neither Broomfield nor Mistress Raven will back down. She explains her motives: 'I think it totally outrageous that you can do a documentary about something you have never experienced first hand.' When he excuses himself by saying he doesn't like pain she scolds him for poor research: 'You should be trying to portray that pain is not the only outlet here – it can be psychological, sexual, any fantasy. It's about the transfer of power and control. There's not just pain involved. However, in your case I'll make sure there is' (laughs). She wins in the end. Broomfield fails to get the key bit of film that he wants (or says he wants). The film ends with the women ganging up on him. They tie him up and haul him up to hang from the ceiling on a pulley while the women playfully lash him with whips. 'And that is the closest I got to doing a session with Mistress Raven' is Broomfield's closing comment. Then the credits role and the editors are listed as Nick Broomfield and Betty Bukhart (remember that she didn't like to be called Betty). Not only did Broomfield (reluctantly?) submit to being strung up, but did making the film also require Broomfield as auteur to relinquish editorial control? Was this the deal that allowed him access? Paradoxically, rather than undermining his control over the subject of the film, it cleverly enacts the transfer of power and control that is at the root of sadomasochistic pleasure. This is no less of a performative film than his earlier work, and so, I would argue, he avoids the charge of prurient exploitation the topic incites.

Despite the obvious 'quality' of *Fetishes*, Brian Winston (2000: 147–8) considers Broomfield's 'forays into the world of commercial sex ethically suspect'. I disagree, and I think Winston is not entirely clear about his own reasons for making this judgement. The film meets all the criteria for quality production and ethical practice that he advocates. It is carefully researched, it shares editorial control with the participants and it doesn't rely on the participants' naivety for giving their consent. Indeed, they show a sophisticated understanding of how the film will be received and its potential consequences for them. It neither positions the sex workers as 'victims' nor attempts to 'save' them from their life of 'immorality', nor does it gloss over the complex effects on their personal lives of the work that they do. It enhances our understanding of a practice that remains largely taboo, regarded by many as a dangerous and violent sexual perversion, a sign of depravity in the people involved.

Critical practice would ideally have the film-maker as 'enabler' to the women's own project. But this would inevitably reduce its 'illocutionary force' (Lara 1998). The case for justice and recognition requires persuasiveness, enabling the audience to connect with the experiences that form the basis for the claim. Broomfield's skill and celebrity as a film-maker make his authorship the more effective strategy, in my view. I think it is a work of great subtlety that contributes a sympathetic portrayal of a stigmatized form of sexual expression in such a way as to engage a mainstream audience's empathy. Like Broomfield, we can be sceptical at first, but like him be persuaded that the mistresses are justified in thinking that they give 'clients a needed service that isn't being provided elsewhere'; and that they themselves are not being exploited in the process.

Conclusion

To return to the questions posed at the beginning of this chapter, these examples show, in my view, that not all documentaries about the sex industry are inevitably exploitative, but some certainly are. The difference is a question of aesthetics as much as it is a question of the power relations between the participants and the film-makers. Indeed, the two cannot be easily separated. It can be seen how the influence of feminist interventions on the politics of sex work has been taken up in ways that have contributed positively to the complex debates about the regulation of the industry and to a better understanding of and empathy with the women involved, which destabilizes the rigid boundary between 'us' and 'them'. Despite the caveat over the representation of foreign sex workers, feminist critique of the generic codes of current affairs and documentary can be seen to have allowed for aesthetic innovations in narrative form and mode of address, enabling new ways of understanding and relating to the issues. When it comes to docuporn, however, a spurious appeal to feminist legitimacy is undermined by the restricting codes of its limited erotic vocabulary and its institutionalized relations of consumption that are characteristic of this type of sex industry documentary. It can only be hoped that these hybrid forms become a historical relic, to be looked back on as a passing stage in the development of truly diverse 'quality' provision of erotic entertainment on television.

Note

1 The data on which this statistical analysis is based were collated by Dr Sherryl Wilson. For the terrestrial trends between 1995 and 2001 the information was drawn from the British

Universities Film and Video Council's database of documentary television programmes. These are incomplete data, because of the lack of complete coverage provided by the database. However, they do provide some indication of the annual trends, which confirm the public perception, noted by the BSC, that there was a marked increase in sex documentaries in 1999. For the more extensive analysis of 1999 the information was drawn from the *Radio Times* listing magazine and covered a range of digital as well as terrestrial channels. Financial support for this research was provided by the School of Cultural Studies at the University of the West of England.

Recommended reading

Feminist Review (2001) Special issue on sex work, 67(1).

Macdonald, M. (2000) Rethinking personalization in current affairs journalism, in C. Sparks and J. Tulloch (eds) *Tabloid Tales: Global Debates over Media Standards*. Lanham, MD: Rowman and Littlefield.

McLaughlin, L. (1991) Discourses of prostitution/discourses of sexuality, *Critical Studies in Mass Communication*, 16/8(3): 249–72.

Rich, B. R. (1983) Anti-porn: soft issue, hard world, in C. Brunsdon (ed.) *Films for Women*. London: BFI.

Winston, B. (2000) *Lies, Damn Lies and Documentaries*. London: BFI.

GAY, LESBIAN AND QUEER
SEXUALITIES IN UK DRAMA

Television drama, in many of its genres, picks up on and dramatizes contemporary social and political issues in order to maintain relevance and credibility in a medium whose appeal is founded on immediacy (Ellis 2000). This chapter identifies the political discourses that have regulated the ways in which homosexuality has been represented on television over recent decades. In particular it maps the transition from secrecy, invisibility and shame to coming out, visibility and pride in the history of gay and lesbian representation in British television. In doing so it engages with the cultural debates arising from liberation movements of the 1970s, the politics of hybridity in the 1980s and queer activism in the 1990s.

As well as this historical trajectory, the chapter is structured around the institutional spaces for gay, lesbian and queer drama in the UK, from the relatively constrained opportunities for politically progressive representations in the mainstream to the less inhibited approaches that have emerged in 'quality' drama on minority channels. This includes the trend towards more commercial definitions of 'quality' through their appeal to an international niche market. Shifting definitions of 'quality' and the cultures of taste from which they derive are explored in relation to the emergence of multistrand serial forms to replace the single plays and art films that previously defined this category. These changes raise questions about audience reception and the increasingly ambivalent ideological effects of postmodern narrative forms. The chapter begins with a brief overview of the changing political and aesthetic discourses regulating gay and lesbian representation before moving on to the discussion of specific examples.

Coming out of the closet

The roots of a twenty-first century understanding of gay and lesbian sexuality as an 'identity' lie in late nineteenth-century medical and sexological discourses in which homosexuality moved from being a category of sin, as defined by the Christian Church, to a psychosexual disposition. As a sinful act it had been assumed that anyone could be tempted. The deterrent for 'sodomy', up to the middle of the nineteenth century in the UK, was the death penalty. The stigmatization and secrecy attached to male homosexual identity throughout the twentieth century derived from legal prohibition (the Criminal Law Amendment Act of 1885). Lesbianism was not criminalized in the same way, though it has shared a similar social stigma. The law didn't change in the UK until the liberal reforms in 1967, following from the recommendations of the Wolfenden Committee Report of 1957, which legalized homosexual acts between men over 21 years old in certain contexts (Weeks 1989).

The key change in these reforms was the distinction that was made between sexual behaviour in public and in private. The concern to maintain 'public decency' went along with a liberal conviction that the state had no business interfering in the private expression of sexuality, as long as no one was harmed. This meant that the closeted male homosexual remained fearful of the scandal that followed from exposure. Homosexuality was legitimate only to the extent that it remained invisible. A secretive, private subculture developed at the same time that criminal prosecutions increased for sexual activity in public places, such as 'cruising' in parks or 'cottaging' in public toilets. Publicity that followed from these scandals kept the issue of homosexuality in the public domain, but always as 'deviance' and 'criminality'. Lesbians, on the other hand, were not subject to prosecution and this had the effect of making them even more invisible. This sharp distinction between the public and the private gave impetus to the gay liberation movement of the 1970s and its demand for full citizenship rights. Visibility, an end to 'the closet', was central to their political campaign – only through this connecting of the private with the public, it was argued, could they gain self-respect. The issue of visibility in the mass media was an important strand of this campaign as a means for the shame of a hidden and stigmatized identity to be converted into a public declaration of pride (Plummer 1995: 81–96). Gay and lesbian citizenship rights eventually became widely debated in the public sphere, including on television news and current affairs.

The political campaigns intensified in the 1980s in response to two developments: the election of a morally conservative government (in both the UK and USA) and the onset of the AIDS epidemic. This combination helped to fuel a moral panic over AIDS as 'the gay plague'. Emblematic of the political backlash that ensued in the UK was a clause in the Local Government Bill (1988), the now notorious Section 28, banning the promotion of homosexual relationships by local authorities. The controversy provoked by this measure served to fuel the debates over citizenship rights, thus drawing even more public attention to the issue (Stacey 1991). It was a period in British politics that was sharply divided between the conservative moralists who dominated the government and radical political activists fighting against them. The polarity of these positions was undermined, however, by two other factors. The first was the neo-liberal economic ideologies of the conservatives, whose free market rhetoric worked against the long-term viability of their imposition of 'family values'. The second was the circulation of government advertisements and education campaigns promoting safe sex practices to counteract the AIDS crisis. These helped to bring representations of an embodied homosexuality into the public sphere on an unprecedented scale (Watney 1997; Wilton 1997). In the crossfire of these competing cultural and economic forces homosexuality became a highly visible and contentious political issue that was taken up by television drama in line with its commitment to addressing contemporary concerns.

The homophobia of the 1980s conservative backlash therefore helped to produce the more confrontational 'queer' politics of the 1990s. This was characterized by a suspicion of state legislation as a means for achieving sexual liberation on the grounds that the state is too deeply implicated in a heteronormative model of citizenship to which the family is central. In order to be accepted as 'good' citizens, gays and lesbians are required to imitate this model, with the right to marriage or the legal adoption of children being seen as a means to be assimilated into the dominant culture. In the changed political context of the late 1990s, with a centre-left government, adoption rights have been approved and a civil union for same sex couples promised by 2006. The figure of the 'respectable' gay or lesbian in a stable domestic relationship has emerged as an acceptable public figure, with exposure no longer a cause for scandal and resignations. The boundary has shifted so that now it is the 'unrespectable' queer who indulges in public cruising and promiscuous sex who is the (intentionally) scandalous figure.

Queers refuse the state-defined model of the good homosexual and instead celebrate the transgressive potential opened up by the commodified spaces of the urban gay village and new forms of distribution for pornography on the Internet. These spaces allow for the expression of an embodied sexuality that resists the policing of desire. This includes the policing inherent in an identity politics that draws boundaries between hetero- and homosexual identities. In a queer world sexual desire is mobile and identity a matter of performance. Both are therefore open to transformation (see discussion of Butler 1990 in the Introduction). Queer politics has been criticized in turn for being a sexual politics for young, white, male, urban trendies. Indeed, some argue that it is hardly a politics at all, in that it works outside the mechanisms by which citizenship rights are fought for and won. Rosemary Hennessy (1995), for example, regards the flight from identity categories as a retreat from sexual politics, leaving a hedonistic individualism in its wake. The continuous subdivision and subversion of existing categories is complicit, in her view, with the tendencies of the market towards stimulating consumption through constant innovation and individualization – a tendency that postmodern aesthetics and queer politics simply reflect. Moreover, the queer emphasis on spectacle and visibility is, in her view, symptomatic of its integration into the commodified spaces of consumer culture. As such it is a product of the capitalist hegemony that characterizes the present and is complicit with its class, race and gender exclusions.

Distinctions in taste and the politics of aesthetic form

'Quality' drama has been an important institutional space on public service television for the expression of sexual subjectivities that lie outside the 'respectable' norm. Oppositional, political dramas have existed alongside the more conformist and 'respectable' costume dramas, which themselves have become more sexually adventurous in recent years (Nelson 2001b). The leeway in sexual censorship began with the live studio dramas broadcast as the *Wednesday Play* (BBC 1964–84), whose style and content were influenced by the social realist films of the time, as well as by a writer-led, theatrical tradition. Their reputation for engaging with serious political issues was matched by their willingness to risk sexual scandal (Creeber 2001b: 13). Their social realist aesthetic brought non-metropolitan working-class lives into television drama in plays that engaged with, among other things, the rise of 'the permissive society'. One of the most notorious was *Up the Junction* (BBC 1965, director Ken Loach), adapted by Nell Dunn from her own book. 'Mixing elements of montage, voice-over and location filming, it built on and helped to establish the medium's unique capabilities for the representation of the social real' (Caughie 2000: 122). Its open acknowledgement of back street abortion offended many people but also contributed to the climate of opinion that produced a change in the law. The political context for public service broadcasting at this time positively encouraged this engaged approach. The Pilkington Committee Report in 1962, which preceded the setting up of BBC2, declared that 'it is television's moral responsibility to shun triviality and risk challenge and controversy' (Caughie 2000: 78–87). Among the controversial topics addressed was the legalization of homosexuality.

   Quality drama is accorded the status of art despite its presence on a mass medium and as such is protected to some degree from the censorship regimes that regulate the majority of television's output. Complaints from viewers about sex in television drama are usually expressed as an objection to 'gratuitous sex' unmotivated by these higher purposes (Millwood Hargrave 1992). Moreover, licence is also given where drama is clearly addressed to a minority audience with the cultural capital to cultivate an 'aesthetic disposition' (Bourdieu 1984). In other words, controversial sexuality is fine in television drama as long as it only appeals to a relatively small group of middle-class liberals. Some forms of quality drama can, therefore, act as a kind of vanguard, testing the boundaries of the acceptable on television, from where it might move into the mainstream in response to more widespread cultural change. These are distinct from the 'respectable' middle-brow tastes of the dominant business class, for whom costume dramas based on literary novels have more appeal.

Literary adaptations have long been an important strand of quality drama on British television. These mostly uncontroversial costume dramas, often based on nineteenth-century novels, have sumptuous production values that have formed the basis for their success in the global market. Perhaps surprisingly, however, it was in this generic tradition that lesbian and gay sexuality first emerged from the shadows of invisibility and the indignities of negative stereotyping. Examples such as *Brideshead Revisited*, *Portrait of a Marriage*, *Tales of the City* and *Oranges Are Not the Only Fruit* are credited with providing the only available portrayals of physical affection between same-sex lovers on US as well as British television in the early 1990s (Capsuto 2000: 317–25). Ideally suited to limited run serials, these adaptations of famous (twentieth-century) novels combine the artistic credibility derived from their source with the aesthetic values of their sumptuous *mise-en-scène* and a historical setting that allows for a certain distance from the events depicted.

It was also significant that all these dramas could be read through a liberal humanist perspective, which values pluralism and freedom of speech, while avoiding any sense of homosexuality as a politicized sexual identity. *Oranges Are Not the Only Fruit* (BBC2 1990), for example, Jeanette Winterson's adaptation of her own highly regarded novel, was potentially very controversial, given that the lesbian sexuality of Jess, the main protagonist, was a primary theme. Set in the north of England, it offers a critical perspective on Christian religious fundamentalism and the institutional norms of patriarchy. Of course, the pre-publicity for the serial highlighted its literary credentials and its status as art (Nelson 1997: 138). But in Hilary Hinds's view, its favourable reception was also an accident of timing. In the two years preceding the broadcast, liberal fears about the protection of free speech had been provoked not only by the passing of Section 28 but also by the Islamic death threat against Salman Rushdie for his novel *The Satanic Verses*, which criticized Islamic fundamentalism. The liberal inclination to defend homosexual authors against censorship therefore coincided with an animosity towards religious fundamentalism. This created a public mood in which any hostility to lesbian sexuality was deflected on to the fundamentalist religion against which the main character rebelled. The liberal humanist reading meant that the serial was interpreted as being about 'the family' or 'religion' or 'the pains of growing up', but never 'lesbianism' (Hinds 1997).

The association of the single play or literary adaptations with 'quality' is derived from hierarchies of taste established in relation to cultural forms that predate television, such as theatre or literature, and is based on distinctions in class cultures (Brunsdon 1990). The differing value given to the narrative forms of realism and melodrama also works to underpin this hierarchy (Hallam and Marshment 2000). Winterson, for example, deliberately adapted her novel to conform to the traditions of realism in serious television drama by reducing the elements of fantasy and the carnivalesque found in the novel (Nelson 1997). However, the forms of television drama have been transformed since debates about the politics of realism first emerged in the 1980s (Bennet *et al.* 1981). The single play has all but disappeared (since 1984), while the continuous soap opera, initially despised for its association with cheap day-time serials for women, has extended its influence across the whole of the schedules, expanding and diversifying as it demonstrates its power to attract broad segments of the audience. The cultural status of melodrama has also shifted as its emotional 'excess' became appropriated as postmodern 'irony' by the new middle classes, a mode of reading long familiar in 'camp' gay subcultures (Ross 1989) but with a very different political significance (Medhurst 1997).

Although for some commentators, such as John Caughie (2000), these changes have presaged a decline in quality and a depoliticization of television drama, others have sought to validate the cultural worth of a popular and feminized tradition. In this view the hybrid forms of serial television drama have enabled a progressive exploration of the politics of sexuality in which the norms of heterosexual masculinity have been decentred by a diverse range of political challenges from the margins (Carson and Llewellyn-Jones 2000; Creeber 2001a). Their structure works against the modernist ideal of the 'progressive text' in that their multiple narratives and episodic structures allow for the exploration of shifting and marginal social identities, thereby bringing previously hidden aspects of social existence into view and redefining the boundary between the public and the private. However, no form in itself can be labelled as either reactionary or progressive, art or trash. A drama's meaning and worth will depend on particular audiences and their activation of the text, as was the case with *Oranges Are Not the Only Fruit*. The investments audiences make in fictional worlds preclude an exclusive focus on textual structures and shift our attention to the importance of context and pleasure in these processes. This is par-ticularly true of postmodem dramatic forms in which intertextuality and multiple narratives, the blurring of boundaries between realism and melodrama, the highbrow and the popular, undermine any unambiguous ideological positioning of the viewer (Carson and Llewellyn-Jones 2000; Creeber 2001a).

The feminist focus of much of this debate receives more extended attention in the next chapter, where it is taken up in relation to US television drama. But here I explore its relevance to the politics of gay representation and compare the potential offered by the diverse forms of the art film, literary adaptations and limited run serials. First, I consider the place assigned to homosexual identities within main-stream heteronormative drama. Then I track the emergence from the mid-1980s to the mid-1990s of new forms of gay representation on BBC2 and Channel 4, which also challenged the prevailing hegemony of white identities in British drama. The final section looks at the issues raised by the commodification of gay sexuality in the serial drama *Queer as Folk* (Channel 4 1999 and 2000; Showtime 2000–). This was hailed by many as a landmark in the history of gay representation, and its focus on white, gay, urban men draws attention to their greater visibility at the expense of other less affluent sexual minorities in the consumer culture of the 1990s.

Popular drama: sexuality as a social issue

The processes of regulation set limits to ensure that mainstream drama conforms to normative assumptions about sexual behaviour. If broadcast before the 9.00 p.m. watershed, it must be deemed suitable for family viewing. For drama this has meant an almost exclusive focus on heterosexual relationships as a result of the expressions of disgust and moral condemnation that have greeted the few examples of homosexual relationships to appear. Research in 1992 by the Broadcasting Standards Commission (Millwood Hargrave 1992) showed that for about a third of viewers any depiction of homosexuality was unacceptable, while for two-thirds showing physical contact between gay men would be offensive. These proportions had reduced by 1999, especially among younger viewers, but still under half of the sample agreed that scenes of men kissing are acceptable before 9.00 p.m. There were fewer objections to women kissing (Millwood Hargrave 1999: 62–71).

On those few occasions before the 1980s when gay or lesbian characters were explicitly portrayed they were based on established stereotypes: camp queens and butch lesbians to be laughed at in comedies, sinister objects of fear in thrillers or figures of pity in social problem dramas. They were positioned as marginal characters in heterosexual plots. 'Heterocentric narrative construction will structure the plot to revolve around how straight characters respond to lesbians, gays and queers. We therefore see them through a straight gaze' (Doty and Gove 1997: 88). It wasn't until 1975 with the dramatized portrayal of Quentin Crisp's life in *The Naked Civil Servant* (Thames 1975) that a sympathetic and complex characterization of a gay protagonist was placed at the centre of a television drama on British television. It won many awards but remained an isolated example.

The main problem with gay and lesbian representation in television drama hasn't been a plethora of negative stereotypes but their invisibility (Munt 1992; Doty and Gove 1997: 86). This absence explains why 'queer' reading strategies have developed to read nominally 'straight' characters as gay or lesbian through gesture, dress, double entendres or narrative role (Graham 1995; Doty and Gove 1997; Medhurst 1997). In some cases these characters have been deliberately double-coded to offer subcultural appeal without offending the mainstream audience. There is also a tradition of 'camp' appropriation by gay men of female stars whose 'excessive' melodramatic or comic performances can be read as gender artifice (Babuscio 1984). In other cases extensive 'rewriting' by viewers has extended characters' textual connotations. The homosocial bonds of 'buddy' characters are especially open to being appropriated in this way, as the lesbian following for *Cagney and Lacey* demonstrated (D'Acci 1994). Elaborate creative responses have been developed in the fan cultures surrounding 'cult' television series, such as the 'slash fiction' written by women fans of *Star Trek* (NBC 1966–69), which refigure it as a gay romance between Spock and Captain Kirk (Jenkins 1995; Penley 1997). More recent US serials addressed to teenage audiences, alive to the potential offered to fan cultures by the Internet, have deliberately encouraged these practices by incorporating lesbian themes and connotations in fantasy dramas such as *Xena Warrior Princess* (MCA/Universal 1995–2001) (Gwenllian Jones 2000; Pullen 2000) and *Buffy the Vampire Slayer* (Fox 1997–2003) (Parks and Levine 2003). The pleasurable playfulness of these forms of appropriation has made some viewers impatient with the more 'serious' attempts at politically correct representations addressed to gay and lesbian audiences, which have been criticized for creating a minority ghetto (Richardson 1995).

The representation of homosexuality has emerged in a 'socially responsible' form in the mainstream soap operas that dominate prime time viewing in the UK. All of the early evening soaps have now included gay and lesbian characters and the shocked response that greeted homosexual kisses in the 1980s has subsided, although it is still the case that only certain kinds of 'respectable' gays and lesbians in stable domesticated relationships can be shown. The pedagogic use of soap operas as a form of social education has long been recognized and exploited because of their focus on the family and sexual relationships that constitute the subject matter and setting of this genre. David Buckingham and Sarah Bragg's (2004) research on young people's responses to sexuality on television reveals the extent to which these serials allow children to watch and talk about normally hidden adult sexual behaviour, including adultery and homosexuality. The open-ended serial form allows a diversity of perspectives on these 'transgressions' to be presented, and openly talked about in the family and among friends. Soap operas, along with teenage magazines, offer a less embarrassing way of learning about sexual relationships than is possible in school. Nor are they limited by the 'biological' approach that characterizes these more explicitly 'educational' settings.

Problems still remain as to how to integrate lesbian and gay characters into long-running soaps. The inclusion of one or two into a predominantly heterosexual milieu has the effect of creating characters isolated from any lesbian or gay community. This makes it difficult to sustain the characters in the long term as the variety of story lines and interactions is severely curtailed. The other problem is the taboo on showing embodied sexual encounters, especially between gay men. 'Camp' remains the preferred form for gay male expression on mainstream television (as the success of Graham Norton as a presenter confirms), where sex is displaced into innuendo and gay identity expressed as feminine excess. In soaps this translates as the appropriation of sexually active, peroxide blonde, middle-aged women, such as Bet Lynch in *Coronation Street* or Peggy Mitchell in *Eastenders*, as gay icons.

Quality drama: the politics of difference

The institutional space for lesbian and gay drama on Channel 4 is distinct from that on BBC2, the other minority channel on terrestrial television in the UK. It was based from the beginning on a very different conception of public service broadcasting from the

BBC. Discussing the Annan report that preceded the formation of Channel 4 in 1982, Caughie comments on the contrast with Pilkington: 'Just as the Pilkington committee had established a discourse about the place of broadcasting which can be identified by certain key terms – "seriousness of purpose", "the sins of trivialization", "challenging" – so the Annan committee seemed to initiate a new discourse which had as its central terms "openness", "plurality", "diversity"' (Caughie 2000: 186). The *Wednesday Play* had acquired its worth from criteria based in class distinctions, as part of a strategy for bringing challenging theatre to a wider audience via live studio recordings, whereas Channel 4's differentiated address has always been defined in relation to other forms of social difference, and in relation to *film* rather than theatrical or literary traditions (Caughie 2000: 179–202). Channel 4's remit was to cater for audiences not served by the mainstream commercial channel, to encourage innovation and experimentation, to encourage wider access to programme-making for underrepresented groups.

During the 1980s, Channel 4 was sheltered from the full effects of its free market structure by its uncommercial remit, and a system of finance in which its advertising space was sold by ITV, which financed Channel 4 with a levy, thus guaranteeing a minimum level of funding. This freed Channel 4 to experiment. With no studio space to fill and with cameras becoming ever more portable, there was the chance for a new television aesthetic to be developed, one influenced by the traditions of art film and experimental video. The channel's first gay season of programmes, called *In the Pink* (1986), included two art films by the gay film director Derek Jarman: *Jubilee* and *Sebastion*. Channel 4's structure of independent production companies bidding for commissions from the channel allowed an influx of people who had never worked in television before. Among these the Franchised Workshops, set up with joint funding from the Greater London Council, were often based around the notion of speaking from a particular community, whether defined by sexuality, ethnicity or gender. One of these, *Sankofa*, was a collective of black British film-makers with a background in art who explored ways to portray hybrid ethnic identities, especially those of black British gay men. Their ambitious but only partially successful low-budget film, *Passion of Remembrance* (Blackwood and Julien 1986), uses an avant-garde aesthetic to question the stereotypes of black masculinity in ways that were completely outside the mainstream of racial and sexual politics at that time (Mercer 1988; Parmar 1990; Hall 1996).

It mixes a stylistic heritage from the modernist avant-garde with acts of remembering that are part of the movement to reclaim a black history. Three quite different narrative strands are juxtaposed. One shows a black woman arguing with a black man in an abstract desert, questioning her exclusion from the black power movement as they are circled by a 360-degree camera pan. Another presents scenes from the everyday lives of a black household and traces their differences – including those created by the younger generation's gay sexuality. A third is a montage of video images taken of political demonstrations that various characters watch and comment upon. It exposes the differences within the black 'community' and it signals a new 'politics of articulation' to replace the 'politics of identity'; that is, political alliances based on shared political interests rather than on essentialized categories. 'Maggie is it true you're a lesbian? What have gay marches got to do with black struggle?' someone asks as they watch the video images of a demonstration. This differentiation among the characters expresses the concern of the film-makers to speak *from*, rather than *for*, the black community. They draw attention to differences *within* ethnic groups, including differences in gender and sexual orientation, while still seeking the grounds for a shared politics of resistance (Williamson 1986).

Experimental forms do not attract large audiences. Broadcast in the 'graveyard slot' of 11.00 p.m. on Monday, these films were on the margins of the schedule, a space that disappeared in the 1990s when the workshop funding ceased. 'They became a charitable anachronism in a market economy' (Caughie 2000: 200). In Caughie's view, their loss marked the end of an alternative form of television drama that enabled experimentation and complexity freed from commercial constraints – a truly oppositional space. Judith Williamson, writing in 1988, was more ambivalent about the political usefulness of these spaces. Her doubts presaged a transition in left-wing cultural politics, a move away from experimental forms that appeal to a minority. Williamson (1988) dared to question the point of these films when no one watches them except an educated elite with the acquired cultural capital. She argued for the left to 'reclaim certain kinds of pleasurable cinematic experience' in order to communicate with more people (*ibid.*: 111–12).

The film she used as a comparison was *My Beautiful Laundrette* (directed by Frears 1985, broadcast on Channel 4 1987), written by Hanif Kureishi. It was a huge success at the box office and helped to establish the reputation of Film on Four, a company owned by Channel 4, for quality films about contemporary British society. It combines political relevance with popular accessibility in its focus on the hybrid sexual and ethnic identities of an entrepreneurial Asian family. At the centre of the story is the relationship between Omar, who manages one of the family businesses (a laundrette) in South London, and Johnny, an old school friend turned 'skinhead' whose racist friends eventually provoke violence. It places these personal stories in the precise political context of Thatcherism and explores the ambivalent position inhabited by Asian businessmen in a simultaneously racist and entrepreneurial culture. The complexity of this politics of race, sexuality and enterprise in contemporary British society is expressed through a mixture of naturalism, comedy and the surreal in a loosely resolved episodic narrative. Arguably, this hybrid and open narrative form is what enables the expression of hybrid subject positions without the impenetrability or didacticism of modernist aesthetics. The bigger budget also allows for the sort of visual pleasures that attract a much wider audience and, potentially, international distribution (Carson and Llewellyn-Jones 2000). It uses the visual and narrative traditions of sexual portrayal in film romance. 'In some ways it's an absolutely classic romance. You're just dying for those people to kiss, but they're both men and one is black and the other is white' (Williamson 1988: 111).

A few years later the BBC produced *The Buddha of Suburbia* (BBC2 1993), a four-part serial adapted from Hanif Kureishi's novel, which also includes scenes of inter-racial gay sex in a rescripting of romance conventions. This follows the 'coming of age' adventures of a young man, Karim, of mixed 'race' parentage, whose ambitions to be an actor take him away from the suburban milieu of his family home and into the bohemian cultures of London's theatre scene. It presents a simultaneously critical and nostalgic parody of the sexually permissive bohemian culture of the 1970s in which there is an oscillation between emotional empathy and intellectual distance from the characters and events portrayed. It also mildly satirizes the colonial ideologies that underpin British fascination with Indian culture, as portrayed in the 'heritage' dramas that had emerged in the 1980s. Its suburban London setting emphasizes the ludicrousness of the encounter, not only on the part of the English, but in the ways that Karim's Indian father plays up to his role as mystic guru and lover. In fact, by playing off the two worlds against each other, it offers the kind of carnivalesque parody that Bakhtin (1984) admired for its levelling effect, in which everyone's pretensions are reduced by laughter. 'Every parody is an intentionally dialogised hybrid. Within it language and styles actively and mutually illuminate one another' (Rose 1993: 154).

The political ambivalence of the drama is apparent in the debates that have emerged around Karim, the main character. The drama is open to very different readings depending on which aspects are emphasized. Bruce Carson (2000), for example, argues that in the television version, the loss of the first person perspective and the effect of the camera reduce the novel's satiric distance and instead reproduce rather than satirize our fetishistic relation to Karim's racialized sexual allure. Carson draws on the post-colonial critique of the racialized power relations of colonialism, which have had such a strong effect on film and photographic conventions and how we read them. In his view, it is Karim's exoticized 'otherness' that allows him to be positioned as the passive sexualized object of a more powerful white gaze. This position is enhanced by his feminized dress as he takes on the stylistic flamboyance of an androgynous 1970s bohemianism. This is in a context where the erotic gaze at white male bodies is still very rare outside adverts, music videos and gay male pornography. My own reading, however, is that this fetishization is then subjected to an explicit critique of this viewing relation. We are invited to laugh at the 'right on' white theatre director, who despite his professed radicalism positions Karim as an exoticized and erotic projection of his own imaginings about Indian culture. This culminates in a scene where Karim is persuaded to join him in a group sex encounter with his wife.

David Oswell (1998), on the other hand, offers a reading of *Buddha of Suburbia* as 'a postmodern romance'. He emphasizes its 'queer' portrayal of a fluid sexuality, unconstrained by the boundaries of race, class, gender or, indeed, geography. This undermines any sense that his sexual allure has rendered him powerless. Karim's journey of discovery opens up the possibility of self-fashioning in a spirit of post-modern openness of potential identities. Karim's 'queer' indeterminacy of sexual orientation – he declares at one point 'I'll fuck anyone', and, as Oswell comments, 'we do indeed see that this is the case' – is related to his racial positioning as 'in between' Indian and white identity, in a hybrid mix that unsettles his gender position as well as his sense of ethnic belonging.

Karim, in Oswell's view, is on a flight *from* identity, and the boundaries that constrain who he can be and whom he can love. This includes the geographical boundaries of the city, as Karim finds a world of metropolitan sophistication once he becomes a theatre actor. But this isn't presented as an antithesis to the suburbs. Here too he has to fight against being racially stereotyped, not only in a production of Kipling's *Jungle Book* but also in the improvised experimental theatre work he then moves into. We are also encouraged to stand back from the stereotypical view of the uniform suburbs. Although the city is full of sexual possibilities, including the rather comically presented group sex scene, Karim's experience of sex in the suburbs is equally diverse. His homosexual encounter with Charlie takes place in the attic of the suburban home Charlie shares with his mother. It forces a recognition of suburbia as visibly hybrid in its sexual practices, rather than secretive, uniform and normalized (Oswell 1998: 166–9).

The question that arises with Karim, and with queer politics more generally, is whether his resistance to categorization and conformity is reduced to an individualism that rejects any politics of group identity. Karim certainly seems uncomfortable with each of the communities he encounters and by the end his endless reinvention of the self is itself subject to critique. Oswell points to the final episode where Jamila confronts Karim for not attending an anti-fascist demonstration. 'Where are you going Karim – as a person?' she asks him. In his final conversation with the now successful pop star Charlie, Karim realizes he no longer admires or loves him. When Charlie declares, in a presaging of the Thatcher era, 'Money is all there is', he replies, 'I used to think that pleasure was all there was – when my father talked about the spirit I thought it was all bullshit.' In these exchanges, Oswell argues, the drama recognizes the limitations and costs of being queer – all the people left behind and all the failures to commit to anything or anyone beyond the self in the journey to self-realization – that in the end produces no resistance to the pleasure-seeking, materialist values of consumer capitalism (Oswell 1998: 171).

In the same way as Karim, we as viewers are encouraged to be critically reflexive and open to forming new identifications, as when our fetishizing gaze at the racialized other is followed by a critical awareness of that position. This mix of possible erotic and political investments makes any prediction of the text's ideological effects problematic and historically contingent. Oswell cites Joseph Bristow's notion of texts as a 'cruising zone' that allows audiences to make a series of imaginative identifications and form themselves in the process. But this openness raises the same questions for us as for Karim. In the depoliticized discourse of postmodern culture is there a failure to commit to anything or anyone beyond our own pleasure? In this way *Buddha of Suburbia* explores whether the rejection of essentialized identities simply leads back to a depoliticized individualism rather than a politics of identity that recognizes the complex articulation of multiple identifications.

Politically incorrect: queer lifestyle drama

During the latter half of the 1990s, Channel 4 as a fully fledged commercial company selling its own advertising sought to capitalize on its 'alternative' image in a branding exercise designed to attract youthful and affluent audiences to its platform of channels. These now included E4 and the subscription film channel FilmFour. Caughie's (2000: 192–7) assessment is that Channel 4 in the 1980s provided a space for serious, oppositional drama that the prevailing conditions of market-led commissioning couldn't deliver. In his view *My Beautiful Laundrette* would struggle to get commissioned today. As well as the fact that it didn't have an established star name as writer or performer, 'it is too untidy in its shape, too uncertain in its narrative focus, too many themes are pursued and too few conclusions reached . . . Its ambivalent, complex politics . . . dissolves the boundaries between the good guys and the bad guys' (*ibid.*: 198–9). Yet this description is very like the multinarrative forms of postmodern serial drama developed in the US commercial system that are designed to appeal to up-market audiences. In the UK these 'quality' serials have been the site for 'progressive' constructions of gay and lesbian sexuality in a market-oriented context for drama. When it comes to sexual diversity commercial channels are now at the forefront of cultural innovation as they develop their distinctive 'brands'.

Queer as Folk originated as an eight-part serial followed by a two-part sequel (Channel 4 1999 and 2000). Its portrayal of a range of 'queer' identities and a no-holds-barred attitude to the embodied performance of gay sexuality was perfect not only as a late night draw on its main channel, where it achieved four million viewers, but also for repeats on the newly launched E4. Its status as a 'quality' product was further enhanced by showings at international film festivals around the world. A longer version remade for the US market (Showtime 2000–) is based on the original but written by a team of American writers. In both these forms it has acquired 'cult' status, as the extensive merchandising, via the web, of mementoes of the series confirms. The significance of *Queer as Folk* as a landmark in the representation of gay sexuality in television drama arises from its relation to the preceding twenty years of debates on the representation of gay and lesbian sexuality. The emphasis on simply wanting a presence or on 'positive' characters to counteract negative stereotyping was joined by a desire for characters who weren't 'bland, saintly, desexualised mainstream figures who might as well be heterosexual' (Doty and Gove 1997: 87). The impact of queer politics was a reaction to 'politically correct' images in favour of openly sexual portrayals that dared to transgress heteronormative standards of decorum and acknowledged the range of 'queer' sexual practices that fell outside the assimilated gay or lesbian couple. It was a challenge that posed serious problems for an institution in which the passionate kiss still defined the limits of homoeroticism.

Queer as Folk had been preceded by *This Life*, a 32-episode, post-watershed serial about a group of young lawyers, produced by Tony Garnett's independent company World Productions for BBC2 (1996 and 1997). This had aspired to be a 'drama of recognition' for twenty-something professionals (Garnett 2001). A tolerant attitude to gay sexuality is foregrounded from the start, when Warren is appointed to a job at a law firm despite having 'come out' during the interview. It was also marked by a more general permissiveness in the language used and in the explicit, non-judgemental portrayal of recreational drug use. In the characterization of Warren and a bisexual character, Ferdy, *This Life* suggests that casual and promiscuous sex is the norm for gay men. The final episode, for example, shows two men having anal sex in the toilets while attending a wedding party. But the inclusion of one or two gay characters in a drama where the majority of characters are heterosexual cannot stand in for the whole gay and lesbian community. It is in this respect that *Queer as Folk* is different. All the main characters are gay.

Queer as Folk was undoubtedly shocking to many people but the effect was to generate huge amounts of publicity for the serial without any long-term negative repercussions for the channel, despite all the complaints. The admonishments from the regulators and Channel 4's response are interesting for the way that they mobilize competing discourses of sexual regulation to justify their positions. The BSC picked out three isolated 'acts' that it considered 'obscene'. The most serious objection was to the explicit and graphic gay sexual encounter involving a 15-year-old boy in episode one. The ITC was more concerned with the overall context within which these scenes were consumed; that is, they were shown without sufficient warning, without respon-sible educative follow-up on subjects such as safe sex, young people and sexuality. The ITC was also concerned about the celebratory tone of the first episode; it lacked a critical perspective on the acts depicted within the narrative. Channel 4's response was to declare itself extremely proud of the series, and to argue that illegal under-age gay sex was as legitimate a topic for drama as any other illegal activity, such as murder or theft. Moreover, it defended its mission as a channel 'to put alternative viewpoints on screen' (Gibson 1999b).

Not surprisingly, even within the gay and lesbian 'community' views about the series differed, views based on differences in political strategy between the lesbian and gay movements and queer activism. From the perspective of the liberal politics of gay liberation, working for the political rights of inclusion as equal citizens, the decision to show sex between a promiscuous and charismatic 29-year-old and a 15-year-old virgin in the first ten minutes of the first episode was politically foolhardy. Stuart's seduction of the schoolboy, Nathan, is filmed with them lying at the very front of the scene, allowing us to see every detail of the encounter, including ejaculation, a (literally) 'in your face' defiance of television's standards of sexual decorum. This was especially provocative at a time when the British Parliament was debating the equalizing of the age of consent to 16 and when homophobic prejudice that gay men are driven by an uncontrollable desire to seduce young boys legitimized the unequal age of consent.

Yet the assumption that *Queer as Folk* promotes promiscuous and irresponsible gay sex as a desirable lifestyle depends on a reading of the drama that neglects the serial's

Figure 5 Stuart (Aidan Gillen) cruises Canal Street in *Queer as Folk* (CH4, 1999)

complexity and ambivalence. Sally Munt (2000) and Peter Billingham (2000) both show how the drama explores the contradictions and repression that structured gay identity in the late 1990s in ways that evade a neat ideological reading based on notions of positive and negative images. It presents a gay lifestyle rarely seen on television before, in which everything else is incidental to 'going out and looking for a shag', thereby deliberately replacing the mainstream stereotype of the 'gay man as a lone, desexualised helpmate whose function is to service heterosexual plots' (Munt 2000: 532). The focus is on three gay men placed in relation to their families and friends as well as in relation to each other. Stuart's confrontational, sexually excessive and risk-taking queer identity is contrasted with Vince's ethical, placatory, love-sick persona, a contrast that leads Stuart to accuse Vince of being 'a straight man who happens to fuck men'. But the multiple narrative strands resonate with each other in unpredictable ways as the drama unfolds, undermining any fixed position from which to evaluate their behaviour. It even dares a shift in modality in the final episode, where the naturalistic, if glossy, style transforms into an ironized utopian fantasy parodying the cult film *Thelma and Louise* (Scott 1991), where love conquers all as Stuart and Vince drive off into the sunset.

The desire to transform the imposed shame of homosexuality into gay pride is shown to be not just a matter of political conflict but also a process full of psychological complexity. Sally Munt reads *Queer as Folk* as an exploration of the ambivalence, the displacements and the exclusions that are produced by reversing the shame/pride dichotomy in the fight against homophobia. The rhetoric of pride in the lesbian and gay movement is premised on leaving the 'closet', a secretive prison of shame. In *Queer as Folk* this is shown to depend on a process in which shame is displaced to produce other forms of exclusion based on 'race', class and gender.

The portrayal of Manchester's club scene in the commodified gay quarter of Canal Street makes homosexuality into a desirable 'have-it-all lifestyle' where the ethos of 'find 'em, fuck 'em, forget 'em' seems untainted by any post-AIDS restraint or ethical judgements on sexual excess and hedonism. Yet Munt points out the extent to which Stuart is motivated by shame. This is most obvious in his 'coming out' speech to his parents, in which all the insults he has ever endured are listed and reclaimed as positive signifiers of his identity. In a more dispersed way throughout the text, she argues, the pain experienced by living in a homophobic society is repudiated through projection, in violent fantasies of revenge on the perpetrators. These scenes lie outside the boundaries of the newly desirable, gentrified spaces of an attractive and aspirational gay scene. They blow up the car of a suburban mother to avenge one of Stuart's gay friends for her rejection of him. Nathan's new-found confidence from his liaison with Stuart enables him to answer back to the homophobic black teacher at his school. Stuart and Vince force the 'white trash' figure, who calls them faggot, to apologize in the fantasy ending. 'Homophobia is now located in non-white and working class cultures who are thus perceived as enemies' (Munt 2000: 538).

In Munt's view the text consciously acknowledges these displacements. Nathan, the 15-year-old embroiled in fighting homophobia in his school, laments his oppression, to which his friend Donna retorts, 'I'm black and I'm a girl. Try that for a week.' Vince's lack of gay chic in his naff obsession with *Dr Who* videos, his petty bourgeois aspirations to be manager of a supermarket and his impoverished but selfless family is a counterpoint to Stuart's effortless and selfish affluence. While Stuart is the focus for the scopophilic gaze, it is Vince's unrequited love for him that is the conduit for the viewer's desire. Stuart's splitting of love and desire, from this point of view, can be seen not as an identity to be envied but as psychological damage that needs to be healed. The deleterious effects of shame must be acknowledged, in order to be transcended. Sally Munt (2000: 541) argues that *Queer as Folk* is part of that process. Fictional narratives are one way in which we can inhabit the split-off characters of our inner life: 'Narratives can move us to restitution through the passage of time that reading, and grief, requires.' *Queer as Folk*'s focus on the promiscuous gay scene 'did dangerously break boundaries, but in unpredictable ways which contained ambivalent consequences for the reformulation of gay identity after shame' (*ibid.*: 541).

Conclusion

Television has lagged behind the developments in sexual storytelling in other cultural fields as a result of its preoccupation with avoiding offence to its majority audience. Gay and lesbian narratives in television drama remain relatively scarce and are still very constrained by the requirements for 'respectability' in the popular forms of prime time. Nevertheless, on the margins, we have seen how dramas addressed to a minority, for whom the taboos on homosexuality are no longer as potent, have begun to emerge. Changing cultural tastes attuned to a postmodern aesthetic have also affected the forms in which these stories are told. No longer constrained by linear narratives that tell the 'truth' of sexual identity and the realist quest for authenticity, postmodern drama is able to explore the shifting identifications and ambivalent experiences that constitute a field of sexual possibilities. These are for an audience used to playful and ironic modes of 'queer' reading in which pleasurable fantasy and excess have an accepted role.

The complaint that this constitutes a retreat from political and ethical engagement with the 'real world', in which gays and lesbians outside the confines of a privileged urban elite continue to suffer from discrimination and homophobic prejudice, is only partially true and, in some respects, is misplaced. The 'real world' of consumer culture has changed the cultural context in which even the most closeted of homosexuals lead their lives. I would argue that equality of cultural provision for sexual minorities should acknowledge what drama does best: being a space for psychological complexity and pleasurable fantasy that goes beyond the demand for citizenship rights in an 'oppositional public sphere'. These fictional forms do interact with social and political change but we shouldn't fall into the trap of assuming they must always therefore be 'politically correct'.

Recommended reading

Bell, D. and Binnie, J. (2000) *The Sexual Citizen: Queer Politics and Beyond*. Cambridge: Polity Press.

Caughie, J. (2000) *TV Drama: Realism, Modernism and British Culture*. Oxford: Oxford University Press.

Oswell, D. (1998) True love in queer times: romance, suburbia and masculinity, in L. Pearce and G. Whisker (eds) *Fatal Attractions: Rescripting Romance in Contemporary Literature and Film*. London: Pluto Press.

Munt, S. (2000) Shame/pride dichotomies in *Queer as Folk, Textual Practice*, 14 (3): 531–46.

Nelson, R. (1997) *TV Drama in Transition: Forms, Values and Cultural Change*. London: Macmillan.

8 | POSTFEMINIST DRAMA IN THE USA

This chapter considers the ways in which postfeminist discourses have been incorporated into 'quality' drama in the commercial television industry, with a particular focus on *Sex and the City* (HBO 1998–2004). For Home Box Office, the makers of the serial, 'quality' drama has been used successfully to enhance both its visibility and its reputation in a context where cable television has had to struggle to gain any cultural status at all. In 2001 *Sex and the City* won the Emmy for 'Outstanding Comedy Series' – the first time a cable TV show has ever taken top honours for best series in any category (http://www.hbo.com/city/insiders_guide/news) and since then it has been showered with awards. News items and features relating to *Sex and the City* appear regularly in the print media and work to maintain its visibility and status as 'must see TV'. Its success, I will argue, has been achieved by generic innovation to address a niche market. Rather than offering a mixed schedule or hybridized genres for family viewing, as the networks do, HBO's brand name acts as an umbrella for multiple channels that separate out programmes designed for specific audiences. It has a whole channel addressed to women: HBO Signature, 'smart, sophisticated entertainment for women'. The creation of a successful brand in a competitive market, as was explained in Chapter 2, depends on the ability to innovate within a pattern of predictable pleasures to create a recognizable identity for a product that appeals to a commercially attractive audience. The novelty of *Sex and the City* lies in the migration of a woman-centred and explicit sexual discourse into television drama, enabled by the differentiated taste cultures of a multichannel environment.

The success of this long-form drama serial is symptomatic of the forces shaping programmes in the digital, multichannel era of television and its integration with the interlocking circuits of global markets. HBO is owned by America Online/Time Warner, which merged with IPC (International Publishing Corporation), the magazine publisher, in 2001. This economic convergence has produced an international media conglomerate covering the Internet and print media, as well as television. HBO has to sell itself first to its subscribers in the USA, on the basis of its appeal to a sufficiently affluent group of consumers, before syndicating to other distributors in a global market. In the UK, on Channel 4, it developed a regular fan base among the 'AB viewers' that advertisers are keen to attract. Its global 'cosmopolitan' appeal also extends beyond English-speaking audiences. In Brazil, for example, it is shown on the Multishow cable channel, owned by the Globo conglomerate. Again this example reveals an audience skewed towards the affluent classes: 94 per cent of viewers are classed as AB (Neves 2003). In the USA, as a show distributed on subscription cable, it is relatively free from government regulations and the restraints imposed by advertisers in comparison to the networks. Arguably this makes it more responsive to the tastes and values of emergent social groups, such as the 'independent career woman' made possible by feminism (Lury 1993: 40–51).[1]

How should this development be understood in the light of debates about the politics of postfeminist culture? The labelling of television drama as postfeminist more often than not signifies ambivalence in its gender politics; it is certainly no guarantee of approval from feminist critics. It is applied to woman-centred dramas that, in the wake of second wave feminism, selectively deploy feminist discourses as a response to cultural changes in the lives of their potential audience, an audience that is addressed as white, heterosexual and relatively youthful and affluent. These dramas emerged out of a hybridization of genres driven by a desire to maximize audiences by creating drama that appealed to both men and women. The feminization of crime genres, such as cop shows (*Cagney and Lacey*, CBS 1982–88) and legal dramas (*LA Law*, NBC 1986–94; *Ally McBeal*, Fox 1997–2003), allowed for an exploitation of the generic pleasures associated with the masculine, public world of work and the feminized, private world of personal relationships (Gamman 1988; D'Acci 1994; Dow 1996; Mayne 1997; Nelson 2000, 2001a; Lotz 2001; Moseley and Read 2002). This allowed an engagement with liberal feminist issues arising from women's relation to the law and to work. A focus on women as protagonists, whose actions drive the narrative, replaced the marginal and narrow range of roles available previously to women characters in these genres (see Chapter 1).

Although it shares their incorporation of feminist themes and their focus on the liberal, heterosexual, white, metropolitan, career woman, *Sex and the City* is very different from these networked dramas. These differences arise, I would argue, from the institutional conditions of its production and distribution as niche market, subscription cable television that encourages a polarization between men's and women's programming (Compaine and Gomery 2000: 524). *Sex and the City* draws on the 'feminine' address established in women's glossy magazines with their consumer-oriented advice on beauty and fashion and on sexual relationships. This reverses the trend towards the hybridization of masculine and feminine genres that has characterized primetime drama on network television. This chapter considers the consequences this has for the portrayal of women's sexuality.

I take up these issues in more detail by drawing comparisons between *Sex and the City* and previous examples of postfeminist drama on US television; discussing how the programme adapts the content and address of women's magazines for television and the Internet; showing how its brand identity is established across the interlocking circuits of the media, celebrity and fashion; and identifying the instability in its comedic mode of address as it oscillates between complicity and critique of a consumer lifestyle.

'Having it all' in postfeminist drama

Postfeminism is an ambiguous term in that it can imply both a continuity and a break with the second wave feminism that preceded it. 'Post' means 'after', and we can therefore simply understand the term as the multiple responses to the political challenges posed by the feminist movement of the 1970s. Generation is one of the key dynamics structuring this debate. For a younger generation born in the 1970s and 1980s, feminism, instead of appearing radical, has become associated with their parents' generation and can therefore be perceived as an establishment ideology whose codes restrict their freedom of expression. This generational dynamic creates fertile ground for the backlash rhetoric that emerged in the right-wing political context of Reaganite America in the 1980s. The key term around which this backlash was organized was 'political correctness', which rapidly became established as a term of abuse. Objections to political correctness focused especially on the feminist critique of fashion, beauty and representational practices that, it was argued, constructed women as disempowered objects of the male gaze and male sexual desire. Younger women began to assert their right to dress to be sexually attractive. When combined with an emerging postmodern aesthetic of parody in popular culture, excessive femininity was performed as an assertive form of feminist fashion (the singer Madonna was a significant influence). The complicit critique this offers to the male gaze has been a matter of furious disagreement among feminist writers but it is a fashion trend that is still going strong.

Another main focus for postfeminist revisionism has been women's role in the workforce as equals with men. In liberal feminism the rights of women to work outside the home and to be able to compete on equal terms with men have been central. In most developed economies not only do women now make up more than 50 per cent of the workforce, but also they are working in careers previously dominated by men. In postfeminist discourses, however, women question whether it was worth it. The personal cost for professional women of competing in a man's world is represented as making it more difficult to find a man to marry. The emotional misery this causes is closely linked to the ticking biological clock that makes women in their thirties the particular focus for these concerns (Dow 1996). In fictional versions of this discourse the emotional tone tends towards melodrama, with the emphasis on the impossibility of a woman getting what she wants – she is a figure of pathos. Or the tone is comedic, where the plight of the thirty-something single girl is a sign of her woeful inadequacy as a woman and to be laughed at in rueful recognition (Whelahan 2000). It has been argued that the unhappy career woman is part of the backlash discourse and is a construction designed to deliver women to the advertisers: these are the women who have disposable income and the dissatisfaction that drives consumption (Dow 1996; Whelahan 2000). Alternatively, it can be seen as a response to a misguided liberal feminist strategy of seeking parity with, rather than valuing women's difference from, men. In these terms, postfeminism is a necessary corrective to a mistaken devaluation of the private domestic world of the feminine where women excel in their ability to nurture and care for others. The realignment between feminism and femininity, in ways that avoid setting up a binary split between feminists and ordinary women, is one of the principal projects of postfeminism (Brunsdon 1997; McRobbie 1997; Hollows 2000).

In the hybrid, women-centred drama characteristic of postfeminist television in the 1980s and 1990s, the division between the public world of work and the private world of the domestic sphere that prevents women 'having it all' has become blurred. This is achieved in *Sex and the City* because the world of work largely disappears from view as a distinct space and set of hierarchical relations, although the women's autonomy from men is underwritten by their economic independence. Work is collapsed into the private sphere and becomes another form of self-expression, alongside consumption, thereby side-stepping the postfeminist problematic. The sex life of the series' central character, Carrie, and those of her friends, act as research for her weekly newspaper column, which she writes from home. Samantha works in public relations, a job where her physical attractions and personal charm are intrinsic to her success. Charlotte manages an art gallery in a manner that suggests it is more of a hobby. This does indeed reflect the changing nature of work in which flexible working and 'knowledge-based' careers have reduced the rigid separation of the public and private spheres. Only Miranda feels the contradiction between her private life and her career success as a lawyer, where long hours and a competitive ethos conflict with her life as a single mother in later seasons of the show.

The generic expectation is that postfeminist drama will be about single women wanting to get married. *Sex and the City* was initially marketed as such to feed into those expectations. The video blurb for the first season states 'Sexy, hip, smart and sassy, *Sex and the City* charts the lives and loves of four women and their quest to find the one thing that eludes them all – a real, satisfying and lasting relationship. Is such a thing possible in New York?' But unlike in other postfeminist narratives, in *Sex and the City* the responsibility for single women's unhappiness isn't laid at the door of feminist women choosing a career over a man. Of the four women only Charlotte is unequivocal in her desire to get married, but she is quickly disillusioned when she does. The traditional romance narrative is still there but as a residual sensibility, a slightly old-fashioned version of femininity that doesn't work in practice. Charlotte's belief in romance is undercut by her new husband's impotence on their wedding night and her discovery that he can be aroused only by a porn magazine in the bathroom (Episode 45, 'Hot Child in the City').[2] She eventually remarries but the wedding day is a comic disaster and her longed-for pregnancy still doesn't materialize. When Carrie and friends visit a former New Yorker for her baby shower (Episode 10, 'The Baby Shower') they aren't shown envying the woman her home in the country, her husband and her coming baby – instead it accentuates the gulf that separates them from her – and they return to their single lives in New York with a huge sigh of relief. Miranda does finally marry her baby's father in the final season of the show, and, with great misgivings, buys a house in Brooklyn. In the final episode Carrie is reunited with Big, the love of her life, when he at last realizes he can't live without her. Nevertheless, these conventional outcomes do not change the fact that the series as a whole was predicated on their being single.

The women's single state is a necessary precondition for their central preoccupation – sexual relationships and how to achieve sexual satisfaction, not previously considered a suitable topic for television drama. The series publicly repudiates the shame of being single and sexually active in defiance of the bourgeois codes that used to be demanded of 'respectable' women. It self-reflexively interrogates media representations of the single woman, although the emotional power of these residual stereotypes is acknowledged. For example, when Carrie appears looking haggard and smoking a cigarette on the front of a magazine under the strap line 'Single and Fabulous?' it sparks a discussion among the four women about why the media want to persuade women to get married (Episode 16, 'They Shoot Single People Don't They?'). Despite their intellectual critique the rest of the episode explores the emotional vulnerabilities of their situation before concluding that it is better to be alone than faking happiness with a man. There is no shame attached to being alone. It ends with Carrie eating by herself in a restaurant, with no book to read as armour, to assert her belief that she really is 'Single and Fabulous!'

This exploration of women's sexuality is enabled by changes in the regulatory regime of television as a consequence of digital convergence. It has moved closer to the freedoms enjoyed by the print media and the Internet as compared to the sensitivity to religious Puritanism historically shown by the television networks. This enables *Sex and the City* to exploit fully the glossy women's magazines' consumerist approach to sexuality, in which women's sexual pleasure and agency is frankly encouraged as part of a consumer lifestyle and attitude. In this respect, *Sex and the City* has moved a long way from the kind of family-centred or wholesome peer-group sitcoms that have previously dominated the network schedules, in which embodied desire provided the repressed subtext rather the primary focus of the dialogue and action. Hybridization of the discourse of women's magazines with the codes of the television sitcom has provided the 'licensed space' that comedy allows for an exploration of sexual taboos and decorum (Neale and Krutnick 1990; Arthurs 1999).

This hybridization has also allowed for the consumer attitude to be lightly satirized, a response that is argued to be characteristic of an aestheticized relation to the self. It is this sensibility that allows for the adoption of ironic ways of consuming and a self-reflexive attitude to one's own identity, appearance and self-presentation. Mike Featherstone characterizes the aestheticized relation to the self as one in which consumers enjoy the swings between the extremes of aesthetic involvement and distanciation, a sensibility, he argues, that is characteristic of the new middle classes of postmodern culture (Featherstone 1991b). It is a form of controlled hedonism that oscillates between complicity with the values of consumer culture and critique. This allows the simultaneous satisfaction of the sensual pleasures allowed by material success and the placating of a guilty, liberal conscience. It emerged in the 'Yuppie TV' of the work-obsessed 1980s, where both envy and guilt, in *LA Law* (NBC 1986–94), for example, were deliberately evoked in response to the affluent lifestyles of its protagonists. The guilt was differentiated by gender. For men it was guilt at their material success whereas for women it was guilt at their lost opportunity for marriage and children (Feuer 1995; Mayne 1997).

This instability in perspective can also be seen in *Ally McBeal* (Fox 1997–2003), another woman-centred postfeminist drama about lawyers. Robin Nelson (2001a) describes its 'flexi-narrative' form as combining conventions from comedy, pop video, melodrama and court room dramas, which produces a complexity of tone and point of view that actively precludes a stable viewing position. Ally herself is 'double coded . . . at once an independent professional woman in charge of her destiny and a vulnerable waif like figure waiting for Mr Right to come along' (*ibid.*: 43). Through its blurring of the boundaries between the public world of work and the private world of the emotions it negotiates the tension between feminism and femininity, but without presenting these as mutually exclusive categories (Moseley and Read 2002). The programme constantly returns to feminist issues in its legal cases – sexual harrassment is a recurring issue – but the legal gains made by feminist activism are sometimes upheld and at other times criticized for having 'gone too far': the comic mode opens them to ridicule. Similarly, the melodramatic excessiveness of Ally's vulnerability tips over into its opposite in that her reactions are sufficiently intense to require accommodation. She doesn't simply fit into a masculinized workplace predicated on rationality; in fact her emotional excess becomes the dominant office code for her male colleagues as well. In the mirror-ridden walls of the unisex toilet, people contemplate their own and other people's faces as they work through the latest emotional trauma, or overhear a secret conversation from the stalls. It is the space where the collapse in the divisions between male and female, masculine and feminine, is most potently symbolized. It is here that the public and private, the personal and the professional, converge to melodramatic and comic effect. This is quite unlike *Cagney and Lacey*, in which the women's toilets formed a refuge, a woman's space, in the hostile terrain of the masculine workplace (see Chapter 1).

The widespread popular success of *Sex and the City* and *Ally McBeal* suggests that contradictory and unstable texts steeped in melodramatic and comedic excess are usable precisely because they allow people to explore the contradictions and instabilities of their own subjectivity. This is predicated on a poststructuralist theory of subjectivity that emphasizes the ways in which we are formed by multiple discourses whose influence is felt in differing ways depending on the context (Morley 1980; Brooks 1997).

Remediating women's magazines

The 'new' media depend for their success on their ability to 'remediate' – that is, 'adapt to a new medium' – the forms that are already established in the 'old' media. The relationship also works in the opposite direction, with earlier technologies 'struggling to maintain their legitimacy by remediating newer ones' (Bolter and Grusin 1999: 61). We can see how this interrelationship works in the way that *Sex and the City* has been used to enhance the visibility and status of cable television, drawing on successful formats established in network television and the print media, and exploiting on its website the new potential offered by the Internet.

The form of *Sex and the City* is very influenced by the print media. Adapted from a book written by Candice Bushnell, a New York journalist, it is structured around the fictionalized writing of a weekly newspaper column. It retains the first person mode of direct address, using Carrie's voice-over to comment on the action in which a question is posed, journalistic research is undertaken and some conclusions are proposed in a personalized, witty and aphoristic style. The questions range from the frivolous to the taboo. They can be serious but not too serious – they don't deal with rape or sexual harassment as in *LA Law* or *Ally McBeal*. Can women have sex like a man? Are men commitment phobes? In New York has monogamy become too much to expect? Is motherhood a cult? Can sex toys enhance your sex life? Does size matter? Each of the ensemble cast provides a different perspective on the question. Their stories are told as alternatives for viewers to weigh up, just as articles in women's magazines offer a variety of personal anecdotes to their readers to exemplify a particular issue and how different people have responded in practice. These are loosely tied together by Carrie's final voice-over in a provisional conclusion that is often tentative in tone. 'Maybe . . .' The bulletin board on the *Sex and the City* website (http://www.hbo.com/ city_community) invites viewers' comments on the episode, asking questions like 'What do you think of the new men in Carrie's life? Talk about it with other fans on the Bulletin Board.' 'Do you identify with Carrie? Talk about it with fellow fans.' Thus multiple perspectives are actively encouraged within a tightly structured, repetitive format in which the characters are bound into a relatively unchanging situation in order to guarantee continuation of the pleasures offered by the brand (Lury 1993: 86–7).

Sex and the City's treatment of sexuality can be understood as an updated version of the 'Cosmo' woman who is dedicated to self-improvement and economic independence

(Ballaster *et al.* 1991). This is a figure who can be related back to the rise of the post-war 'new petit bourgeoisie' whose 'liberated' attitudes to sex, combined with an ethic of 'improvement', were discussed in Chapter 3 in relation to pornography. The four main characters' signature cocktail is called a 'cosmopolitan', signalling this sorority. The show's title echoes that of a book, *Sex and the Single Girl*, written by Helen Gurley Brown, who went on to be the founding editor of *Cosmopolitan* magazine in 1965. The function of sexual imagery and talk in *Sex and the City* is quite different from that in pornographic magazines and cable channels, where sexual arousal is assumed as the purpose for consumption. Instead it dramatizes the kind of consumer and sexual advice offered by women's magazines. This is a sphere of feminine expertise in which it has been argued that women are empowered to look – not only at consumer goods but also at their own bodies as sexual subjects (Radner 1995). Sexuality is presented in this context as a source of potential pleasure for which women should make themselves ready, whether through internalizing the beauty and fashion advice that will attract the right men, or through following advice on sexual technique. Carrie's billboard slogan advertising her newspaper column draws attention to this pedagogic function: 'Carrie Bradshaw *knows* good sex' (my emphasis). It is an expertise rooted in everyday life and experience. When called upon to give a lecture to a roomful of women on how to get a date, Carrie fails miserably. But she succeeds brilliantly the following week when she takes the women to a bar where she guides them in how to work the room by reading the sexual signals, giving them the confidence and expertise to act on their desires (Episode 46, 'Frenemies').

The series is able to go beyond the catalogue function of magazine fashion spreads, or the list of ten tips on how to improve foreplay. A consumer lifestyle is presented not as a series of commodities to be bought but as an integrated lifestyle to be emulated. The clothes and shoes become expressions of the different moods and personalities of embodied, empathetic characters in an authentic setting. This function is in fact most explicit on the programme's website, which differs in tone and emphasis from the television series and more closely matches the look and address of a woman's magazine. It relies on the relationship fans already have with the programme, guiding viewers in how to convert their knowledge about the series into knowledge they can use in their own lives, as discerning consumers of fashion, as creators of 'a look' and a lifestyle. This is represented as a set of active choices that are an expression of individual character and mood. We are invited to conceive of emotional states as a trigger for particular types of consumption and clothing choices, such as the photograph of Carrie that is captioned 'the dress that shows she is finally going to split from Mr Big' (http://www.hbo.com/city_style). The site anticipates, encourages and attempts to shape fan behaviour that will convert into consumerism (Rivett 2000).

Bourgeois bohemians

The almost exclusive focus on sexual relationships and consumption in *Sex and the City* speaks to the cultural influence in the 1990s of the 'bourgeois bohemians'. This class fraction has, David Brooks (2000) argues, replaced the yuppies as the new culturally dominant class in the USA (and other developed economies). The key feature of this new class fraction is their ability to reconcile the contradictions between bourgeois and bohemian values and lifestyles. Sexual permissiveness, which in the bohemian movements of the 1960s was articulated with radical anti-capitalist political values, has been rearticulated to conform not only with the materialist priorities of consumer culture, but also with the emancipatory politics of the 1970s and 1980s. One effect has been to free white, middle-class women from the sexual constraints required by bourgeois respectability. This attention to sexual freedom and pleasure in second wave feminism is culturally specific and arises from the dominance of that movement among white, middle-class women. A quite different political agenda around sexuality arises from the historical positioning of black and working-class women as the embodied 'other' of the white bourgeoisie (Haraway 1990).

A scene from the first season of *Sex and the City* (Episode 6, 'Secret Sex') encapsulates this brand identity; that is, the emotions, attitudes and lifestyle with which it is associated and the specificity of its address. In an episode that explores the shame that some sexual experiences can provoke, Carrie gathers a group of her friends together for the launch of a new publicity campaign promoting her weekly newspaper column called 'Sex and the City'. They wait on the sidewalk for a bus to pass by carrying the poster for her brand on its side. They are in a mood of excited anticipation, marred only by the regret that Mr Big, the new man in her life, has failed to show up to share this proud moment. The revealing dress she is wearing in the poster is the dress that she had worn on their first date, when, despite her best judgement, they had sex. As the bus approaches, the excitement turns to dismay, and Carrie hides her face in shame. There is the poster with Carrie's body stretched in languorous pose along the full length of the bus, under the strapline 'Carrie Bradshaw knows good sex'. But as we pan across her body, next to her seductively made-up lips, a crudely drawn graffiti image of a large penis is revealed.

This short scene exemplifies the series' dramatic terrain, namely the exploration of women's sexuality in a postmodern consumer culture. It is a culture produced by capital's restless search for new and expanded markets, and characterized by the commodification of the individual's relation to the body, self and identity, just as we see here in the relation of Carrie to her billboard image. The scene also exemplifies the programme's tone and style, which mixes the display of celebrity lifestyles for our emulation, as in women's magazines, with a comic puncturing of these aestheticized images. The idealized image of bourgeois perfection in the image of Carrie on her billboard is momentarily satirized by the obscene graffiti. It is an eruption of the repressed 'other' to bourgeois femininity in a deliberate disruption of its codes of sexual decorum. This, plus Big's absence, is a reminder of women's vulnerability to loss of self-esteem when it relies too exclusively on body image and its sexual appeal to men. The presence of Carrie's friends is important, though, in providing the support and reassurance she needs to regain her composure. Their shared culture of femininity offers an alternative to heterosexual dependence.

As a successful brand *Sex and the City* influences the continuing transformations in fashion that characterize consumer culture. News stories about fashion regard it as an important influence. Sarah Jessica Parker (who plays Carrie) is a fashion icon in women's magazines and in newspaper columns; celebrity exposure is rapidly replacing catwalk shows and supermodels as the way to sell high fashion. The British fashion journalist who tracked down and bought Sarah Jessica Parker's handbag in the shape of a horse's head and then wrote about it in a British national newspaper provided publicity for the TV show, the makers of the bag and Parker as a celebrity (Lambert 2001). It also contributed to New York's reputation as a city 'brand' in the global system of capitalism as a source of new fashion ideas. A report on the New York fashion shows in the *Guardian* was headed 'Fashion in the city: cult show underpins style' (Porter 2001). It commented on the 'power of the cult drama' to create a fashion trend, whether for Manolo Blahnik stiletto heels, corsages or purses in the shape of a horse's head. The report focused on the House of Field, which acted as stylist for *Sex and the City*. Theirs is a bohemian look, made newly respectable as mainstream fashion, but retaining in the thrift-store elements reference to the anti-materialist values that characterized the hippie bohemianism of the 1960s. It incorporates the psychedelic patterns of that era and an individual eclecticism achieved by mixing retro and new clothing, the avant-garde and the mass-produced.

The horse's head handbag works within this kitsch aesthetic, in which objects are redefined as 'cool' through a process of irony. It reminds the *Daily Telegraph* journalist of My Little Pony and her nine-year-old self, and it is cheap to buy in comparison to most designer handbags ($165). The HBO website (www.hbo.com/city/insiders_guide/news) offers *Sex and the City* merchandise for sale, but they have no pretensions to be designer goods. They are cheap items, T-shirts, mugs and glasses printed with the *Sex and the City* logo and New York skyline (doubly ironic now). The trash aesthetic of *Sex and the City* anticipates the ironic response that, in the 1980s, for example, was developed as a subcultural, camp response to *Dynasty*, the first prime time television programme to have a resident fashion designer and its own line of fashion merchandising (Feuer 1995). In the decade or so that separates *Dynasty* from the incorporated irony of *Sex and the City*'s trash aesthetics, camp irony has moved from the margins to the centre. It exemplifies the way in which a camp and ironic attitude to mass culture, originating in a gay response to their cultural marginalization, has been appropriated by the mainstream media in order to address niche markets in the affluent middle classes. *Sex and the City* is simply part of a wider cultural trend, the commodified aesthetic of postmodernism in which irony is a central component.

The style also expresses a bohemian attitude to women's sexuality. But the clothes do not simply replicate the rather demure look for women of the hippie era, when sexual liberation, enabled by the separation between sex and reproduction that the pill made possible, still meant women responding to men's sexual initiatives. The *Sex and the City* version of bohemian fashion is post-punk, post-Madonna; it incorporates an assertive sexualized imagery for women that consciously plays with the transgressive sexual connotations of leather, bondage and underwear as outerwear. One garment, 'open to below the navel before swooping under the crotch, had an immaculate cut, even if the look was purposefully wanton . . . you could easily see Carrie giving the look a try, maybe out at the Hamptons.' 'Wantonness' combined with 'a perfect cut' epitomizes the reconciliation of bourgeois with bohemian values in the aesthetics and lifestyle that *Sex and the City* expresses and promotes.

The specificity of this taste culture is made clear in the series itself through the way the four main characters' style and codes of sexual behaviour are defined against other social groupings. There are the restrained (and boring) bourgeois women, untainted by bohemian values, in whom sexual expression is kept under strict control. These are exemplified by the women who look increasingly scandalized as Charlotte, the most 'preppy' one of the four, at a reunion dinner with her university fraternity friends, reveals the fact of her husband's impotence and her own frustration. 'Don't you ever feel like you want to be fucked really hard?' she enquires as they recoil in disgust (Episode 46, 'Frenemies'). Or by Natasha, Big's wife. His boredom with her is defined by her taste in interior design: 'Everything's beige'. Then there are the people who live outside the city, and whose adherence to traditional gender roles is an indicator of their being either low class or simply old-fashioned. On a trip to Staten Island (the ferry marking the boundary) 'real men' offer a tantalizing sexual fantasy for Samantha, but when faced with the reality in the cold light of a working day, her liaison with a firemen doesn't seem such a good idea (Episode 31, 'Where There's Smoke . . .').

In traditional bourgeois cultures unbridled sexual appetites or loose speech are a mark not only of the lower classes but of the unruly woman, who inverts the power relations of gender and has sex like a man (Russo 1995; Arthurs 1999). Samantha's guilt-free promiscuity is exemplary here, although even she has her limits. She is shocked by a new acquaintance who dives under the restaurant table to 'give head' to a man they have just met (Episode 36, 'Are We Sluts?'). Indecorum is a sign of lack of respectability, which for women has been a sexual as well as class category associated with prostitution. *Sex and the City* works through the problem of establishing the boundaries of respectability in a postfeminist culture where women share many of the same freedoms as men, but in which the residual effects of the double standard are still being felt. It strives to be sexually frank without being 'vulgar'.

These women are of a generation old enough to have been influenced by feminism (in their thirties and forties) but too old to participate in a newly fashionable queer culture, despite their appropriation of camp as a style. They are resolutely heterosexual, despite occasional short-lived encounters with gays, lesbians and bisexuals that simply reconfirm it. 'I'm a trisexual' says Samantha jokingly, 'I'll try anything once'. Indeed, she does, briefly, have one lesbian lover. Carrie's relationship with a 26-year-old bisexual founders when she can't handle the thought that he's been with a man; nor does she feel comfortable with his gender-bending friends. 'I was too old to play this game', she tells us in the voice-over (Episode 34, 'Boy, Girl, Boy, Girl . . .'). These episodes, like the one where Samantha dates an African-American, simply mark where their sexual boundaries are drawn. Thus the women's particular mix of bourgeois bohemianism is 'normalized'.

Their transgression of bourgeois sexual decorum marks the foursome as 'unruly', a challenge to patriarchal structures of power, but their adherence to the sleek control of the commodified body makes this compatible with capitalism. Unlike Edina or Patsy, the unruly women in *Absolutely Fabulous* (BBC2 1992–94, BBC1 1995–96, 2000, 2003–), a British comedy that is located in a similar cultural milieu, if the women are made to *look* ridiculous it is a momentary aberration that causes embarrassment (as in the billboard scene). In contrast, the British comedy persistently satirizes consumer culture and the feminine world of fashion, PR and women's magazines, through a farcical exaggeration of fashion styles. Its slapstick mode of comedy undermines the bodily control and discipline that underpins glamour, often as a result of drug-taking or excessive drinking (Kirkham and Skeggs 1998; Arthurs 1999). This aspect of the bohemian legacy of the 1960s in contemporary consumer society plays a very minor role in *Sex and the City* in comparison. The comedy in *Sex and the City* depends instead on verbal wit and ironic distancing, a more intellectual, and in class terms a more bourgeois, form than slapstick. It also enables the complicit critique that is considered to be characteristic of postmodernism (Lash 1990; Featherstone 1991b; Feuer 1995; Klein 2000).

The aestheticized self and sexual relations

Feminist evaluations of *Sex and the City* have conflated it with other examples of postfeminist culture in which comedy and satire has replaced any serious, ethical commitment to challenging the power relations of patriarchy, a challenge that they argue is undermined by complicit critique. The postfeminist irony in texts such as *Bridget Jones* or *Ally McBeal* allows for a constant emphasis on women's appearance and sexual desirability as a source of worth, while simultaneously subjecting this attitude to ridicule (Greer 2000; Whelehan 2000). In this view, the ironic oscillations in our relation to the bourgeois women who people the fictional world of *Sex and the City* are complicit with the aestheticized values of consumer culture and its unequal structuring of the 'look'. It assumes that women in the audience are invited to share this male gaze to the extent that it is internalized in women's narcissistic relation to their own bodies. This objectifies women's bodies and renders them powerless. In a counter-argument, feminine cultures of consumerism and fashion have been considered as a source of pleasure and power that is potentially resistant to male control. Indeed, they can offer women an alternative route to self-esteem and autonomy that overcomes the damaging division that second wave feminism constructs between feminism and femininity (see Lury 1996; McRobbie 1997; Hollows 2000 for overviews of these debates).

These contradictory evaluations need not be presented as alternatives. Part of the problem for academic feminism is to develop arguments that capture the complex contradictions of postfeminism in popular culture. In her discussion of the emphasis on the spectacle of women's bodies in women's magazines, Hilary Radner (1995) draws attention to the way this is counteracted by a textual commentary that variously endorses or asks us to question the extent to which women's worth resides in their looks. In arguing the limitations to metacritical feminist discourse in capturing women's reading practices in everyday life, Radner highlights the potential of feminine culture to 'displace the political onto the minute decisions of a contingent day to day practice in which absolute categories cannot be maintained from moment to moment' (*ibid.*: 178). Consumption is thereby redefined as an active process that has unpredictable ideological consequences. In Lash's (1990) view, the ubiquity of images in postmodern consumer culture in itself produces contradictory juxtapositions that undermine any secure position from which to interpret the world. This, he argues, has the potential to produce self-reflexive, nomadic identities in which gender, for instance, is open to redefinition (*ibid.*: 185–98). *Sex and the City* self-consciously explores the instability of feminine identity in a postfeminist, postmodern consumer culture.

A straightforward celebration of the feminist potential of consumer culture is precluded, however, by its commodity form. This promotes, according to Susan Willis (1991), an alienated and fetished relationship between people, defined by the exchange of commodities. Moreover, the codification of class, 'race' and gender differences in the stylistic details of commodities normalizes and perpetuates notions of inequality and subordination (*ibid.*: 162–3). The professional middle classes, she argues, have been duped by the signs of privilege into confusing the individualized freedom to consume with real political power. 'The production of resistant meanings will always be assimilated by capitalism for the production of fresh commodities' (*ibid.*: 175–9). *Sex and the City* exemplifies these features of the commodity. Its stylistic features contribute to the cultural hegemony of the incorporated resistance of the bourgeois bohemians. Its culture of femininity provides an alternative to heterosexual dependence, but its recurring promise of a shameless utopia of fulfilled desire always ends in disappointment, for the cycle of consumption to begin again next week.

The advert for Bailey's Cream, corporate sponsors of *Sex and the City*, exemplifies how in consumer culture the body as the bearer of sensation replaces the ethical self as an ideal. It presents a sensuous image of swirling, creamy liquid with the slogan 'Let your senses guide you'. Rachel Bowlby (1993: 23) refers to the ideal modern consumer as 'a receptacle and bearer of sensations, poser and posed, with no consistent identity, no moral self'. In this aestheticized culture the question has become does it look good or feel good, rather than is this a good thing to do? Although *Sex and the City* rejects the traditional patriarchal dichotomy of virgin and whore, insisting in its explorations of the women's multiple sexual experiences their right to seek sexual satisfaction without shame, this doesn't mean that there are no limits. Aesthetic boundaries replace moral boundaries so that men who can't kiss very well, who smell, who are too short or whose semen tastes peculiar are rejected on those grounds.

Despite the radical roots of this bohemian attitude, developed in opposition to the rationalist, puritan ethos of nineteenth-century industrial capitalism (in Romanticism and Surrealism as well as Dandyism), it is now fully integrated into consumer marketing and its appeal to our hedonistic impulses and imaginings.

> But an important part of this calculating hedonism is an emotional and cognitive distancing on the part of the individual since it is this distance which introduces the possibility of reflection on consumption and facilitates the adoption of playful and ironic ways of consuming.
>
> (Lury 1996: 76)

For women this relation to an aestheticized, self-reflexive identity in which commodities are used creatively to re-fashion the self is more problematic than for men. Celia Lury (1996: 118–55) argues that this is because they occupy an unstable position in relation to the aestheticized self, an instability that is enacted in the oscillations in tone that characterize *Sex and the City* and its exploration of women's sexuality in a consumer culture.

For the women in *Sex and the City*, it often appears as though hedonism and narcissism have displaced the masochist position that they occupy in patriarchal structures of desire. The grotesque 'other' of sadistic masculinity has been repressed (and displaced into *The Sopranos*, another HBO drama series). In this economy of desire the city streets have lost the danger of a sadistic or reproving masculine gaze. Instead of intimating the dark dangers that kept 'respectable' women off the streets, New York is shown to be a place of freedom and safety – the worst that can happen is that their clothes might be splashed by a passing car (as happens to Carrie in the title sequence). These women move freely around the cafés and boutiques, with a confident sense of possession, enjoying the multiple pleasures of consumption in the company of other women and gay men. In this way their dependence on male lovers for emotional and sensual satisfaction is displaced; they always disappoint or disempower, as Mr Big does in the billboard scene by not showing up. A designer stiletto shoe, Carrie's trade mark obsession, is different. It is always there to be possessed, offering a fetish substitute for the satisfactions denied by men. The autoeroticism legitimated by the narcissistic structure of the look in consumer culture offers the possibility of doing without men at all. The show's promotion of vibrators as a route to sexual satisfaction (Episode 9, 'The Turtle and the Hare') resulted in a huge increase in sales of the 'rabbit' model that was featured (Smith 2002).

The programme's representation of the women's dissatisfaction with their male lovers could be seen as encouraging a rejection of men as a source of emotional and sexual satisfaction in favour of a feminine culture of gossip and shopping. It is the tight-knit relationship of the four women that is the only constant in the series. But they don't live together as in the cosy but adolescent comedy series *Friends*. The recurring message that for grown-ups living in Manhattan means living alone constructs the single household as the norm – a trend that has been cited as one of the major stimuli to consumption in modern cities (Lury 1996).

Sex in this context becomes like shopping: a marker of identity, a source of pleasure. Knowing how to choose the right goods is crucial. But men in *Sex and the City* are the only objects of desire that create consumer dissatisfaction. The women treat men as branded goods: the packaging has to be right but the difficulty is to find one whose use value lives up to the image. The quest becomes one in which they are looking for the phallus that would bring an end to a seemingly endless chain of desire. 'In a city of infinite options there can be no better feeling than that you only have one' is the aphorism Carrie offers at the end of one episode (Episode 7, 'The Monogamists'). Yet there is a recognition that the phallus will never live up to its promise of satisfaction and fulfilment. 'In a city of great expectations is it time to settle for what you can get?' wonders Carrie (Episode 9, 'The Turtle and the Hare'). The women try men out to see if they 'fit for size', as Carrie tells a potential husband. This is literally the case when promiscuous Samantha unexpectedly falls in love (Episode 12, 'Oh Come All Ye Faithful'). When she has sex with her new boyfriend after two weeks of uncharacteristic abstention, she is devastated. His dick is only three inches long! In *Sex and the City* size *does* matter.

Sex and the City incorporates the ambivalence in feminist evaluations of the aestheticized self, showing it to be a source both of confident autonomy and of disempowerment in its unstable oscillations. For instance, Carrie's performance is constructed around her role as a successful and famous journalist researching her newspaper column, which bears the same name as the TV show. She is shown as a detached observer of her own and her friends' sexual desires and experiences. She self-reflexively and playfully deliberates on their consequences, not in terms of some overarching ethical position but from an aesthetic point of view of someone who has to write a witty, readable column that will enhance her professional status. Sexual ethics are converted into a controlled display of witty aphorisms and the comedy of embarrassment. The same is true of the show's address to its viewers. As an audience we are positioned as detached observers of this sexual play, not as we would be in pornography for physical arousal and the satisfactions of masturbation, nor as lessons in morality, but to be amused.

When the oscillation swings back to close involvement, the mood is one of unsatisfied yearning, not playfulness. Carrie's emotional involvement with Big, the main man in her life, produces the feeling that she is out of control: her desire for him can never be fully satisfied. Again this is considered characteristic of a consumer lifestyle in which consumers 'experience moderate swings from being in control to being out of control and back again. Their lives are balanced between feelings of completeness and incompleteness' (Hirschmann 1992, quoted in Lury 1996: 77). Here the consequences of an aestheticized relation to sexual relations are shown to be debilitating – for women. Carrie craves authenticity, and constantly wants to establish whether her relationship with Big is real or not. In one episode, where she is particularly distressed by her powerlessness in relation to Big, Carrie offers a poignant critique of the masquerade as a strategy of female empowerment.

> I think I'm in love with him, and I'm terrified in case he thinks I'm not perfect . . . you should see what I'm like round him – it's like – I wear little outfits. I'm not like me. Sexy Carrie. Casual Carrie. Sometimes I catch myself actually posing – it's exhausting!
>
> (Episode 11, 'The Drought')

Later that evening Big visits her flat for the first time. She is nervous about this as another test of her self-presentation, but is reassured: 'I like it just the way it is', he says. On seeing a couple having sex in the flat opposite, offering a distanced but explicit spectacle, Big turns to her and says, 'Hell – we can do better than that!' The voice-over from Carrie, 'And then he kissed me', places the scene in the realm of a Mills and Boon erotic fiction for women: the unobtainable object of the heroine's desire succumbs when he recognizes her true worth. Yet it also marks a return to the distancing that characterizes the dominant, comic mode of the series. Carrie's worries about her unstable and inauthentic identity are resolved through the aestheticized pleasures of erotic spectacle and generic parody. And there is no end to these oscillations: its serial form doesn't provide the plenitude of narrative closure; instead its repetitions offer the consumer satisfactions of 'diversity within sameness that is comfortable and comforting to most people' (Hirschman 1992, quoted in Lury 1996: 77).

Conclusion

The fragmentation of the television market has allowed a sexually explicit and critical feminist discourse into television comedy, albeit within the parameters of a consumer culture and the limitations this imposes. In my view, this is a welcome innovation in women's representation on television in that it assumes and promotes women's right to sexual pleasure and validates women's friendship and culture. At the same time the contradictions of its comedic and serial form expose this culture to interrogation and critique, thereby encouraging intellectual analysis. The analytic approaches used in this chapter are not confined to an academic elite but are available to a broad segment of educated people. An ability to see ourselves in these characters works not simply to confirm our sense of self but to question the costs as well as the benefits of living in a postfeminist consumer culture. It is in the messy contingencies of the everyday that feminism is produced or inhibited in practice, and it is this quality that *Sex and the City* is able to capture.

This establishes a space in popular culture for interrogation of our own complicity in the processes of commodification – women's narcissistic relation to the self, the production of fetishistic and alienated sexual relations – that continue to undermine our self-esteem and contentment. Whether this has the power to translate into political action is a matter of debate, and beyond the scope of this book (see Willis 1991; Klein 2000; Whelehan 2000 for scepticism in this respect). What remain more hidden from view are the global and class inequalities on which the freedom to pleasurable consumption rests, in which women are often the most disadvantaged (Willis 1991; Klein 2000). The majority lack the economic resources to participate in a globalized consumer culture. From this perspective, the programme can be taken as evidence of the consequences of economic liberalism in a society where moral and religious values are in decline, with no alternatives to the hedonistic values of a hegemonic capitalism. In a post 11 September context, however, the connotations of *Sex and the City*'s logo of the Manhattan skyline have changed, making previous preoccupations seem trivial. The guiltless triumph of consumer values no longer seems so secure.

Notes

1 This is not to say that these are the only people who watch and enjoy the show. There is evidence of its wider appeal, to men and to teenagers of both sexes, drawn by the combination of sexual explicitness and well-written comic scripts. Indeed, in Brazil the statistics show a slight majority of men in the audience (Neves 2003).
2 The numbering follows the HBO website episode summaries (www.hbo.com/city/episode) rather than the video compilations, which start again at one for each season.

Recommended reading

Brunsdon, C., D'Acci, J. and Spigel, L. (1997) *Feminist TV Criticism: A Reader*. Oxford: Oxford TV Studies.

Dow, B. (1996) *Prime-time Feminism: Television, Media Culture and the Women's Movement Since 1970*. Philadelphia: University of Pennsylvania Press.

Feuer, J. (1995) *Seeing through the Eighties: Television and Reaganism*. Durham, NC: Duke University Press.

Lotz, A. (2001) Postfeminist television criticism: rehabilitating critical terms and identifying postfeminist attributes, *Feminist Media Studies*, 1(1): 105–21.

Lury, C. (1996) *Consumer Culture*. Cambridge: Polity Press.

CONCLUSION

Drawing conclusions when writing about television is a seemingly impossible task. It eludes any comprehensive overview. Its ubiquity can only be viewed from a very limited perspective and its open-ended flow makes conclusions inevitably provisional. This book is best understood in the same way as the programmes it has been discussing; that is, in relation to the time and place of its production and within the limits of selection produced by my own interests and purposes and the imagined audience I have in mind. My background in feminist cultural studies has been the primary influence on this; as someone who first engaged with feminist ideas through their portrayal in film and television I am interested in how cultural identity is discursively formed through popular culture. With this in mind I have demonstrated how, in the cases selected, the portrayal of sexuality can be shown to have resulted from the discursive context in which the programme has been made – the sexual norms, codes of taste and decency, genre conventions and hierarchies of taste that regulate what can be said or shown. These discourses are mobilized in the attempts by television companies to address a varied range of consumer-citizens with differentiated aesthetic tastes, political convictions, moral beliefs and sexual identities that will affect their orientations towards sexual portrayal. There is no exact fit between what is produced and how it is consumed but neither are they entirely disconnected. Both are selectively and reflexively formed in relation to the larger discursive context.

Generic inertia and innovation

I have argued that television clearly has a significant role to play in the development of sexual citizenship and that there is a legitimate 'public interest' in the forms of representation made available that shouldn't simply be left to market relations.

The historical formation of taste means that generic conventions constrain the production and consumption of sexual representations in ways that cannot quickly be undone. Nevertheless, we need to recognize, and challenge, the limitations in what is currently in circulation. Diversity of sexual representations on the margins cannot be equated with a generalized shift towards more 'progressive' portrayals in the mainstream. The rhetoric of choice obscures the effects of generic inertia as producers look for predictable audiences based on established categories of consumers that normalize and restrict what programmes are made. I will offer a brief overview of what has emerged from my detailed examination of the television of the recent past before offering a few comments on where television in the future might be heading.

There is plenty of evidence for a continuing conservatism in the mainstream of television that works to maintain the sexual exclusions that have characterized modern industrial societies. Those genres associated with the 'respectable' public sphere, which carry cultural weight as conveyors of 'truth', such as news and science programmes, tend towards normative constructions of gender and sexuality, understood as a fixed category of being based on biological difference, and an assumed heterosexuality. In science and nature programmes this is linked to the hegemony of sociobiology as an explanatory framework that reproduces these normative conceptions of masculine and feminine gender identities. The embedded conventions of visual spectacle also work to position the body of the 'other' as subject to male power, whether this is in 'respectable' documentary of various kinds or in the pornographic forms that exist on the margins. Sexual diversity is most often defined as 'deviance' in the scandal discourses of the mainstream, where the pleasures of concealment, exposure and moral condemnation can be enjoyed as a means to disavow sexual wishes that cannot be acknowledged. A space for carnivalesque 'licence' does exist in scandal and comedy but the ideological ambivalence of these forms makes it easy for people to be confirmed in their prejudices as they distance themselves in their laughter from the rule-breaking object of the humour.

This is not to deny that public service remits and the search for new markets have stimulated generic innovations that have allowed for new citizenship claims to be recognized. New, more pluralistic 'ways of telling' have emerged that don't conform to 'rationalist' models of political debate and that give voice to subordinated 'others'. The widespread adoption of a feminized aesthetic of subjective perspectives, emotional empathy and the open-ended forms of serial narrative, across both factual and fictional genres, has contributed to new forms of 'recognition' that are an important component of sexual citizenship. The address to a post-war generation, who have challenged the relegation of sexuality to the private sphere, has allowed for a relaxation of 'bourgeois' respectability and a broadening of 'legitimate' sexual identities, especially for women and gay men. The equation of emancipation with visibility has contributed to a greater diversity of sexual identities finding expression, in 'quality' drama and documentary, for example.

The normalizing and disciplining effects of discourse are as true for these 'progressive' representations as for more traditional 'stereotypes', such as the boundary that has emerged between the respectable gay citizen and his transgressive queer 'other'. The right to privacy is also an issue, in a culture where visibility is pervasive, to protect the powerless from voyeuristic intrusions, especially for the sexually 'marked' bodies of women and minorities. The ways in which feminist, bohemian, queer and postcolonial identities have been taken up in contemporary forms of postmodern consumer culture are double-edged politically. Only certain kinds of sexual identity are compatible with consumerism and new exclusions are created that disadvantage the poor. There is a gap between images of the self-fashioning consumer and the reality of most people's lives, especially if the global circulation of these programmes is taken into account. Who will be included and excluded from the system of global communications and consumption?

Looking towards the future

The transition to digital television is taking place across the globe, albeit in diverse local contexts. For those countries with a tradition in public service television fears of a rampant commercialism accompany these changes. The UK is developing its digital services ahead of many of its global competitors, making, perhaps, the British response to these changes of wider interest, especially in the way that new regulatory regimes are being tried out. At the start of 2004 the television industry moved into a new period of regulation, as OfCom took over as the new regulator for the converging communications industries. The emphasis is on economic regulation to promote competition and to oversee the transition to a fully digital service by 2010. OfCom retains the duty, however, to protect the public interest, promote plurality and protect audiences from offensive or harmful content, and from unfairness and invasions of privacy. What is not clear at the time of writing is how it is going to do this. In its first six months of operation it is planning to revise every industry code, as part of a more general review of the purposes of public service broadcasting, leading up to the renewal of the BBC's charter in 2006. As part of this process a national consultation exercise is planned, instead of relying on a committee of establishment figures as previous reports on broadcasting policy have done (Brown 2003).

This is consistent with a 'consumer' model of citizenship. What is already apparent is that there is an inherent tension in this model of the citizen-consumer. When decisions have to be made, whose views will eventually prevail? How will the 'public interest' be decided? And how will this be balanced against the increased power of commercial interests as British terrestrial television is opened to foreign ownership? Nevertheless, there does seem to be an attempt to encourage 'cultural citizenship' in order to offset the potentially overweening power of the global media conglomerates to decide for us what we will watch. As Nick Stevenson (2003: 152) explains, 'Cultural citizenship aims to promote conversation where previously there was silence, suspicion, fragmentation or the voices of the powerful.' In using the language of citizenship, there is a concern for rights and responsibilities that goes beyond a simple reliance on consumer 'choice'.

In thinking through the consequences of these changes for the way in which sexual discourses are regulated on television I want to focus on the figure of the child and the rhetoric that is emerging. The paternalistic approaches of the past, designed to protect the child audience from harm and their parents from embarrassment, shows signs of being replaced. The final report from the old regime of regulators shifted the policy agenda towards recognition of children's citizenship rights as active 'self-regulating' consumers of culture and to the support they and their families will need to exercise these responsibly (Buckingham and Bragg 2003). It provided a framework of research to support this transition based on extensive focus group interviews with children and their parents, supplemented by diary entries from the children on their viewing, and a sceptical review of existing 'effects' research from a cultural studies perspective (Buckingham and Bragg 2002).

Reporting on this research, David Buckingham and Sarah Bragg (2003) emphasize that television and the media more generally are an important source of learning 'what it means to be sexual' and can work to broaden the rather narrow contexts in which children learn about sex in their everyday lives. This research was conducted during the same period as this book, but starting from the other end of the communicative cycle in which audiences produce meanings from the programmes they watch. The extent to which the conclusions match mine is significant, I think. The viewing patterns of children differ from those of adults, of course, especially in their lighter viewing late at night when much of the less mainstream sexual content is shown, but the continuing force of 'traditional' ideas about sexual identity among this generation of viewers is evident. Calls by the report for education in 'media literacy' to empower children to be critical viewers are intended to enable them to deconstruct the normative discourses that make up the bulk of their viewing, if future generations are to look beyond the categories and boundaries that currently limit their sense of who they are and what they might become. I would endorse this aim and hope that this book might also contribute to its fulfilment.

Popular television needs to be taken more seriously as an important influence on identity formation and understanding of the 'other'. To finish on this issue, I want to suggest how rethinking the concept of 'cosmopolitanism' might help towards this process. The 'market-led' definition of cosmopolitan identities is of affluent mobile consumers in a global market, for whom the self-fashioning images of postmodern television have been designed. Nick Stevenson (2003: 5) offers another way of defining cosmopolitanism that envisages a more egalitarian future to which television could contribute. Cosmopolitanism, he argues, is a way of viewing the world that:

dispenses with national exclusions, dichotomous forms of gendered and racial thinking and rigid separations between culture and nature. Such a sensibility would be open to the new spaces of political and ethical engagement that seeks to appreciate the ways in which humanity is mixed into intercultural ways of life.

Living together harmoniously in a globalized world, he argues, requires us to develop the emotional capacity to live with the 'other', within the self as well as 'out there'. Recognizing the 'stranger within' – our own internal contradictions, unruly desires and emotions – while developing the ability to respect and learn from those who are different from us, is something television can help us to do, but only if we develop 'an understanding of the discourses, codes and narratives that make such political understandings possible' (*ibid.*: 5).

This understanding will only emerge out of an 'informed citizenship' to which formal education can contribute. It also requires a more developed 'national conversation', to which journalism could contribute if it moved beyond scandalized headlines in reaction to 'explicit sex', and developed a critical reviewing practice that engages with television as a complex cultural form. Despite its utopianism, I think this way of thinking about cultural citizenship has a value. It moves us beyond the twin poles of state paternalism and the narcissistic individualism of the market, and offers a model for balancing the competing demands of pleasure and responsibility in the formation of our sexual selves.

GLOSSARY

Aesthetics   A set of principles of good taste and the appreciation of beauty (*Oxford English Dictionary*). It is used to describe and evaluate the form and style in which representations are embodied – in semiotic terms the 'signifiers' as opposed to the 'signified'. In cultural studies the emphasis is on how these criteria of aesthetic value are established and reproduced.

Avant-garde   Innovative artistic movements that are ahead of the mainstream ideas of the time. Associated most strongly with the modernist movement of the twentieth century in which the 'new' replaced artistic tradition as the primary criterion of value. Indeed, it involved dismantling and deconstructing those traditions.

Broadcasters Audience Research Board Ltd (BARB)   A company that sells audience statistics to broadcasters in the UK. Less detailed information is provided free on the website http://www.barb.co.uk.

Bohemian   A socially unconventional person. Associated with the Romantic ideal of the artist as 'outsider' who rejects the conformist values of **bourgeois** society. It has come to be associated with a form of middle-class rebellion linked to sexual permissiveness and a rejection of materialist values. It re-emerged in the post-war period as a strong component in the hippie movement.

Bourgeois   The economic class that owns or manages the means of production in industrial capitalism. Used pejoratively to describe people who are conventional, unimaginative and materialistic to the extent that they put profit-making and the maintenance of the social order, from which they materially benefit, above all other values.

Carnivalesque   A term that describes the kind of licentious behaviour that emerges on festive occasions when the norms of behaviour that govern everyday life are temporarily suspended. It emerged as a concept of cultural analysis following Michael Bakhtin's (1984) theorization of its significance in the work of the writer Rabelais.

Citizen   Member of a political community usually defined in relation to national forms of belonging. This involves inclusion in the rights that are offered to citizens, such as the right to vote in political elections, but also responsibilities such as the legal requirement to pay taxes.

Class   This term is often used in everyday language to mean social status; that is, where people are placed in a hierarchy of esteem. In Marxist analysis, however, it is used to designate an economic relation to wealth creation in capitalism. In these terms there are two classes, those who own the means of production and those who are paid wages. However, the middle classes, in professional and managerial roles that help to reproduce the system but who are still dependent on wages, occupy a contradictory position in terms of their interests between these two classes. The connection between social and economic classes, in Bourdieu's (1984) analysis, is that social hierarchies, which are reproduced through cultural and educational institutions, work to legitimate and reproduce the economic classes.

Codes   The socially produced rules that govern the selection and combination of signs in symbolic forms and whose shared understanding facilitates communication between the participants in a cultural community.

Commodity   A product that can be bought or sold in a market. Commodification is the process by which experiences, services or goods are turned into a form in which they can be exchanged in this way.

Conglomerates   Large, usually multinational, organizations resulting from mergers between smaller firms. In capitalism there is a tendency for firms to merge in this way in order to remain profitable by reducing competition and monopolizing the market.

Consumer culture/society   Used to designate the cultural and social consequences of what is variously described as 'late' or 'postmodern' capitalism. It indicates an emphasis on the stimulation of consumption in order to sustain the cycle of production and consumption in a system that can produce more goods than are needed for basic survival.

Deviant   In sexual terms, this refers to those acts, and the people who perform them, that fall outside a culturally defined 'norm'. I place it in inverted commas to indicate that it is not an intrinsic quality of the person or act but is produced through these cultural processes and is subject to challenge and change.

Digital   The technical form in which information is encoded and transmitted as binary code. This allows for the transfer and sharing of data between differing media technologies, such as computers, radio, televisions, films and print media. It is gradually replacing older forms of 'analogue' broadcasting based on 'wave' transmission rather than binary code.

Disavowal   A term used in psychoanalysis to indicate when a wish is expressed in the act of denial but not acknowledged because it is too painful, threatening or shameful to do so. This depends on unconscious psychological processes that are by definition not amenable to conscious control. These unconscious wishes are brought to consciousness in order to be denied. In Freudian theory this originates in the castration complex where the knowledge of sexual difference between the boy child and his mother stimulates desire that is then repressed because of the prohibitions on incest.

Disinterested   I am fighting a losing battle here to retain the use of this term not to mean 'uninterested' as is its most common usage today, but in its original sense of there being no personal gain or financial reward for promoting a particular case or state of affairs. This is an important concept in weighing up the 'public interest' as opposed to the profit incentive that underwrites the commercial media.

Diversity   In relation to culture it is used as a term to describe the range of identities that arise in complex modern societies, with their dynamic mix of ethnicities, sexual orientations and class interests, for example.

Ethics   Used to indicate where personal actions are based on weighing up choices between what is right and wrong. The values that underpin those choices may originate in a specific community, such as religious values. The attempt to find common grounds for ethical choices that negotiate between the specific interests and value systems of these diverse groupings is one of the purposes of political discussion in the public sphere.

Ethnicity   Forms of belonging that derive from recognition of shared cultural values, customs, beliefs and a common history and destiny that give a sense of collective solidarity. This may also be embodied in a shared language or national identity. People may identify with more than one group where individuals have a mixed cultural heritage. It may also change over time.

Exchange value   A Marxist concept that refers to the monetary value of a commodity in a market.

Feminism   A diverse set of political and cultural discourses that share the aim of overcoming the relative powerlessness that women experience in comparison to men. The causes and therefore the solutions to this inequality are much disputed and form the basis for different 'schools' of feminist theory and activism. For example, liberal feminists see the problem as wanting to improve women's position within the existing political and economic order, while socialist feminists see that order as part of the problem and in need, therefore, of more fundamental change before women can achieve equality. 'Second wave feminism' refers to the intense period of political activity and polemical writing during the 1970s and 1980s, often also referred to as the 'women's liberation movement'. This is to distinguish it from the 'first wave' of feminist activism when the 'suffragettes' campaigned for women to get the vote early on in the twentieth century.

Fetishism   In Freudian theory this refers to the sexual satisfaction that men can gain from objects that stand in for the female genitalia, such as shoes, fur or stockings. In film theory it has been used to explain the obsessive return to the image of the glamorized woman in which her sexual allure is presented through a transfixed camera gaze at parts of her body or face or clothing. Explanations for female fetishism need a revision of the Freudian version, based as it is on the displacement provoked by castration anxiety.

Heteronormative   The assumption of a universal heterosexual orientation, which works to marginalize and exclude same-sex forms of desire.

Hybridization   The bringing together of two distinct cultural identities or forms to create a new one. This sense is derived from the practice of grafting two different plants together to produce a new type of plant.

Identity   We create our sense of self out of the interrelation between who we imagine we are, or want to become, and the way in which we are positioned by existing subject positions constructed through discourse and social experience. These produce multiple identifications based on, among other things, nationality, gender, class, ethnicity, sexual orientation and the jobs that we do. The notion of self-fashioning foregrounds the degree to which our identities are open to transformation over time, while more traditional sociological theory emphasizes the degree to which we are positioned by relatively slow-to-change social structures and the discourses to which they give rise.

Imagined community   This concept captures the degree to which our identifications are base on an imagined relation to others with whom we feel an affinity and to whom we attribute an identity.

Individualism   The belief that the individual is the primary source of agency and values, rather than the social groups to which we belong.

Interests   In some cases this word is used not in its common meaning of being enthusiastic about something but to mean having some existing advantage, often monetary or political, at stake.

Market   Means by which goods and services are exchanged for money, which is based on the belief that prices respond to the balance between supply and demand.

Marxism   A political theory derived from Karl Marx's analysis of the way that capitalist markets exploit the labour of workers to extract surplus value in the forms of profits for the owners of the means of production. In this theory the fundamental division in society is between wage labourers and the owners of capital.

Modernity   The condition of living in a modern world in which innovation and progress is valued over tradition and continuity. The 'creative destruction' produced by capitalist markets contributes to this condition.

Narcissism   The love of one's own self-image. In Freudian theory this is one of the primary drives (for survival of the self) that is shaped by the formation of the ego. It underlines fantasies of omnipotence but can also be expressed through autoeroticism.

Neo-liberalism   A political ideology that became dominant in the 1980s, based on the belief that capitalist markets should be free to operate with as little government interference as possible.

New social movements   The social liberation movements that emerged in the 1960s and 1970s with an emphasis on collective identities, values and lifestyles rather than, or in addition to, developed ideologies, and that tended to emerge more from middle- than working-class constituencies. Examples include women's, gay and lesbian, environmentalist and anti-racist movements.

Nielsen Media Research   A global ratings company. In the United States, Nielsen sells television audience estimates for broadcast and cable networks, television stations, national syndicators, regional cable television systems, satellite providers, advertisers and advertising agencies.

Normative   A sociological term meaning the way in which certain common expectations are established about how we ought to behave and what values we should hold.

Paternalism   Well-meaning policies based on an assumption that people need to be protected rather than having the freedom to make their own choices.

Patriarchy   Societies that are based on the power men hold over women, both in the private sphere of the family and in public institutions such as the church, law, government and business.

Pedagogy   The theory and practice of education.

Performative   A linguistic term in which the words perform an action. The example often cited is the words 'I do' at a marriage ceremony, which in their enunciation seal the contract. It has been taken up more widely to describe the way in which identity is formed through discursive practices.

Petit-bourgeoisie   The lower middle classes.

Popular   Used in cultural studies to refer to cultural practices that arise from 'the people' rather than originating in the dominant classes, but that in modern societies, more often than not, arise from their interaction with the mass-produced media.

Postmodern   Used to describe a transformation in the conditions of modern societies in the post-war period, and to the forms of culture to which this period has given rise. In both cases a greater uncertainty, ambivalence and loss of faith in 'grand narratives' of explanation have been argued to characterize the transition.

Psychoanalysis   A set of psychological theories and practices originating in the work of Sigmund Freud (1856–1939), based on a belief in the existence of unconscious motivations and desire. We can only discover these indirectly through the interpretation of bodily symptoms and other symbolic manifestations, such as dreams or fictional narratives.

Puritanism   A form of Protestant Christianity in which great emphasis is placed on austerity and the sinful nature of sensual pleasures.

Queer   Originally used as a term to denigrate homosexuals but then reappropriated as a term of political defiance against the policing of sexual identities and behaviour. In political and theoretical discourses it emphasizes the transgression of culturally produced identity boundaries that limit sexual expression.

Race   Used in inverted commas to indicate the ideological nature of the common assumption that 'race' is a description of groups of people separated by biological differences. There are, in fact, no clear boundaries between humans based on biology; instead they are produced though cultural and political processes. The categories of 'race', and the hierarchies to which they give rise, are thus open to challenge and transformation.

Traditional   Used to describe societies in which social and cultural practices and values are reproduced in a relatively unchanging way from generation to generation.

Use value   A term used by Marx to differentiate the value a product has for its owner based on its usefulness, as distinct from the value it has in exchange for money.

Voyeurism   A Freudian term used in feminist film theory to describe the sadistic pleasure in looking at a character who cannot look back at the spectator. This heightens the potential pleasure in watching sexualized imagery, in that the guilt induced by sexual arousal in these circumstances can be evaded by projecting the guilt on to the object of the look, who is almost always a woman. This objectified woman can then be devalued and punished through the processes of narrative, thereby heightening the viewer's sense of their own power.

APPENDIX: DOCUMENTARIES ABOUT SEX ON UK TELEVISION

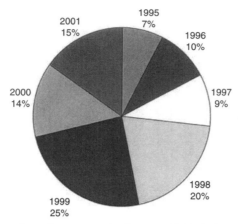

Figure A1 Percentage of sex documentaries by year, 1995–2001
(*Source*: BUFVC television documentaries database)

Animal Planet	1
BBC 1	9
BBC 2	57
BBC Choice	9
BBC Knowledge	3
Bravo	222
Channel 4	101
Channel 5	36
Discovery	6
History	1
ITV	27
ITV 2	4
Living	164
Geographic	1
Sky One	26
UK Arena	1
UK Gold	1
UK Horizons	11

Figure A2 Number of sex documentaries by channel, 1999
(*Source*: *The Radio Times*)

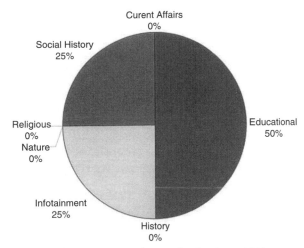

Figure A3 Types of sex documentaries during the daytime, 1999
(*Source*: *The Radio Times*)

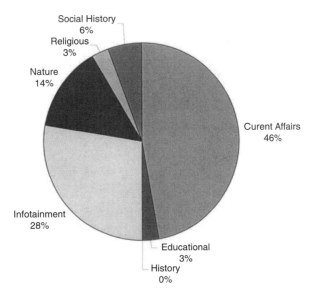

Figure A4 Types of sex documentaries pre-watershed, 1999
(*Source*: *The Radio Times*)

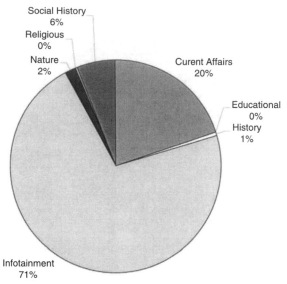

Figure A5 Types of sex documentaries post-watershed, 1999
(*Source*: *The Radio Times*)

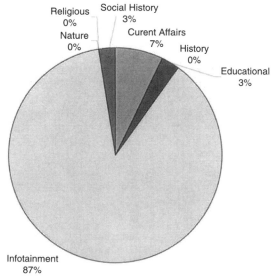

Figure A6 Types of sex documentaries during the nighttime, 1999
(*Source*: *The Radio Times*)

Category and Channel									
Category	Animal Planet	BBC1	BBC 2	BBC Choice	BBC Knowledge	Bravo	Channel 4	Channel 5	Discovery
Affairs	1	3	43	3			38	8	5
Educational			6		3		2		
History	1		3						
Infotainment		7	8	4		217	55	34	2
Nature			3	4			1		3
Religious		1					1		
Social History			12	2			16	2	

Category and Channel									
Category	History	ITV	ITV 2	Living	National Geographic	Sky One	UK Arena	UK Gold	UK Horizons
Affairs		19	1	2		2		1	5
Educational									
History									
Infotainment		14	3	161		25	1	1	8
Nature					1				2
Religious		1							
Social History	1	3	1						

Figure A7 Types of sex documentaries across channels, 1999
(*Source*: *The Radio Times*)

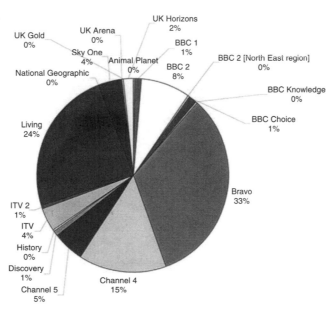

Figure A8 Percentage of sex documentaries by channel, 1999
(*Source*: *The Radio Times*)

BIBLIOGRAPHY

Adorno, T. (1993) The culture industry: enlightenment as mass deception, in S. During (ed.) *The Cultural Studies Reader*. London and New York: Routledge.

Altman, R. (1999) *Film/Genre*. London: British Film Institute.

Ang, I. (1991) *Desperately Seeking the Audience*. London: Routledge.

Ang, I. (1996) *Living Room Wars: Rethinking Media Audiences for a Postmodern World*. London: Routledge.

Ang, I. (1998) *Desperately Seeking the Audience*, 2nd edn. London: Routledge.

Arthurs, J. (1999) Revolting women: the body in comic performance, in J. Arthurs and J. Grimshaw (eds) *Women's Bodies: Discipline and Transgression*. London: Cassell.

Babuscio, J. (1984) Camp and the gay sensibility, in R. Dyer (ed.) *Gays and Film*. New York: Zoetrope.

Backstein, K. (2001) Soft love: the romantic vision of sex on the Showtime Network. *Television and New Media*, 2(4): 303–17.

Bakhtin, M. (1984) *Rabelais and His World*. Bloomington: Indiana University Press.

Ballaster, E., Beetham, M., Frazer, E. and Hebron, S. (1991) *Women's Worlds: Ideology, Femininity and the Woman's Magazine*. London: Macmillan Education.

Bauman, Z. (2003) *Liquid Love*. Cambridge: Polity Press.

BBCi (2001) *Money Programme Home Page* (http://news.bbc.co.uk). Accessed 10 April.

Beck, U. and Beck-Gernsheim, E. (2002) *Individualization: Institutional Individualism and Its Social and Political Consequences*. London: Sage.

Bell, D. and Binnie, J. (2000) *The Sexual Citizen: Queer Politics and Beyond*. Cambridge: Polity Press.

Bell, E. (2003) Souffle and jelly bill won't worry Murdoch. *Guardian*, 11 July.

Bennet, T., Boyd-Bowman, S., Mercer, C. and Woollacott, J. (eds) (1981) *Popular Film and Television*. London: British Film Institute.

Berlant, L. and Duggan, L. (eds) (2001) *Our Monica, Ourselves: The Clinton Affair and the National Interest*. New York: New York University Press.

Berry, C., Hamilton, A. and Jayamane, L. (eds) (1997) *The Film-maker and the Prostitute: Denis O'Rourke's 'The Good Woman of Bangkok'*. Sydney: Power Publications.

Bhattacharyya, G. (2002) *Sexuality and Society: An Introduction*. London: Routledge.

Billington, P. (2000) A Manchester heterotopia? 'Queer as Folk', in *Sensing the City through Television*. Bristol: Intellect.

Bird, E. S. (1997) What a story! Understanding the audience for scandal, in J. Lull and S. Hinerman (eds) *Media Scandals*. Cambridge: Polity Press.

Bocock, R. (1997) Choice and regulation: sexual moralities, in K. Thompson (ed.) *Media and Cultural Regulation*. London: Sage/Open University.

Bolter, J. and Gruisin, R. (1999) *Remediation: Understanding New Media*. Cambridge, MA: MIT Press.

Bourdieu, P. (1984) *Distinction – A Social Critique of the Judgement of Taste*. London: Routledge.

Bowlby, R. (1993) *Shopping with Freud*. London: Routledge.

Bragg, S. and Buckingham, D. (2002) *Young People and Sexual Content on Television: A Review of the Research*. London: Broadcasting Standards Commission.

Bristow, J. (1997) *Sexuality*. London: Routledge.

Broadcasting Standards Commission (1999) Finding: *Sex and Shopping* (www.bsc.org.uk). Accessed 12 June 2001.

Broadcasting Standards Commission (2002) Finding: *Brass Eye Special* (www.bsc.org.uk). Accessed on 15 September 2002.

Brooks, A. (1997) *Postfeminisms: Feminism. Cultural Theory and Cultural Forms*. London: Routledge.

Brooks, D. (2000) *Bobos in Paradise: The New Upper Class and How They Got There*. New York: Simon and Schuster.

Brown, M. (2003) Countdown to a new order. *Guardian*, 1 December.

Brunsdon, C. (1990) Problems with quality. *Screen*, 31(1): 67–90.

Brunsdon, C. (1997) Identity in feminist television criticism, in C. Brunsdon, J. D'Acci and L. Spigel (eds) *Feminist Television Criticism: A Reader*. Oxford: Clarendon Press.

Bruzzi, S. (2000) *New Documentary: A Critical Introduction*. London: Routledge.

Buckingham, D. and Bragg, S. (2003) *Young People, Media and Personal Relationships*. London: Advertising Standards Authority, British Board of Film Classification, British Broadcasting Corporation, Broadcasting Standards Commission, Independent Television Commission.

Buckingham, D. and Bragg, S. (2004) *Young People, Sex and the Media: The Facts of Life?* Basingstoke: Palgrave Macmillan.

Butler, J. (1990) *Gender Trouble: Feminism and the Subversion of Identity*. London: Routledge.

Capsuto, S. (2000) *Alternate Channels: The Uncensored Story of Gay and Lesbian Images on Radio and Television*. New York: Ballantine Books.

Carson, B. (2000) Cultural hybridity, masculinity and nostalgia, in B. Carson and M. Llewellyn-Jones (eds) *Frames and Fictions on Television: The Politics of Identity within Drama*. Exeter: Intellect Books.

Carson, B. and Llewellyn-Jones, M. (eds) (2000) *Frames and Fictions on Television: The Politics of Identity within Drama*. Exeter: Intellect Books.

Carter, C., Branston, G. and Allan, S. (eds) (1998) *News, Gender and Power*. London: Routledge.

Cartwright, L. (1998) A cultural anatomy of the visible human project, in P. A. Treichler, L. Cartwright and C. Penley, *The Visible Woman: Imaging Technologies, Gender and Science*. New York: New York University Press.

Caughie, J. (2000) *TV Drama: Realism, Modernism and British Culture*. Oxford: Oxford University Press.

Chris, C. (2002) All documentary, all the time? Discovery Communications Inc. and trends in cable television. *Television and New Media*, 3(1): 7–28.

Clark, D. (1990) *Cagney and Lacey*: feminist strategies of detection, in M. E. Brown (ed.) *Television and Women's Culture. The Politics of the Popular*. London: Sage.

Coles, R. (1998) Feelin's, in M. Merck (ed.) *After Diana: Irreverent Elegies*. London: Verso.

Compaine, M. and Gomery, D. (2000) *Who Owns the Media? Competition and Concentration in the Mass Media Industry*. Mahwah, NJ: Lawrence Erlbaum Associates.

Couldry, N. (2003) *Media Rituals: A Critical Approach*. London: Routledge.

Creeber, G. (2001a) Intimacy, continuity and memory in the TV drama serial. *Media, Culture and Society*, 23(4): 439–53.

Creeber, G. (2001b) The Wednesday Play and Play for Today, in G. Creeber (ed.) *The Television Genre Book*. London: British Film Institute.

Creeber, G. (ed.) (2001c) *The Television Genre Book*. London: British Film Institute.

Critcher, C. (2003) *Moral Panics and the Media*. Buckingham: Open University Press.

Crowther, B. (1995) Towards a feminist critique of television natural history programmes, in P. Florence and D. Reynolds (eds) *Feminist Subjects: Multimedia: Cultural Methodologies*. Manchester: Manchester University Press.

Curran, J. (1996) Mass media and democracy revisited, in J. Curran and M. Gurevitch (eds) *Mass Media and Society*. London: Arnold.

Curran, J. and Seaton, J. (1997) *Power without Responsibility*. London: Routledge.

D'Acci, J. (1994) *Defining Women: Television and the Case of Cagney and Lacey*. Chapel Hill: University of North Carolina Press.

D'Acci, J. (2002) Gender representation and television, in T. Miller (ed.) *Television Studies*. London: British Film Institute.

Doezema, J. (2001) Ouch! Western feminists' wounded attachment to the Third World prostitute. *Feminist Review*, 67(1): 16–29.

Donnelly, K. (2001) Discovery Channel and Walking with Dinosaurs, in G. Creeber (ed.) *The Television Genre Book*. London: British Film Institute.

Doty, A. and Gove, B. (1997) Queer representation in the mass media, in A. Medhurst and S. Munt (eds) *Lesbian and Gay Studies Reader*. London: Cassell.

Dovey, J. (2000) *Freakshow: First Person Media and Factual Television*. London: Pluto Press.

Dow, B. (1996) *Prime-time Feminism: Television, Media Culture and the Women's Movement since 1970*. Philadelphia: University of Pennsylvania Press.

Elias, N. (1994) *The Civilizing Process. Volume 1: History of Manners*. Oxford: Blackwell.

Ellis, J. (2000) *Seeing Things: Television in the Age of Uncertainty*. London: I. B. Tauris.

Epstein, D. and Johnson, R. (1998) *Schooling Sexualities*. Buckingham: Open University Press.

Featherstone, M. (1991a) The body in consumer culture, in M. Featherstone, M. Hepworth and S. Turner (eds) *The Body: Social Process and Cultural Theory*. London: Sage.

Featherstone, M. (1991b) *Consumer Culture and Postmodernism*. London: Sage.

Feminist Review (2001) Special issue on sex work, 67(1).

Feuer, J. (1995) *Seeing through the Eighties: Television and Reaganism*. Durham, NC: Duke University Press.

Foucault, M. (1988) *The Care of the Self. History of Sexuality, Volume 3*. Harmondsworth: Penguin.

Foucault, M. (1990) *The History of Sexuality, Volume 1, An Introduction*. Harmondsworth: Penguin.

Fraser, N. (1995) Politics, culture and the public sphere: towards a postmodern conception, in L. Nicholson and S. Seidman (eds) *Social Postmodernism: Beyond Identity Politics*. Cambridge: Cambridge University Press.

Freud, S. (1991) *Jokes and Their Relation to the Unconscious*. London: Penguin (first published 1916).

Friday, N. (1976) *My Secret Garden: Women's Sexual Fantasies*. London: Quartet Books.

Friday, N. (1991) *Women on Top: How Real Life Has Changed Women's Sexual Fantasies*. London: Hutchinson.

Frith, S. (1996) Entertainment, in J. Curran and M. Gurevitch (eds) *Mass Media and Society*. London: Arnold.

Frow, J. (1995) *Cultural Studies and Cultural Value*. Oxford: Oxford University Press.

Gamman, L. (1988) Watching the detectives: the enigma of the female gaze, in L. Gamman and M. Marshment (eds) *The Female Gaze*. London: The Women's Press.

Gamson, J. (2001) Jessica Hahn, media whore: sex scandals and female publicity. *Critical Studies in Media Communication*, 18(2): 157–73.

Garnett, T. (2001) Interview with Tony Garnett on *Taboo*, BBC2, 26 November.

Garnham, N. (1990) The political economy of the production of culture, in F. Inglis (ed.) *Capitalism and Communication*. London: Sage.

Garnham, N. (2000) *Emancipation, the Media and Modernity: Arguments about the Media and Social Theory*. Oxford: Oxford University Press.

Gauntlett, D. (2002) *Media, Gender and Identity: An Introduction*. London: Routledge.

Gauntlett, D. and Hill, A. (1999) *TV Living: Television, Culture and Everyday Life*. London: Routledge.

Gibson, J. (1999a) Get your kit on. *Guardian* (G2 Supplement), 8 June.

Gibson, J. (1999b) Gay programme upsets viewers. *Guardian*, 22 June.

Giddens, A. (1992) *The Transformation of Intimacy: Sexuality, Love and Eroticism in Modern Societies*. Cambridge: Polity Press.

Gitlin, T. (1994) *Inside Prime Time*. London: Routledge.

Glyn, K. (2000) *Tabloid Culture: Trash Taste, Popular Power, and the Transformation of American TV*. Durham, NC: Duke University Press.

Graham, P. (1995) Girl's camp: the politics of parody, in T. Wilton (ed.) *Immortal, Invisible: Lesbians and the Moving Image*. London: Routledge.

Greer, G. (2000) *The Whole Woman*. London: Doubleday.

Gronbeck, B. E. (1997) Character, celebrity, and sexual innuendo in the mass-mediated presidency, in J. Lull, and S. Hinerman (eds) *Media Scandals: Morality and Desire in the Popular Culture Marketplace*. Cambridge: Polity Press.

Gross, L. (1989) Out of the mainstream: sexual minorities and the mass media, in E. Seiter, H. Borchers, G. Kreutzner and E. Warth (eds) *Television, Audiences and Cultural Power*. London: Routledge.

Gunter, B. (2002) *Media Sex: What Are the Issues?* Mahwah, NJ: Lawrence Erlbaum Associates.

Gwenllian Jones, S. (2000) Histories, fictions, and Xena: Warrior Princess. *Television and New Media*, 1(4): 403–18.

Gwenllian Jones, S. (2002) Gender and queerness, in T. Miller (ed.) *Television Studies*. London: British Film Institute.

Habermas, J. (1991) *The Structural Transformation of the Public Sphere*. Cambridge, MA: MIT Press.

Hall, S. (1990) Cultural identity and diaspora, in J. Rutherford (ed.) *Identity: Community, Culture, Difference*. London: Lawrence and Wishart.

Hall, S. (1996) New ethnicities, in D. Morley and K.-H. Chen (eds) *Stuart Hall: Critical Dialogues in Cultural Studies*. London and New York: Routledge (first published 1988).

Hallam, J. and Marshment, M. (2000) *Realism and Popular Cinema*. Manchester: Manchester University Press.

Haraway, D. (1990) Investment strategies for the evolving portfolio of primate females, in M. Jacobus, E. Fox Keller and S. Shuttleworth (eds) *Body/Politics: Women and the Discourse of Science*. London: Routledge.

Haraway, D. (1991) A cyborg manifesto: science, technology and socialist feminism in the late twentieth century, in *Simians, Cyborgs and Women: The Reinvention of Nature*. New York: Routledge.

Haraway, D. (1992) The promise of monsters: a regenerative politics for inappriopriate/d others, in L. Grossberg, C. Nelson and P. Treichler (eds) *Cultural Studies Reader*. New York: Routledge.

Haraway, D. (1997) The virtual speculum in the new world order, *Feminist Review*, 55: 22–72.

Harding, J. (1998) *Sex Acts: Practices of Femininity and Masculinity*. London: Sage.

Hartley, J. (1999) *Uses of Television*. London and New York: Routledge.

Hartley, J. (2002) The constructed viewer, in T. Miller (ed.) *Television Studies*. London: British Film Institute.

Harvey, S. (1998) Doing it my way – broadcasting regulation in capitalist cultures: the case of 'fairness and impartiality'. *Media, Culture and Society*, 20(4): 535–56.

Hennessy, R. (1995) Queer visibility in commodity culture, in L. Nicholson and S. Seidman (eds) *Social Postmodernism: Beyond Identity Politics*. Cambridge: Cambridge University Press.

Herman, E. S. and McChesney, R. W. (1997) *The Global Media: The New Missionaries of Corporate Capitalism*. London: Cassell.

Hewett, P. and Jowell, T. (2002) *A New Future for Communications* (http://www.com-municationsbill.gov.uk/policy_narrative/550800.html). Accessed 17 June 2002.

Hills, M. (2002) *Fan Cultures*. London: Routledge.

Hinds, H. (1997) Fruitful investigations: the case of the successful lesbian text, in C. Brunsdon, J. D'Acci and L. Spigel (eds) *Feminist Television Criticism: A Reader*. Oxford: Clarendon Press.

Hinds, H. and Stacey, J. (2001) Imaging feminism, imaging femininity: the bra burner, Diana and the woman who kills. *Feminist Media Studies*, 1(2): 153–77.

Hinerman, S. (1997) (Don't) leave me alone: tabloid narrative and the Michael Jackson child-abuse scandal, in J. Lull and S. Hinerman (eds) *Media Scandals*. Cambridge: Polity Press.

Hirschmann, E. C. (1992) The consciousness of addiction: towards a general theory of compulsive consumption. *Journal of Consumer Research*, 19: 155–79.

Hollows, J. (2000) *Feminism, Femininity and Popular Culture*. Manchester: Manchester University Press.

Holt, L. (1998) Diana and the backlash, in M. Merck (ed.) *After Diana: Irreverent Elegies*. London: Verso.

Independent Television Commission (n.d.) *The ITC Programme Code* (http://www.itc.org.uk).

Jacobus, M., Fox Keller, E. and Shuttleworth, S. (eds) (1990) *Body/Politics: Women and the Discourses of Science*. London: Routledge.

Jankovich, M. (2001) Naked ambitions: pornography, taste and the problem of the middlebrow. *Scope: An Online Journal of Film Studies*, June (http://www.nottingham.ac.uk/film/journal). Accessed 15 July 2003.

Jankovich, M. and Lyons, J. (eds) (2003) *Quality Popular Television*. London: British Film Institute.

Jenkins, H. (1995) Out of the closet and into the universe: queers and Star Trek, in J. Tulloch and H. Jenkins (eds) *Science Fiction Audiences*. London: Routledge.

Jenkins, H. (ed.) (1998) *The Children's Culture Reader*. New York: New York University Press.

Johnson, M. L. (2002) *Jane Sexes It Up. True Confessions of Feminist Desire*. New York: Four Walls Eight Windows.

Jones, P. (2001) The best of both worlds? Freedom of communication and 'positive' broadcasting regulation. *Media, Culture and Society*, 23(3): 385–96.

Juffer, J. (1998) *At Home with Pornography: Women, Sex and Everyday Life*. New York: New York University Press.

Kellner, D. (2003) *Media Spectacle*. London: Routledge.

Kelly, K. (2003) Digital convergence: dead, dying or delayed. Paper presented to the Media in Transition 3 conference, MIT, Cambridge, MA, 2–4 May.

Kertz, L. (2002) Morals and markets: deviance. Paper presented to the Media in Transition 2 conference, MIT, Cambridge, MA, 10–12 May.

Kidd, M. (1999) The bearded lesbian, in J. Arthurs and J. Grimshaw (eds) *Women's Bodies: Discipline and Transgression*. London: Cassell.

Kilvington, J., Day, S. and Ward, H. (2001) Prostitution policy in Europe: a time of change. *Feminist Review*, 67(1): 78–93.

Kinkaid, J. R. (1998) Producing erotic children, in H. Jenkins (ed.) *The Children's Culture Reader*. New York: New York University Press.

Kinsey, A. (1953) *Sexual Behavior in the Human Female*. Philadelphia: W. B. Saunders.

Kinsey, A. C., Pomeroy, W. B. and Martin, C. E. (1948) *Sexual Behavior in the Human Male*. Philadelphia: W. B. Saunders.

Kipnis, L. (1999) *Bound and Gagged: Pornography and the Politics of Fantasy in America*. Durham, NC: Duke University Press.

Kirkham, P. and Skeggs, B. (1998) *Absolutely Fabulous*: absolutely feminist?, in C. Geraghty and D. Lusted (eds) *The Television Studies Book*. London: Arnold.

Kitzinger, J. (2001) Transformations of public and private knowledge: audience reception, feminism and the experience of childhood sexual abuse. *Feminist Media Studies*, 1(1): 91–104.

Klein, N. (2000) *No Logo*. London: Flamingo.

Kuhn, A. (1982) *Women's Pictures: Feminism and Cinema*. London: Routledge and Kegan Paul.

Lambert, V. (2001) Horseplay with a handbag, *Daily Telegraph*, 4 July.

Langer, J. (1998) *Tabloid Television: Popular Journalism and the 'Other News'*. London: Routledge.

Laqueur, T. (1990) *Making Sex: Body and Gender from the Greeks to Freud*. Cambridge, MA: Harvard University Press.

Lara, M. P. (1998) *Moral Textures: Feminist Narratives in the Public Sphere*. Cambridge: Polity Press.

Lash, S. (1990) *Sociology of Postmodernism*. London: Routledge.

Liepe-Levinson, K. (2002) *Strip Show*. London: Routledge.

Lindahl-Elliot, N. (2001) Signs of anthropomorphism: the case of natural history television documentaries. *Social Semiotics*, 11(3): 289–305.

Lotz, A. (2001) Postfeminist television criticism: rehabilitating critical terms and identifying postfeminist attributes. *Feminist Media Studies*, 1(1): 105–21.

Lull, J. and Hinerman, S. (eds) (1997) *Media Scandals: Morality and Desire in the Popular Culture Marketplace*. Cambridge: Polity Press.

Lupton, D. (1994) *Medicine as Culture: Illness, Disease and the Body in Western Societies*. London: Sage.

Lury, C. (1993) *Cultural Rights: Technology, Legality and Personality*. London: Routledge.

Lury, C. (1996) *Consumer Culture*. Cambridge: Polity Press.

McCabe, J. (2000) Diagnosing the alien: producing identities, American 'quality' drama and British television culture in the 1990s, in B. Carson and M. Llewellyn-Jones (eds) *Frames and Fictions on Television: The Politics of Identity within Drama*. Exeter: Intellect Books.

McChesney, R. (1998) The political economy of global communications, in R. McChesney, E. Woods and J. Foster (eds) *Capitalism in the Information Age*. New York: Monthly Review Press.

Macdonald, M. (2000) Rethinking personalization in current affairs journalism, in C. Sparks and J. Tulloch (eds) *Tabloid Tales: Global Debates over Media Standards*. Lanham, MD: Rowman and Littlefield.

McGuigan, J. (1996) *Culture and the Public Sphere*. London: Routledge.

McLachlan, S. and Golding, P. (2000) Tabloidization in the British press: a quantitative investigation into changes in British newspapers, 1952–1997, in C. Sparks and J. Tulloch (eds) *Tabloid Tales: Global Debates over Media Standards*. Lanham, MD: Rowman and Littlefield.

McLaughlin, L. (1991) Discourses of prostitution/discourses of sexuality. *Critical Studies in Mass Communication*, 16(3): 249–72.

McLaughlin, L. (1998) Gender, privacy and publicity in 'media event space', in C. Carter, G. Branston and S. Allan (eds) *News, Gender and Power*. London: Routledge.

McLean, G. (2001) We've seen it all before, *Guardian*, G2 Supplement, 17 April.

McNair, B. (1996) *Mediated Sex: Pornography and Postmodern Culture*. London: Arnold.

McNair, B. (2002) *Striptease Culture: Sex, Media and the Democratisation of Desire*. London: Routledge.

McQuail, D. and Siune, K. (eds) (1998) *Media Policy: Convergence, Concentration and Commerce*. London: Sage.

McRobbie, A. (1997) Bridging the gap: feminism, fashion and consumption. *Feminist Review*, 55: 73–89.

Mayne, J. (1997) LA Law and prime time feminism, in C. Brunsdon, J. D'Acci and L. Spigel (eds) *Feminist Television Criticism: A Reader*. Oxford: Oxford University Press.

Medhurst, A. (1997) Camp, in A. Medhurst and S. Munt (eds) *Lesbian and Gay Studies Reader*. London: Cassell.

Meehan, E. R. (1990) Why we don't count: the commodity audience, in P. Mellencamp (ed.) *The Logics of Television: Essays in Cultural Criticism*. London: British Film Institute.

Meehan, E. R. (2001) Gendering the commodity audience: critical media research, feminism, and political economy, in E. Meehan and E. Riordan (eds) *Sex and Money: Feminism and Political Economy in the Media*. Minneapolis: University of Minnesota Press.

Mellencamp, P. (1992) *High Anxiety: Catastrophe, Scandal, Age and Comedy*. Bloomington: Indiana University Press.

Mercer, K. (1988) Race, sexual politics and black masculinity, in R. Chapman and J. Rutherford (eds) *Male Order: Unwrapping Masculinity*. London: Lawrence and Wishart.

Merchant, C. (1989) *The Death of Nature: Women, Ecology and the Scientific Revolution*. San Francisco: HarperCollins.

Merck, M. (2000) *In Your Face: 9 Sexual Studies*. New York: New York University Press.

Miller, T. (ed.) (2002) *Television Studies*. London: British Film Institute.

Millwood Hargrave, A. (1992) *Sex and Sexuality in Broadcasting*. London: Broadcasting Standards Commission.

Millwood Hargrave, A. (1999) *Sex and Sensibility*. London: Broadcasting Standards Commission.

Mistress L (2001) A Faustian bargain: speaking out against the media. *Feminist Review*, 67(1): 145–50.

Morley, D. (1980) *The Nationwide Audience*. London: British Film Institute.

Morrison, T. (1992) *Raceing Justice, En-gendering Power*. New York: Pantheon.

Morrison, T. (1997) *Birth of a Nation Hood: Gaze, Script and Spectacle in the OJ Simpson Case*. New York: Vintage.

Moseley, R. and Read, J. (2002) 'Having it Ally': popular television (post)feminism. *Feminist Media Studies*, 2(2): 231–49.

Mulgan, G. (1990) Television's holy grail: seven types of quality, in G. Mulgan (ed.) *The Question of Quality*. London: British Film Institute.

Munt, S. (1992) Sex and sexuality, in A. Millwood Hargrave (ed.) *Sex and Sexuality in Broadcasting*. London: Broadcasting Standards Commission.

Munt, S. (2000) Shame/pride dichotomies in QAF. *Textual Practice*, 14(3): 531–46.

Neale, S. and Krutnick, F. (1990) *Popular Film and Television Comedy*. London: Routledge.

Nelson, R. (1997) *TV Drama in Transition: Forms, Values and Cultural Change*. London: Macmillan.

Nelson, R. (2000) Performing (wo)manoeuvres: the progress of gendering in TV drama, in B. Carson and M. Llewellyn-Jones (eds) *Frames and Fictions on Television: The Politics of Identity within Drama*. Exeter: Intellect Books.

Nelson, R. (2001a) Ally McBeal, in G. Creeber (ed.) *The Television Genre Book*. London: British Film Institute.

Nelson, R. (2001b) Costume drama, in G. Creeber (ed.) *The Television Genre Book*. London: British Film Institute.

Neves, S. (2003) Information supplied by the Multishow's advertising department based on figures from 2002. Translated and forwarded by personal e-mail.

Newcombe, H. (2004) *Cagney and Lacey* (http://www.museum.tv/archives/etv/C/htmlC/cagneyandla/cagneyandla.htm). Accessed 1 February 2004.

Nicholls, B. (1994) The ethnographer's tale, in *Blurred Boundaries*. Bloomington: Indiana University Press.

Ostergaard, B. S. (1998) Convergence: legislative dilemmas, in D. McQuail and K. Suine (eds) *Media Policy: Convergence, Concentration and Commerce*. London: Sage.

Oswell, D. (1998) True love in queer times: romance, suburbia and masculinity, in L. Pearce and G. Whisker (eds) *Fatal Attractions: Rescripting Romance in Contemporary Literature and Film*. London: Pluto Press.

O'Toole, L. (1998) *Pornocopia: Porn, Sex, Technology and Desire*. London: Serpent's Tail.

Parks, L. and Levine, E. (eds) (2003) *Red Noise: Critical Writings on Buffy the Vampire Slayer*. Durham, NC: Duke University Press.

Parmar, P. (1990) Black feminism: the politics of articulation, in J. Rutherford (ed.) *Identity: Community, Culture, Difference*. London: Lawrence and Wishart.

Penley, C. (1997) *Nasa/Trek: Popular Science and Sex in America*. London: Verso.

Plummer, K. (1995) *Telling Sexual Stories: Power, Change and Social Worlds*. London: Routledge.

Plummer, K. (1996) Intimate citizenship and the culture of sexual storytelling, in J. Weeks and J. Holland (eds) *Sexual Cultures: Communities, Values and Intimacy*. Basingstoke: Macmillan.

Poovey, M. (1990) The representation of prostitution in Britain in the 1840s, in M. Jacobus, E. Fox Keller and A. Shuttleworth (eds) *Body/Politics: Women and the Discourses of Science*. London: Routledge.

Porter, C. (2001) Fashion in the city: cult show underpins style, *Guardian*, 10 September.

Pullen, K. (2000) I love Xena.com: creating online fanzine communities, in D. Gauntlett (ed.) *Web Studies: Rewiring Media Studies for the Digital Age*. London: Arnold.

Radner, H. (1995) *Shopping Around: Feminine Culture and the Pursuit of Pleasure*. New York: Routledge.

Rich, B. R. (1986) Anti-porn: soft issue, hard world, in C. Brunsdon (ed.) *Films for Women*. London: British Film Institute.

Richardson, C. (1995) TVOD: The never bending story, in P. Burston and C. Richardson (eds) *A Queer Romance*. London: Routledge.

Richardson, S. (1986) *Clarissa*. London: Penguin.

Rickard, W. (2001) 'Been there, seen it, done it, I've got the T-shirt': British sex workers reflect on jobs, hopes, the future and retirement. *Feminist Review*, 67(1): 111–32.

Rivett, M. (2000) Approaches to analysing the web text: a consideration of the web site as an emergent cultural form, *Convergence*, 6(3): 34–60.

Robertson, C. (2001) Sky One back to basics. *Broadcast*, 19 January.

Root, J. (1984) *Pictures of Women: Sexuality*. London: Pandora Press/C4.

Rose, J. (2003) The cult of celebrity, in *On Not Being Able to Sleep: Psychoanalysis and the Modern World*. London: Chatto and Windus.

Rose, M. (1993) *Parody: Ancient, Modern and Postmodern*. Cambridge: Cambridge University Press.

Ross, A. (1989) *No Respect: Intellectuals and Popular Culture*. London: Routledge.

Ross, A. (1993) The popularity of pornography, in S. During (ed.) *The Cultural Studies Reader*. London: Routledge.

Rowe, K. (1995) *The Unruly Woman: Gender and the Genres of Laughter*. Austin: University of Texas Press.

Russo, M. (1995) *The Female Grotesque: Risk, Excess and Modernity*. London: Routledge.

Sedgwick, E. K. (1990) *Epistemology of the Closet*. Berkeley: University of California Press.

Segal, L. (1994) *Straight Sex: The Politics of Pleasure*. London: Virago.

Segal, L. (1997) Sexualities, in K. Woodward (ed.) *Identity and Difference*. London: Sage/Open University.

Segal, L. and Mackintosh, M. (eds) (1992) *Sex Exposed: Sexuality and the Pornography Debate*. London: Virago.

Seidman, S. (1995) Deconstructing queer theory or the under-theorisation of the social and the ethical, in L. Nicholson and S. Seidman (eds) *Social Postmodernism: Beyond Identity Politics*. Cambridge: Cambridge University Press.

Shattuc, J. M. (1997) *The Talking Cure: TV Talk Shows and Women*. London: Routledge.

Shaw, C. (1999) *Deciding What We Watch: Taste, Decency and Media Ethics in the UK and USA*. Oxford: Clarendon Press.

Shome, R. (2001) White femininity and the discourse of the nation: re/membering Princess Diana. *Feminist Media Studies*, 1(3): 323–41.

Siune, K. and Hulten, O. (1998) Does public broadcasting have a future?, in D. McQuail and K. Suine (eds) *Media Policy: Convergence, Concentration and Commerce*. London: Sage.

Skibre, M. L. (2001) Norwegian massage parlours. *Feminist Review*, 67(1): 67–73.

Smith, C. (2002) From oppression to the jelly rabbit. Paper presented at the Third Wave Feminism conference, Exeter University, 13–15 July.

Sparks, C. and Tulloch, J. (2000) *Tabloid Tales: Global Debates over Media Standards*. Lanham, MD: Rowman and Littlefield.

Stabile, C. (1998) Shooting the mother: fetal photography and the politics of disappearance, in P. A. Treichler, L. Cartwright and C. Penley (eds) *The Visible Woman: Imaging Technologies, Gender and Science*. New York: New York University Press.

Stacey, J. (1991) Promoting normality: Section 28 and the regulation of sexuality, in S. Franklin, C. Lury and J. Stacey (eds) *Off-centre: Feminism and Cultural Studies*. New York: HarperCollins.

Steemers, J. (1999) Between culture and commerce: the problem of redefining public service broadcasting for the digital age. *Convergence*, 5(3): 44–66.

Stevenson, N. (2003) *Cultural Citizenship*. Maidenhead: Open University Press.

Stones, R. (2002) Social theory, documentary and distant others: simplicity and subversion in *The Good Woman of Bangkok*. *European Journal of Cultural Studies*, 5(2): 217–37.

Straayer, C. (1993) The seduction of boundaries: feminist fluidity in Annie Sprinkle's art/education/sex, in P. Church Gibson and R. Gisbon (eds) *Dirty Looks: Women, Pornography and Power*. London: British Film Institute.

Thompson, B. (1994) *Soft Core: Moral Crusades against Pornography in Britain and America*. London: Cassell.

Thompson, J. (1997) 'And besides, the wench is dead': media scandals and the globalization of communication, in J. Lull and S. Hinerman (eds) *Media Scandals: Morality and Desire in the Popular Culture Marketplace*. Cambridge: Polity Press.

Thompson, J. (2000) *Political Scandals: Power and Visibility in the Media Age*. Cambridge: Polity Press.

Thumin, J. (ed.) (2001) *Small Screens, Big Ideas: Television in the 1950s*. London: I. B. Tauris.

Tomlinson, J. (1999) *Globalization and Culture*. Cambridge: Polity Press.

Treichler, P. A., Cartwright, L. and Penley, C. (eds) (1998) *The Visible Woman: Imaging Technologies, Gender and Science*. New York: New York University Press.

Vance, C. (ed.) (1992) *Pleasure and Danger: Exploring Female Sexuality*. London: Pandora.

Walkerdine, V. (1998) Popular culture and the eroticization of little girls, in H. Jenkins (ed.) *The Children's Culture Reader*. New York: New York University Press.

Walkowitz, J. (1992) *City of Dreadful Delight: Narratives of Sexual Danger in Late-Victorian London*. London: Virago.

Watney, S. (1997) *Policing Desire: Pornography, AIDS and the Media*. London: Cassell.

Weeks, J. (1989) *Sex, Politics and Society: The Regulation of Sexuality since 1800*. Harlow: Longman.

Weeks, J. (2003) *Sexuality*. London and New York: Routledge.

Wells, M. (2002) The great contender. *Guardian*, 25 March.

Wells, M. (2003a) Talk to me. *Guardian*, 22 January.

Wells, M. (2003b) Channel Five programming stripped bare of pornography. *Guardian*, 14 July.

Whelahan, I. (2000) *Overloaded: Popular Culture and the Future of Feminism*. London: The Women's Press.

Williams, L. (1990) *Hard Core: Power, Pleasure and the 'Frenzy of the Visible'*. London: Pandora.

Williams, L. (1993) A provoking agent: the pornography and performance art of Annie Sprinkle, in P. Church Gibson and R. Gisbon (eds) *Dirty Looks: Women, Pornography and Power*. London: British Film Institute.

Williamson, J. (1986) A world of difference. *New Statesman*, 5 December.

Williamson, J. (1988) Two kinds of otherness: black film and the avante garde. *Screen*, 29(4): 106–12.

Willis, S. (1991) *A Primer for Daily Life: Is There More to Life than Shopping?* London: Routledge.

Wilson, S. (2003) *Oprah, Celebrity and Formations of Self*. Basingstoke: Palgrave.

Wilton, T. (1997) *Engendering AIDS: Deconstructing Sex, Text and Epidemic*. London: Sage.

Wilton, T. (1999) Temporality, materiality: towards a body in time, in J. Arthurs and J. Grimshaw (eds) *Women's Bodies: Discipline and Transgression*. London: Cassell.

Winston, B. (2000) *Lies, Damn Lies and Documentaries*. London: British Film Institute.

Wolf, N. (1993) *Fire with Fire: The New Female Power and How It Will Change the Twentieth Century*. London: Chatto and Windus.

INDEX

Page numbers in *italics* refer to figures

CRITICAL READINGS: MEDIA AND GENDER

Cynthia Carter and Linda Steiner (eds)

Critical Readings: Media and Gender provides a lively and engaging introduction to the field of media and gender research, drawing from a wide range of important international scholarship. A variety of conceptual and methodological approaches is used to explore subjects such as: entertainment; news; grassroots communication; new media texts; institutions; audiences. Topics include:

- Gender identity and television talk shows
- The sexualization of the popular press
- The representation of lesbians on television
- The cult of femininity in women's magazines
- Images of African American women and Latinas in Hollywood cinema
- Pornography and masculine power

This book is ideal for undergraduate courses in cultural and media studies, gender studies, the sociology of the media, mass communication, journalism, communication studies and politics.

Essays by: John Beynon, Mary Ellen Brown, Helen Davies, Elizabeth Hadley Freydberg, Margaret Gallagher, Heather Gilmour, Patricia Holland, Sherrie A. Inness, Robert Jensen, Myra Macdonald, Marguerite Moritz, Carmen Ruíz, Anne Scott, Lesley Semmens, Jane Shattuc, Saraswati Sunindyo, Lynette Willoughby.

Contents

Series editor's foreword – Acknowledgements – The contested terrain of media and gender: editors' introduction – Part one: Gendered texts in context – Readings 1-5 – Part two: (Re)Producing gender – Readings 6-10 – Part three: Gendered audiences and identities – Readings 11-15 – Index.

384pp   0 335 21097 X (Paperback)   0 335 21098 8 (Hardback)